Relational Analytics

This guidebook goes beyond people analytics to provide a research-based, practice-tested methodology for doing relational analytics, based on the science of relational coordination.

We are witnessing a revolution in people analytics, where data are used to identify and leverage human talent to drive performance outcomes. Today's workplace is interdependent, and individuals drive performance through networks that span department, organization and sector boundaries. This book shares the relational coordination framework, with a validated scalable analytic tool that has been used successfully across dozens of countries and industries to understand, measure and influence networks of relationships in and across organizations, and which can be applied at any level in the private and public sectors worldwide.

Graduate students and practitioners in human resource management, health policy and management, organizational behavior, engineering and network analysis will appreciate the methodology and hands-on guidance this book provides, with its focus on identifying, analyzing and building networks of productive interdependence.

Online resources include data appendices and statistical commands that can be used to conduct all these analyses in readers' own organizations.

Jody Hoffer Gittell is Professor of Management at The Heller School for Social Policy and Management, Brandeis University. She founded the Relational Coordination Research Collaborative (now the Relational Coordination Collaborative) in 2011 to bring people together to advance the research and practice of relational coordination, and currently serves on its Board of Advisors.

Hebatallah Naim Ali is a PhD Candidate at The Heller School for Social Policy and Management, Brandeis University. Her research focus is job crafting practices and relational coordination among staff in the health and human service sectors.

"It is rare that a book is of equal relevance and value to both the practice and research communities. *Relational Analytics* is one such book. Grounded in the theory, research and measures of both relational coordination and social network analysis, its major contribution will be in bringing practitioners and researchers closer together in co-producing knowledge to improve organizational performance."

Stephen M. Shortell, Blue Cross of California Distinguished Professor of Health Policy and Research Emeritus and Dean Emeritus, School of Public Health, UC-Berkeley

"*Relational Analytics* offers a fresh interpretation of people analytics; it shows how managers can use analytics to specify role interdependencies and with whom employees need to interact most critically to achieve strategic objectives. This outstanding book should be read by organizational and HR scholars as well as by organizational leaders, HR Directors, and line managers."

Katherine C. Kellogg, MIT Sloan School of Management

"*Relational Analytics* is a wonderful explanation of the power of relationships in driving successful outcomes and a powerful counter to the disproportionate attention given to individual contributions. It organizes the broad literature related to this topic in ways that help students understand it and practitioners use it."

Peter Cappelli, George W. Taylor Professor of Management, Director, Center for Human Resources, The Wharton School, and Professor of Education, University of Pennsylvania

"This is a quite amazing book. It is written for both practitioners and researchers, and accessible to both. It helps practitioners use relational coordination to improve organizational performance and helps researchers and would-be researchers study its effectiveness. It is comprehensive. It includes the fundamental theory of relational coordination and a systematic review of a large number of studies using the approach that strongly establishes its scholarly credentials. It also gives illustrations of how the approach has been used and gives guidance on how it can be used to intervene.

Relational Analytics is the first book in decades (perhaps since Hackman and Oldham's *Work Redesign* in 1980) to give such a comprehensive and accessible treatment of a construct and approach that are important in both theory and practice. It should be a valuable teaching tool for masters and PhD students in the social sciences and a stimulus for creating and studying positive relational interventions in organizations. I strongly recommend it."

Jean M. Bartunek, Robert A. and Evelyn J. Ferris Chair, Boston College

"Relational coordination has been my go-to explanatory frame for interdependence and coordination since the early 2000's, and I have used the relational coordination scale to understand the quality of coordination and teamwork in several real world interdisciplinary care contexts. But how to help students focusing on applied health services research understand and successfully apply the theory, and quickly master the mechanics of properly calculating relational coordination measures? *Relational Analytics* is an expansive and refined text that lays out the necessary theoretical and practical detail for young scholars to successfully delve into the complexity of coordination. What a welcome addition to the suite of doctoral training tools!"

Jill A. Marsteller, Professor of Health Policy and Management, Johns Hopkins Bloomberg School of Public Health

"*Relational Analytics* is firmly grounded in the premise that relationships form the fabric of organizations. While most methods analyze organizations at the group or individual level, Gittell and Ali provide the framework and tools to assess and change the quality of work relationships. With this book, readers will be well-armed to delve into where the action really is. Researchers and practitioners alike will find the "how-to" aspect to be invaluable.

The authors go beyond describing the typical RC Survey deployment, for example, to helping readers customize the survey to their own context. Readers are shown the multiple innovations developed by those who have preceded them. They are guided to create and make sense of data visualizations that are essential for assessing the current state and advancing organizational change. All tools are integrated at the end of the book into the Relational Model of Organizational Change. Anyone should feel comfortable taking these tools and running with them in any context where they're trying to make an impact."

John Paul Stephens, Associate Professor, Organizational Behavior, Weatherhead School of Management, Case Western Reserve University

"*Relational Analytics* addresses very important principles in a very competent way - it is rich in details and gives the reader new inspiration, general guidelines, and hands on suggestions for conducting research and action learning."

Carsten Hornstrup, Director and Chief Consultant, Joint Action Analytics

"We're developing a master's degree in strategic human resource analytics and *Relational Analytics* is exactly the type of book we've been looking for. Well done!"

Daniel J. Brass, J. Henning Hilliard Professor of Innovation Management, LINKS Center for Social Network Analysis, Gatton College of Business & Economics, University of Kentucky

"*Relational Analytics* takes us a step beyond existing methods by offering a powerful tool for analyzing the systems of interdependencies that constitute our work environments. Beginners and seasoned scholars will glean new insights from this accessible guide. Gittell and Ali complement step by step instructions for design and analysis with a rigorous review of empirical applications of the relational coordination model. The rich examples incorporated in this text highlight a signature strength of the instrument - namely the granularity of the data is especially valuable for informing systemic interventions. This analytical approach thus makes a significant contribution towards the integration of scholarship and practice."

Njoke Thomas, Assistant Professor of Management and Organization,
Boston College

Relational Analytics

Guidelines for Analysis and Action

Jody Hoffer Gittell and
Hebatallah Naim Ali

Routledge
Taylor & Francis Group
NEW YORK AND LONDON

First published 2021
by Routledge
605 Third Avenue, New York, NY 10158

and by Routledge
2 Park Square, Milton Park, Abingdon, Oxon, OX14 4RN

Routledge is an imprint of the Taylor & Francis Group, an informa business

© 2021 Taylor & Francis

The right of Jody Hoffer Gittell and Hebatallah Naim Ali to be identified as authors of this work has been asserted by them in accordance with sections 77 and 78 of the Copyright, Designs and Patents Act 1988.

Library of Congress Cataloging-in-Publication Data
Names: Gittell, Jody Hoffer, author. | Ali, Hebatallah Naim, author.
Title: Relational analytics : guidelines for analysis and action / Jody Hoffer Gittell, Hebatallah Naim Ali.
Description: New York, NY : Routledge, 2021. | Includes bibliographical references and index.
Identifiers: LCCN 2020054433 (print) | LCCN 2020054434 (ebook) | ISBN 9780367477462 (hardback) | ISBN 9780367436254 (paperback) | ISBN 9781003036371 (ebook)
Subjects: LCSH: Organizational behavior--Research--Methodology. | Personnel management–Research–Methodology. | Social sciences–Network analysis.
Classification: LCC HD58.7 .G575 2021 (print) | LCC HD58.7 (ebook) | DDC 302.3/5072–dc23
LC record available at https://lccn.loc.gov/2020054433
LC ebook record available at https://lccn.loc.gov/2020054434

ISBN: 978-0-367-47746-2 (hbk)
ISBN: 978-0-367-43625-4 (pbk)
ISBN: 978-1-003-03637-1 (ebk)

Typeset in Sabon
by SPi Global, India

Dedications

To my parents, John and Shirley, for teaching me the importance of mutual respect, and my siblings Sandy, Ed and Rick, for teaching me how to share and care. To Ross and daughters Rose and Grace, for the best support system I could imagine. May all of us be the change we wish to see.

Jody

To my parents, Ahmed and Souzan, for giving me the courage to journey beyond the familiar. To my little sister, Lamia, and my angels, Nadine and Rana, for giving me a hug, a smile, and half a cookie to keep going.

Heba

Contents

About the Authors

Jody Hoffer Gittell is Professor of Management at The Heller School for Social Policy and Management, Brandeis University. She founded the Relational Coordination Research Collaborative (now the Relational Coordination Collaborative) to bring people together to advance the research and practice of relational coordination, and currently serves on its Advisory Board. Earlier in her career, she developed relational coordination theory, proposing that highly interdependent work is most effectively coordinated through high-quality communication supported by relationships of shared goals, shared knowledge, and mutual respect, and proposing a set of structures that support this process. Her research has been published in a wide range of scientific journals and in five previous books including *Transforming Relationships for High Performance: The Power of Relational Coordination* (Stanford University Press, 2016). Dr. Gittell received her MA from The New School for Social Research and her PhD from the MIT Sloan School of Management.

Hebatallah Naim Ali is a PhD Candidate at The Heller School for Social Policy and Management, Brandeis University. Her research focus is on job crafting practices and relational coordination among support staff for adults with disabilities. She worked with the Centers for Disease Control and the Eastern Mediterranean Regional Office of the World Health Organization to implement the 2011–2012 Stepwise Survey for Chronic Diseases in Egypt. She received her MD from the Faculty of Medicine, Suez Canal University and her MS in International Health Policy and Management from The Heller School for Social Policy and Management, Brandeis University.

Preface

We are living in the midst of a revolution in people analytics, where data are used to identify and leverage human talent to drive performance. No matter how talented they are, however, individuals do not drive performance alone. When work is interdependent, individuals drive performance through networks that span functional, departmental, organizational, and even sectoral boundaries. Optimizing performance under these conditions requires relational analytics.

In this book, we extend people analytics in new directions by providing a research-based, practice-tested methodology for relational analytics, based on social network analysis and the science of relational coordination. We share the relational coordination framework, including a validated scalable tool that has been used successfully across dozens of countries and industries to measure, analyze and strengthen networks within and between organizations. We aim:

- To deepen your understanding of relational analytics, based on social network analysis and the science of relational coordination
- To provide you with a methodology and hands-on guidance for doing relational analytics
- To help you strengthen networks within and between organizations to achieve positive outcomes, informed by the results of your analysis

Stepping back, we are concerned about persistent racism, economic inequality, the global pandemic, and the increasing frequency and intensity of natural disasters due to climate change. We are hopeful that relational analytics will nudge people to see themselves as part of an interdependent network of being—and to act accordingly.

Acknowledgements

Many students and colleagues have contributed to this book. In 2005, I began to draft it as a way to capture basic knowledge about the measurement and analysis of relational coordination. Students and colleagues at Brandeis University's Heller School, such as Susan Pfefferle, Taletha Derrington, Farbod Hagigi, Brenda Bond, Dana Weinberg, and Signe Peterson Flieger, read the draft and offered suggestions, helping me to continually clarify and refine the presentation. Over the years, they and others contributed their own innovations for the measurement and analysis of relational coordination.

To provide context for the methods, I added a theory chapter then a systematic review of the published research through years of careful work with Caroline Logan and Rendelle Bolton. At the same time, I was gaining insights about using relational coordination data and principles to create positive change from Saleema Moore, Curt Lindberg, Kenneth Milne, Nancy Whitelaw, Dale Collins Vidal, Thomas Huber, Tony Suchman, Margie Godfrey, Carsten Hornstrup, and others. Building on these insights and in conversation with Ed Schein and Amy Edmondson, I expanded the linear model of performance into a dynamic model of change.

Then it happened—I met Hebatallah Naim Ali when she was a student in my Relational Coordination Research and Analytics course in Spring 2017. Heba immediately visualized relational coordination as a matrix, showing that she intuitively understood the network structure of the construct. The following year she became the teaching assistant for the course, then became the person who many in the community—including me—asked to help with their analyses. Heba was insatiably curious and learned everything she could about social network analysis and factor analysis and other techniques to push the boundaries of relational coordination methods. Whatever she didn't know intrigued her endlessly, so she set out to learn it. She even worked with a small research team to carry out relational coordination interventions in two community-based residences for people with traumatic brain injury. Through this experience, she learned about using relational coordination data and principles in a participatory change process that involved frontline staff, leaders, residents, families, and community members.

In 2019, I decided it was time to turn this working draft into a published book, with online resources to be constantly updated to reflect learning and innovation in the community. Heba was the obvious partner and it has been a joy. In addition to her curiosity and intellect, Heba is a delightfully kind human being with a warm laugh and a deep loyalty to her family, her friends, and her ever-growing circle of beloved colleagues.

Together, we acknowledge with gratitude the hundreds of you who have helped on this journey, whether we've met you, co-authored with you, or simply read your work. Heba and I invite those of you who are new to these methods to join our community of researchers and positive changemakers. We have only just begun!

Jody Hoffer Gittell

Hebatallah Naim Ali

Chapter 1

From People Analytics to Relational Analytics

We are living in the midst of a revolution in people analytics, where data are used to identify and leverage human talent to drive performance. This revolution has occurred in response to a growing desire for evidence-based management (Barends & Rousseau, 2018; Rousseau, 2012), and a desire for new ways to achieve control over the human resources that are critical to every organization's success. But in today's complex world, there is little that individuals can achieve on their own. On the horizon is the next phase of the analytics revolution—relational analytics—that goes beyond a focus on individuals to focus on the relationships between them where value can be either created or depleted.

In this book, we provide researchers, leaders, and consultants with a research-based, practice-tested methodology for doing relational analytics, based on the science of relational coordination. We share relational coordination theory and the validated measurement and analytic tools that have been used in dozens of countries and industries to assess, understand, and shape relational networks within and across organizations. The aim of this book is to help readers to create positive change by using relational analytics to identify and build high-quality networks across functional, departmental, organizational, and sectoral boundaries.

The People Analytics Revolution

People analytics—the application of predictive modeling, big data, and artificial intelligence to human resource management—is increasingly used at every stage of the human resource life cycle, including recruiting, hiring, onboarding, training, compensation, benefits, performance management, advancement, and retention. When HR data from multiple sources are combined into a common format, machine learning can be used to create algorithms to predict outcomes. Based on these algorithms, one can recommend which kinds of training an individual employee should engage in, which kinds of benefits might be attractive to her, and which career moves might be advantageous for both her and her employer (Tambe, Cappelli, & Yakubovich, 2019).

In other words, people analytics can provide an evidence-based methodology to inform managerial decisions about human resource management. One advantage of using people analytics, like data analytics more generally, is to break free of existing theories (Tambe et al., 2019). Rather than testing hypotheses that are generated from existing theories, you can build predictive models that have the potential to go beyond what theory or managers themselves can currently imagine. For example, machine learning can uncover unexpected findings that go against managerial biases.

Because people analytics are based on algorithms, they are more instantaneous, encompassing, interactive, and opaque than previous technologies and their potential to control employees is thereby greatly enhanced, according to Kate Kellogg and her colleagues (Kellogg, Valentine, & Christin, 2020). Employee wearables coupled with people analytics enable employers to better monitor their employees, then incentivize employees to do things that are favorable for the employer (Marr, 2018). Employers can monitor their employees' health behaviors, for example, and reward or penalize them based on the gathered data; or monitor employees to detect potential harm to themselves or others around them. This data can also be shared with workers themselves. Workers with wearables can get feedback on their own physical and psychological states, along with recommendations of how to respond. Workers with wearables can also get updated information constantly to inform their next moves, helping them work smarter and not necessarily harder. For these reasons, connected workers have the potential to be more productive. In addition to getting feedback about their own physical and psychological states, employees can be provided with continuous feedback regarding company performance, allowing them to make better decisions about where to focus and what to do.

Limitations of People Analytics

While big data has been used successfully in multiple fields of management, "the effective application of AI to HR problems presents different challenges than it does in other areas. These challenges range from practical to conceptual, including the fact that data analytics—when applied to decisions about people—can create serious conflicts with what society typically sees as important for making consequential decisions about individuals." Drawing heavily from Tambe, Cappelli and Yakubovitch's seminal paper on this topic, these limitations in our view range from somewhat concerning to severe (Tambe et al., 2019):

> **Lack of standardized data.** HR doesn't have as much standardized data as do fields like accounting, so it is harder to find consistent data over time or across organizations that are needed to conduct analytics. Even when the data do exist, the components that are needed to

develop useful algorithms are often owned by different parts of the organization—for example, hiring data and organizational performance data. One challenge is gathering all the data from these multiple databases and converting them into a common format.

Rare events. Big data analytics work poorly for predicting relatively rare events such as employee terminations.

Gaming. Once employees know which algorithms are being used, they can game the system in an attempt to achieve their own desired outcomes.

Privacy issues. There are clearly privacy issues when analyzing data about people though some argue these can be adequately addressed through methods that allow analysts to learn only about the population, not about individuals.

Lack of causal attribution. It is hard to explain or justify decisions that impact individuals when they are based on patterns identified in a large data set. Knowing which attributes are driving a decision is important in HR and this is typically not possible when using predictive algorithms. "Demonstrably causal algorithms are more defendable in the court of law and thus address at least some legal constraints discussed above. They are fairer due to the explicit specification of causal paths from individual characteristics to performance" (Tambe et al., 2019). Causal explanations are also more readily accepted by those who are involved, both the person who is making the decision and the person who is the target of the decision.

Weakening relationships and commitment to action. It is hard to build a relationship based on decisions that account for the needs of the other when decisions are made by algorithms. Decisions made by algorithms may therefore weaken relationships. Similarly, how willingly will people commit to the outcomes of decisions that they have not been involved in making? And will employees accept outcomes generated by data analytics if they have not been involved in developing the algorithms? "Ensuring employee involvement in the process of building and using algorithms is [therefore] necessary for their success" (Tambe et al., 2019).

Replicating bias. While people analytics can help managers to break free of existing biases, making decisions based on existing data can replicate bias when existing data are based on past discriminatory behavior. For example, if white men have performed best in your organization in the past due to discriminatory practices that have supported their work better than the work of others, the resulting algorithms will wrongly recommend hiring white men. In addition, you can only use data on people who have been hired, so if you continue to hire the same kind of people, thus restricting variation, it will become impossible over time to test the relationship between a wider range of personal attributes and performance.

Strengthening hierarchical control. There are legitimate concerns about the potential to use people analytics as algorithmic methods that control workers even more than previous technical and bureaucratic controls have done. Why? People analytics increase the ability to control employee behavior by enabling new ways of directing, evaluating, and disciplining them (Kellogg et al., 2020). Depending on your perspective, this potential for increased hierarchical control could be seen as either a strength or limitation of people analytics.

Neglecting interdependence. The most important limitation of people analytics is the interdependence of work itself. Does it make sense to use individual data when most desired performance outcomes are in fact based on interdependent behavior?

> *Any reasonably complex* job is interdependent with other jobs, and therefore individual performance is hard to disentangle from group performance. A vast literature documents numerous problems with existing performance systems as well as our field's failure to establish a clear link between individual, team, and organizational performance … . Complex jobs are interdependent with one another, and thus, one employee's performance is often inextricable from the performance of the group: is it sufficient to be a good individual contributor, and if not, how do we measure interactions with others?
>
> (Tambe et al., 2019)

How Well Do Relational Analytics Address Current Limitations of People Analytics?

Arguably, three of the biggest limitations of people analytics are the potential for (1) replicating bias, (2) strengthening hierarchical control, and (3) neglecting interdependence. How well do relational analytics address these limitations? Just as people analytics can replicate bias when used to predict future outcomes based on past outcomes, relational analytics run the same risk. If relational analytics show that surgeons tend to have weak ties with other roles and that these weak ties predict negative patient outcomes, for example, these findings can be used to create a narrative that surgeons are inherently cowboys or even jerks. Alternatively, the same findings can be used to explore the systems that have created a surgeon-led hierarchy and a structure of individual accountability that contributes to dysfunctional ties between surgeons and other roles. Rather than "pointing the finger" at individual causes of behavior, relational analytics tend to foster a mindset of looking for systemic causes of behavior.

Like people analytics, relational analytics also have the potential to be controlling, though in different ways. People analytics can accomplish control by comparing individuals to other individuals and ranking them, then further intensify control by obscuring participant understanding about where data comes from, thereby removing accountability. While competitive ranking can be highly motivating, it also has the potential to motivate behaviors that undermine rather than optimize interdependent systems, as we learned from the founder of improvement science W. Edwards Deming. Relational analytics are excellent for providing data that enable people to reflect on their patterns of interaction to achieve collective self-control, a form of control that is less hierarchical and more mutual, according to early management thinker Mary Parker Follett. Even so, relational analytics can be misused by participants who are accustomed to achieving control and/or being controlled through the use of competitive ranking systems. Skillful facilitation of data sharing is therefore needed to enable participants to achieve collective self-control. In Chapter 10, we will explore multiple approaches to effectively facilitate the sharing of relational data.

The most fundamental limitation of people analytics is the simplest. *No matter how talented they are, individuals cannot drive performance alone.* Interdependence is where relational analytics shine. Because the unit of analysis for people analytics is the individual actor, people analytics are inherently geared toward capturing and optimizing individual behaviors. Because the unit of analysis for relational analytics is the connections between actors rather than the individual actors themselves, relational analytics are inherently geared toward capturing and optimizing interdependent behaviors. Why does this matter? When our work is highly interdependent—when I can't accomplish my tasks without input from you, and vice versa, or my team can't accomplish its tasks without input from your team, or my organization can't accomplish its tasks without input from other organizations in our ecosystem—relational analytics provide insights into the nature and quality of connections that make the difference between success or failure. We can go even further than analyzing the connections between individuals or groups, by visualizing each connection in the context of the larger network in which it is embedded. When we see each part in relation to the whole, we can more readily engage in the systems thinking that is a powerful driver of improvement (Deming, 2000).

Relational Analytics as the New Frontier

In sum, when work is interdependent, individuals drive performance through networks that span department, organization, and sector boundaries. Analytically, you can address this interdependence in multiple ways. For example, you can "include business and financial performance data at the organizational level closest to employee control to have the best chance of seeing how individual performance affects larger business units and the company as a whole" (Tambe et al., 2019). Alternatively, you could "focus on outcomes rather than narrow metrics, i.e. if the company is performing well and individuals are contributing to its success, then they should be rewarded accordingly" (Marr, 2018). You can also address interdependence more directly by collecting data from multiple perspectives, including one's colleagues. The interdependence of work thus helps to explain the move toward frequent evaluations conducted from a 360-degree perspective.

You can also use the big data methods associated with people analytics to uncover collective behaviors or norms (Tambe et al., 2019). You can monitor collective behavior or the culture of a company through the use of natural language processing on data that are gathered from company chat boards, email, social media, open-ended questions in surveys, or open-ended comments in performance reviews, etc. Culture analytics allow you to see how the culture is changing, or to identify different cultures that may exist in the same organization (Marr, 2018). Analysis of real conversations between your staff and customers might be useful, for example, using voice analytics, text analytics, or sentiment analysis tools (Marr, 2018).

The wearable badge introduced above for monitoring individual employees can also be used to monitor employee–employee interactions or employee–customer interactions. These interactive data allow one to predict which teams will be successful, and to identify which employees are most productive, creative, or likely to become great leaders. Analyzing email data can also generate insights about how employees treat each other (Marr, 2018). In addition, Microsoft has been analyzing calendar invites to analyze the impact of employee–employee interactions on the onboarding process. They found for example that if a manager sets up a meeting in week one, the new employee is more likely to stay.

Due to the interdependence between employees in creating performance outcomes, it is advantageous to supplement people analytics with these relational analytics. Matthew Bidwell, Faculty Co-Director of the People Analytics Institute at the Wharton School, notes that companies are using organizational network analysis to better understand the impact of relationships on desired outcomes. According to Isabel Fernandez-Mateo of the London Business School: "What drives group or organizational performance is not just people individually but also the interactions between them. So that's what everyone is trying to understand now."

Exhibit 1.1 shows several foundational articles and books for the field of relational analytics. Relational Analytics goes beyond these previous books by providing a research-based, practice-tested methodology for doing relational analytics that is based on the science of relational coordination. In this book, we offer a validated set of tools to assess relational networks among key stakeholders. These tools can help organizations support the relational coordination—the teaming—that is essential for achieving desired outcomes when work is highly interdependent. These tools can help to ensure that the current revolution in people analytics does not only address the behaviors of individual employees, but also the relationships between them where value can be either created or depleted.

Exhibit 1.1 Some Foundational Articles and Books for Relational Analytics

Granovetter	"The Strength of Weak Ties." *American Journal of Sociology.*	1979
Bourdieu	"The Forms of Capital." *Cultural Theory: An Anthology.*	1986
Putnam	*Bowling Alone: The Collapse and Revival of American Community*	2000
Lin	"Building a Network Theory of Social Capital." *Social Capital.*	2001
Gittell	*The Southwest Airlines Way: Using the Power of Relationships to Achieve High Performance*	2003
Gittell	*High-Performance Healthcare: Using the Power of Relationships to Achieve Quality, Efficiency, and Resilience*	2009
Cross and Thomas	*Driving Results Through Social Networks: How Top Organizations Leverage Networks for Performance and Growth*	2009
Labianca et al	*Contemporary Perspectives on Organizational Social Networks*	2014
Ashcroft, Childs, Myers, and Schluter	*The Relational Lens: Understanding, Managing and Measuring Stakeholder Relationships*	2016
Gittell	*Transforming Relationships for High Performance: The Power of Relational Coordination*	2016
Brass and Borgatti	*Social Networks at Work*	2019

Social Networks and Social Capital as Two Approaches to Relational Analytics

Social networks are perhaps the most common approach to relational analytics. Over the last 40 years, the use of social network analysis has multiplied, crossing over to multiple disciplines and fields. The appeal of social networks is in their ability to map and study the dynamics of interactions, which is further facilitated by digital drawing of the networks. The social network methodology provides a strong set of analytical tools and has offered a fresh perspective to the social sciences. Traditionally social science has used one modal analysis, which samples and investigates individual characteristics to report information about the collective or the population. But if social entities are interconnected networks of living, traditional social science analysis is only studying the nodes and is omitting the influence of the lines that connect those nodes (Borgatti, Brass, & Halgin, 2014).

Despite its obvious appeal, confusion, criticisms, and controversies have followed social network analysis, and many researchers have argued about its limitations as a primarily descriptive form of analysis lacking in theoretical principles. Researchers such as Granovetter and Salancik have called this the *theory gap*, arguing that social network analysis provides a powerful descriptive tool but does not add to the theoretical body of social and relational sciences (Granovetter, 1979). This critique asserts that social networks fail to analyze agency or causal pathways. In scientific terms, they claim that social networks fail to explain independent and dependent variables and fail to provide pathways to explain the origins or outcomes of actors' interactions in the network.

However, this argument has faded as many other theories have integrated social networks into their thinking. Indeed, social networks have grown to become part of almost all areas of organizational inquiry including leadership and power analysis, staff retention, job performance, and relational coordination (Borgatti et al., 2014; De Nooy, Mrvar, & Batagelj, 2018). In other words, while social network analysis is arguably atheoretical, it is easily paired with organizational theories that recognize the interconnected nature of the social world and have causal stories to tell about it.

Social capital is a second promising approach to relational analytics. One common definition, introduced by Robert Putnam, is that social capital includes "features of social organization such as networks, norms, and social trust that facilitate coordination and cooperation for mutual benefit" (Putnam, 1995). Another prominent definition was introduced by Pierre Bourdieu, a French philosopher whose life works focused on social position and status and the resource exclusivity that comes with them. He defined social capital as "the aggregate of the actual or potential resources which are linked to possession of a durable network of more or less institutionalized relationships of mutual acquaintance and recognition" (Bourdieu, 1986). A third prominent definition, and the easiest to measure, was introduced by Nan Lin (Lin, Cook, & Burt, 2001), who defined social capital as "resources embedded in a social structure that are accessed and/or mobilized for purposive actions." Like social networks, however, social capital has been critiqued. Some have argued that social capital is not a form of capital, while others have argued that "social capital" is a redundant term because all types of capital are social (Claridge, 2004; Lin et al., 2001).

Putting these arguments aside, let's draw upon the Lin et al. (2001) definition of social capital as a set of relationships that enables people to access resources, and consider how to measure the value of social capital. First, a clear distinction must be made about the level of the networks we are assessing. Theorists emphasize the difference between collective macro-level networks, which are collectively produced by a particular community. Accordingly, *macro*-level social capital often focuses on measuring cultural norms and community cohesion, with measurement parameters that include trust, owned identity, civil and political integration, quality of democracy, and so on, as in Putnam's work. *Meso*-level social capital is typically evaluated on an organizational level, focusing on networks within and/or between organizations. Finally, *micro*-level social capital analysis quantifies the resources that become available to an individual directly through his or her personal social network. Therefore, individual social capital can simply be identified as an individual's access to social resources, and can be measured through:

- Number of alters in the individual's network
- Numbers of accessible resources directly linked to these alters
- The alters' willingness to purposely mobilize these resources from themselves to the individual in question.

Based on this definition, Flap calculated individual social capital using the following formula (Völker & Flap, 2004):

$$SC = \sum_i \sum_j r_{ij} p_{ij}$$

where SC is the quantification of individual total social capital, i refers to the number of alters in the individual's network, j is the number of resources accessible to each alter, r_{ij} is the quantification of resources of type j in possession of network alter i, and p is the probability of accessing it.

This equation describes the social capital accessible to an individual, but without really considering the context of that social capital and the degree to which it is useful and likely to be utilized. Because not all accessible resources are utilized, the distinction must be made between accessibility and utilization. Hence, researchers often assess the value of social capital in specific contexts: for example, social support, career support, or market success. As Van Der Gaag and Snijders explained: "What is a valuable social resource depends on the needs, goals, and opportunities (including the available economic, intellectual, skill-related, and institutional resources) of the individuals making up the population" (Van Der Gaag & Snijders, 2004). Therefore, most studies that assess individual social capital compare both the resources themselves and their accessibility and usefulness for individuals who share a common location, time, and domain.

Relational Coordination as a Third Approach to Relational Analytics

Relational coordination builds on both social networks and social capital to provide a third promising approach to relational analytics. Relational coordination is a theory about the relational dynamics of coordinating work, the performance consequences of those dynamics, and how organizations strengthen or weaken these dynamics for better or worse through their everyday management practices. Coordination that occurs through high-quality communication supported by relationships of shared goals shared knowledge and mutual respect *creates value* by enabling organizations to more readily achieve their desired outcomes. On the other hand, coordination that occurs through infrequent, delayed, inaccurate, finger-pointing communication, driven by functional goals, exclusive knowledge, and lack of respect, *depletes value* by reducing the ability of organizations

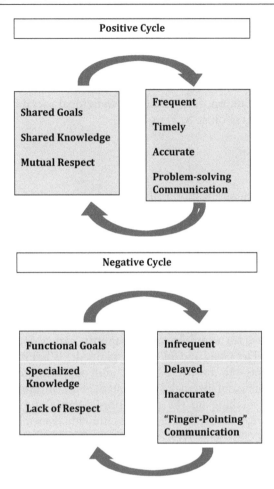

Exhibit 1.2 Mutually Reinforcing Cycles of Relational Coordination, Positive and Negative.

to achieve their desired outcomes. See Exhibit 1.2 for an illustration of these mutually reinforcing cycles of relational coordination, for better or worse.

These mutually reinforcing dynamics were originally discovered through field research carried out in the airline and healthcare industries as reported in *The Southwest Airlines Way* and in *High-Performance Healthcare* (Gittell, 2005, 2009). In these projects, a survey tool was developed to measure relational coordination as a network of ties between interdependent roles, and was later validated (Valentine, Nembhard, & Edmondson, 2015). Exhibit 1.3 shows which roles were involved in these relational coordination networks as conceptualized and measured in the two earliest studies.

Relational coordination is not just about flight departures and patient care, however. Whenever multiple roles need to work *interdependently*, in

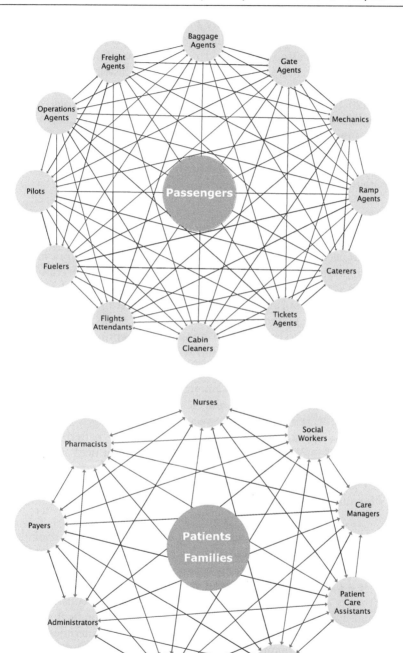

Exhibit 1.3 Visualizing Relational Coordination as a Network of Ties Between Roles. (1) Flight departure process; (2) Patient care process

the context of *uncertainty* and *time constraints*, relational coordination is likely to be important for achieving desired performance outcomes. Relational coordination theory and its analytic methods have now been tested through extensive research in dozens of industries and in dozens of countries around the world. As we will show in Chapter 3, there is now a substantial body of empirical evidence suggesting that strong relational coordination at various levels—between individuals (micro), between functions and departments (meso), and between organizations in the same or different sectors (macro)—helps to improve outcomes for multiple stakeholders. At the same time, weak relational coordination significantly reduces the potential to achieve these outcomes.

Commonalities with Social Networks and Social Capital

Like social networks, relational coordination relies on a network methodology for analyzing and visualizing relationships, including overall network patterns as well as specific dyadic ties within the network. Like social networks, relational coordination can be measured from the perspective of individuals to understand the resources they can access through their networks, and it can also be measured across a larger entity such as an organization or a community. As Gittell and Weiss explained (2004):

> Relations, defined by linkages among actors or units, are the fundamental component of network theories. Actors are interdependent rather than independent; relational ties between actors are channels for transferring resources; and structures are comprised of lasting patterns of relations among actors (Wasserman & Faust, 1994). Thus, the network perspective offers a useful way to understand coordination more deeply, an activity that is fundamentally about connections among interdependent actors who must transfer information and other resources to achieve outcomes.

Relational coordination also has much in common with social capital. Like social capital, relational coordination is an asset, a resource, and a source of value that arises from connections between participants. Relational coordination is a particular form of social capital that is useful for coordinating work that is highly interdependent, uncertain and time constrained. Like relational coordination, social capital is part of a theoretical model that links it to organizational structures and performance outcomes (Leana & Van Buren, 1999; Nahapiet & Ghoshal, 1998).

In sum, relational coordination shares with social networks the conceptualization of social and organizational phenomena as networks of ties. Relational coordination shares with social capital a theoretical framework that explains how it impacts desired outcomes, and how organizations and individuals can shape it to achieve desired outcomes. It is fair to say that relational coordination combines some of the best qualities of social networks with the best qualities of social capital to solve the most challenging problems that people and their organizations face when carrying out interdependent work. It is very practical indeed!

Summing Up

We invite you to read the chapters of this book that are most relevant for your needs. In Chapter 2 you'll dive more deeply into the theory of relational coordination—its communication and relationship dimensions, its impact on desired outcomes, how organizations strengthen it, and why it matters most when work is highly interdependent, uncertain, and time constrained. In Chapter 3, you will discover the evidence for relational coordination based on a systematic review of this growing body of research. In Chapter 4, you will learn about alternative research/evaluation designs you can use to answer specific questions about relational coordination, for the purpose of carrying out research, or helping to improve outcomes for key stakeholders, or both. For example, how strong is relational coordination in one team, organization or ecosystem versus others? Why? What difference does it make for their performance? How effective is a particular intervention for strengthening relational coordination?

In Chapter 5, you will be introduced to the methods and tools for measuring relational coordination, including alternative versions of the Relational Coordination Survey. Chapter 6 shows how to construct your relational coordination variables and carry out basic analytics. Then in Chapter 7 you will learn how to visualize and analyze your relational coordination data using matrices and networks. Chapter 8 shows how you can measure the organizational structures that shape relational coordination, and assess how they are operating in your team, organization, or broader network. In Chapter 9, you will learn modeling techniques to analyze differences in relational coordination between sites, or changes in relational coordination over time. You will also learn causal modeling to assess how management practices are shaping relational coordination. and how relational coordination is driving key outcomes of interest. Finally, in Chapter 10 you will learn how to use relational analytics to create positive change. This chapter shows you how to analyze, reflect upon, and strengthen relational coordination using a multi-stakeholder Relational Model of Organizational Change and a growing set of tools developed by partners of the Relational Coordination Collaborative. In Chapter 11, we send you on your way with key takeaways for both research and action.

References

Barends, E., & Rousseau, D. M. (2018). *Evidence-based Management: How to Use Evidence to Make Better Organizational Decisions*. London, UK: Kogan Page Publishers.

Borgatti, S. P., Brass, D. J., & Halgin, D. S. (2014). Social network research: Confusions, criticisms, and controversies. In *Contemporary Perspectives on Organizational Social Networks* (Vol. 40, pp. 1–29): Bingley, UK: Emerald Group Publishing Limited.

Bourdieu, P. (1986). The forms of capital. In J. G. Richardson (Ed.), *Handbook of Theory and Research for the Sociology of Education* (pp. 241–258). Westport, CT: Greenwood Press.

Claridge, T. (2004). *Social Capital and Natural Resource Management*. Brisbane, Australia: University of Queensland, PhD Dissertation.

De Nooy, W., Mrvar, A., & Batagelj, V. (2018). *Exploratory Social Network Analysis with Pajek: Revised and Expanded edition for Updated Software*. Cambridge, UK: Cambridge University Press.

Deming, W. E. (2000). *Out of the Crisis*. Cambridge, MA: MIT Press.

Gittell, J. H. (2009). *High Performance Healthcare: Using the Power of Relationships to Achieve Quality, Efficiency and Resilience*. New York, NY: McGraw-Hill.

Gittell, J. H. (2005). *The Southwest Airlines Way: Using the Power of Relationships to Achieve High Performance*. New York, NY: McGraw-Hill.

Gittell, J. H., & Weiss, L. (2004). Coordination networks within and across organizations: A multi-level framework. *Journal of Management Studies*, 41(1), 127–153. doi:10.1111/j.1467-6486.2004.00424.x

Granovetter, M. (1979). The theory-gap in social network analysis. In P. Holland and S. Leinhardt (Eds.), *Perspectives on Social Network Research* (pp. 501–518). New York: Academic Press.

Kellogg, K. C., Valentine, M. A., & Christin, A. (2020). Algorithms at work: The new contested terrain of control. *Academy of Management Annals*, 14(1), 366–410. doi:10.5465/annals.2018.0174

Leana, C. R., & Van Buren, H. J. (1999). Organizational social capital and employment practices. *Academy of Management Review*, 24(3), 538–555. doi:10.5465/amr.1999.2202136

Lin, N., Cook, K. S., & Burt, R. S. (2001). *Social Capital Theory and Research*. New York, NY: Aldien de Gruyter.

Marr, B. (2018). *Data-Driven HR: How to Use Analytics and Metrics to Drive Performance*. New York, NY: Kogan Page.

Nahapiet, J., & Ghoshal, S. (1998). Social capital, intellectual capital, and the organizational advantage. *Academy of Management Review*, 23(2), 242–266. doi:10.5465/amr.1998.533225

Putnam, R. D. (1995). Bowling alone: America's declining social capital. *Journal of Democracy*, 6(1), 65–78. doi:10.1353/jod.1995.0002

Rousseau, D. M. (2012). *The Oxford Handbook of Evidence-Based Management*. Oxford, UK: Oxford University Press.

Tambe, P., Cappelli, P., & Yakubovich, V. (2019). Artificial intelligence in human resources management: Challenges and a path forward. *California Management Review*, 61(4), 15–42. doi:10.1177/0008125619867910

Valentine, M. A., Nembhard, I. M., & Edmondson, A. C. (2015). Measuring team-work in health care settings: A review of survey instruments. *Medical Care*, 53(4), e16–e30. doi: 10.1097/MLR.0b013e31827feef6

Van Der Gaag, M., & Snijders, T.. (2004). Proposals for the measurement of indi-vidual social capital. In H. Flap & B. Volker (Eds.), *Creation and Returns of Social Capital: A New Research Program* (pp. 154–169). London; New York, NY: Routledge.

Flap, H. & Völker, B. (2004). *Creation and Returns of Social Capital: A New Research Program*. London; New York, NY: Routledge.

Wasserman, S., & Faust, K. (1994). *Social Network Analysis: Methods and Applications*. Cambridge, UK: Cambridge University Press.

Chapter 2

The Theory of Relational Coordination

What is Relational Coordination?

Relational coordination can be defined as a mutually reinforcing process of communicating and relating for the purpose of task integration (Gittell, 2002b). It is a theory and a set of analytic methods for understanding the relational dynamics of coordinating work within and between organizations. When coordination is carried out through frequent, high-quality communication supported by relationships of shared goals, shared knowledge, and mutual respect, organizations can better achieve desired outcomes for their multiple stakeholders. When coordination is carried out instead through insufficiently frequent, low-quality communication driven by functional goals, exclusive knowledge, and lack of respect, organizations struggle to achieve their desired outcomes.

While other theories have argued for the importance of relationships for coordinating work, relational coordination theory is different from other theories in several important ways. First, relational coordination theory portrays coordination as a network of communicating and relating among participants in a work process, Second, relational coordination theory specifies *which dimensions* of communicating and relating matter for effective coordination. Third, relational coordination theory offers tools to measure communicating and relating through a network of ties. Fourth, the theory explains how these dimensions of communicating and relating help organizations to achieve a wide array of desired outcomes, and how their impact is greatest when work is highly interdependent, uncertain, and time constrained. Fifth, the theory explains how organizational structures can be designed to support relational coordination. Finally, relational coordination theory has been widely tested through empirical research, across dozens of industry contexts, and in dozens of countries around the world.

Overview of Relational Coordination Theory

Mary Parker Follett is the first theorist to have proposed a relational theory of coordination. She accepted the then-prevalent argument that the primary function of organizations was to coordinate work. She argued uniquely, however, that coordination at its most effective is not a mechanical process but rather a process of continuous interrelating between the parts and the whole. In her words:

> It is impossible ... to work most effectively at coordination until you have made up your mind where you stand philosophically in regard to the relation of parts to wholes. We have spoken of the relation of departments—sales and production, advertising, and financial—to each other, but the most profound truth that philosophy has ever given us concerns not only the relation of parts, but the relation of parts to the whole, not to a stationary whole, but to a whole a-making.

(Follett, 1949)

Consistent with Follett's argument, Thompson later suggested that coordination as a process of reciprocal relating, or "mutual adjustment," can indeed be beneficial (Thompson, 1967). But he offered a contingency argument, suggesting that this is true only when tasks are reciprocally interdependent, or in other words, when outcomes from one task feedback to create new information for participants who are performing related tasks. Moreover, Thompson saw mutual adjustment as playing a limited role in organizations. Because mutual adjustment is prohibitively costly, he argued, coordination more commonly occurs through coordinating mechanisms such as supervision, routines, scheduling, pre-planning, or standardization (Kogut & Zander, 1996). These coordinating mechanisms can enable organizations to achieve coordination with less direct interaction among participants. But due to their limited information processing capacity, these coordinating mechanisms were only expected to be effective in settings with low levels of task interdependence and uncertainty (Argote, 1982; Galbraith, 1974; Tushman & Nadler, 1978; Ven, Delbecq, & Koenig, 1976).

Since then, the nature of work has changed. Work is now characterized by even higher levels of interdependence, uncertainty, and time constraints, expanding the relevance of mutual adjustment beyond what Thompson originally foresaw. As a result, organizational scholars have begun to see coordination as a fundamentally relational process. They have responded by developing relational approaches to coordination that build on Follett's vision of coordination, including Weick and colleagues' theory of sensemaking (Weick, 1993; Weick & Roberts, 1993), Faraj and colleagues' theory of expertise coordination (Faraj & Sproull, 2000; Faraj & Xiao, 2006), Argote and colleagues' theory of transactive memory (Liang, Moreland, & Argote, 1995), Quinn and Dutton's theory of coordination as energy-in-conversation (Quinn & Dutton, 2006), Heckscher and Adler's theory of collaborative community (Adler & Heckscher, 2005; Heckscher & Donnellon, 1994), Bechky's theory of role-based coordination, and

Stephens' theory of coordination through esthetic experience of the whole (Bechky, 2006; Stephens, 2020). In the context of this larger body of work, relational coordination theory offers a unique way to conceptualize the dynamics of coordination.

Coordination Based on Roles

Relational coordination differs from many other relationship-based approaches to coordination by focusing on relationships *between roles* rather than on relationships *between unique individuals*. Relational coordination is not the first approach to focus on coordination between roles. Follett's and Thompson's seminal work also focused on role-based coordination, as did Bechky's work (Bechky, 2006). A focus on role-based relationships more generally is found in Meyerson and colleagues' work on swift trust and in Klein and colleagues' work on deindividualization.

Why focus on role-based coordination? Role-based coordination has a practical advantage over coordination that is based on personal ties. In organizations with high levels of relational coordination, employees are connected by relationships of shared goals, shared knowledge, and mutual respect *regardless of whether or not they have strong personal ties*. This feature allows for the interchangeability of employees, allowing employees to come and go without missing a beat, an important consideration for organizations that strive to achieve high levels of performance while allowing employees the scheduling flexibility to meet their commitments outside the workplace. While role-based coordination may require greater organizational investments to foster than personal friendship ties—for example, designing cross-role boundary spanner roles and cross-role performance measurement systems versus (or in addition to) hosting after-work parties—role-based coordination is also more robust to staffing changes that occur over time (Bechky, 2006; Gittell, Seidner, & Wimbush, 2010).

Specific Dimensions of Communication and Relationships

Relational coordination theory also differs from other theories by proposing specific dimensions of communication and relationships that are needed for effective coordination. While many of the more recent theories emphasize the importance of shared knowledge or shared understandings, the theory of relational coordination argues that shared knowledge or shared understandings are necessary but not sufficient. If effective coordination is to occur, participants must also be connected by relationships of shared goals and mutual respect. Together these three relational dimensions form the basis for coordinated collective action (Gittell, 2006).

To summarize, the theory of relational coordination is unique in identifying multiple dimensions of relationships that are integral to the coordination of work, while focusing on the development of these relationships between roles rather than between unique individuals. In the following sections, we describe both the communication and the relationship dimensions of relational coordination, then describe the ways in which these dimensions mutually reinforce one another.

Communication Dimensions of Relational Coordination

Frequent Communication

Organization design and group theorists have explored the characteristics of communication for coordinating work (Ancona & Caldwell, 1992; Argote, 1982; Katz & Tushman, 1979; Tushman & Nadler, 1978; Van de Ven et al., 1976). The frequency of communication between participants is often placed in a central role. But the role of frequent communication is not merely informational. Frequent communication helps to build relationships through the familiarity that grows from repeated interaction. Indeed, in social network analysis, strong ties are defined primarily and sometimes solely in terms of frequency (Granovetter, 1973). By contrast, some argue that high-quality connections can exist independent of the frequency of communication (Dutton, 2003). While recognizing the importance of sufficiently frequent communication for coordinating highly interdependent work, relational coordination encompasses far more than the frequency of communication.

Timely Communication

Communication can be frequent and still be of poor quality. For one thing, it can lack timeliness. In coordinating highly interdependent work, timing can be critical. Delayed communication may result in errors or delays, with negative implications for organizational outcomes. Though timely communication has not been widely recognized as essential to the coordination of highly interdependent work, research by Wanda Orlikowski and Joann Yates, as well as research by Mary Waller, supports the importance of timely communication for successful task performance (Orlikowski & Yates, 1994; Waller, 1999).

Accurate Communication

The effective coordination of work depends not only on frequent and timely communication, but also on accurate communication. If updates are received frequently and in a timely way but the information is inaccurate, either an error will occur, or instead a delay will occur as participants halt the process to seek more accurate information. Consistent with this reasoning, O'Reilly and Roberts showed that accurate communication plays a critical role in task group effectiveness (O'Reilly & Roberts, 1977). The accuracy of communication can also have implications for trustworthiness and therefore affect the likelihood of knowledge seeking, as suggested by Levin and Cross (Levin & Cross, 2004).

Problem-Solving Communication

Task interdependencies often result in problems that require joint problem-solving (Gladstein, 1984; Heckscher & Donnellon, 1994; Pondy, 1967). Hence, effective coordination requires that participants engage in problem-solving communication. But the more common response to interdependence is conflict as well as blaming and the avoidance of blame. As W. Edwards Deming predicted in his work on Total Quality Management, the resort to blaming rather than problem-solving reduces opportunities to solve problems, with negative consequences for performance (Deming, 2000). Stevenson and Gilly have explored more deeply the role that problem-solving communication plays in the coordination of highly interdependent work (Stevenson & Gilly, 1993).

Relationship Dimensions of Relational Coordination

Communication does not occur in a vacuum. Participants' ability to effectively coordinate their work is influenced by the quality of their relationships, particularly the strength of shared goals, shared knowledge, and mutual respect.

Shared Goals

Effective coordination depends upon participants having a high level of shared goals for the work process in which they are engaged. With a set of shared goals for the work process, participants have a powerful bond and can more easily come to compatible conclusions about how to respond as new information becomes available. However, shared goals are often lacking among participants who work in different functional areas. In their classic work on organizations, James March and Herbert Simon described the negative outcomes that occur when participants pursue their own subgoals without reference to the superordinate goals of the work process in which they are engaged (March & Simon, 1958). This subgoal optimization is a fundamental flaw of the bureaucratic organizational form, and it is challenging to overcome. Theorists such as Richard Saavedra and colleagues, and Ruth Wageman, have identified shared goals as playing an important role in the coordination of highly interdependent work (Saavedra, Earley, & Van Dyne, 1993; Wageman, 1995).

Shared Knowledge

Furthermore, effective coordination depends upon participants having a high degree of shared knowledge regarding each other's tasks. When participants know how their tasks fit together with the tasks of others in the same work process, they have a context for knowing who will be impacted by any given change and therefore for knowing who needs to know what, and with what urgency. But shared knowledge is often lacking. Consistent with sociological theories, Deborah Dougherty showed that participants from different functional backgrounds often reside in different "thought worlds" due to differences in their training, socialization, and expertise (Dougherty, 1992). She showed that these thought worlds create obstacles to effective communication and therefore undermine the effective coordination of work. Karl Weick's "sense-making" theory as tested by Weick and Karlene Roberts and by Kevin Crowston and Eve Kammerer suggests that collective mind, or shared understanding of the work process by those who are participants in it, can connect participants from these distinct thought worlds and thereby enhance coordination (Crowston & Kammerer, 1998; Weick & Roberts, 1993).

Mutual Respect

Finally, effective coordination depends upon participants having respect for other participants in the same work process. Disrespect is one of the potential sources of division among those who play different roles in a given work process. Occupational identity serves as a source of pride, as well as a source of invidious comparison. Members of distinct occupational communities often have different status and may bolster their own status by actively cultivating disrespect for the work performed by others, as illustrated by John Van Maanen and Steve Barley (Van Maanen & Barley, 1984). When members of these distinct occupational communities are engaged in a common work process, the potential for these divisive relationships to undermine coordination is apparent. By contrast, respect for the competence of others creates a powerful bond and is integral to the effective coordination of highly interdependent work (Eisenberg, 1990).

Mutually Reinforcing Cycles of Communicating and Relating

To summarize, relational coordination theory states that the coordination of work is most effectively carried out through frequent, high-quality communication and through high-quality relationships among participants. Furthermore, the theory argues that relationships of shared goals, shared knowledge, and mutual respect *support* frequent, high-quality communication and vice versa—and that these dimensions work together to enable participants to effectively coordinate their work. Scholars in the field of communication have found that relationships influence the frequency and quality of communication, and that the frequency and quality of communication in turn influence the quality of relationships. For example, communications scholar Theodore Newcomb argued that frequent, high-quality communication is rewarding for those who engage in it and thus develops the basis for trusting and respectful relations (Newcomb, 1956). Others have argued for the reverse causal path, namely that strong group member relations form the basis for effective communication (Frey, 1996). This mutual influence between communication and relationships is at the heart of relational coordination.

Shared goals motivate participants to move beyond subgoal optimization and to act with regard for the overall work process. Shared knowledge informs participants of how their own tasks and the tasks of others contribute to the overall work process, enabling them to act with regard for the overall work process. Respect for the work of others encourages participants to value the contributions of others and to consider the impact of their actions on others, further reinforcing the inclination to act with regard for the overall work process. This web of relationships reinforces and is reinforced by, the frequency, timeliness, accuracy, and problem-solving nature of communication, enabling participants to effectively coordinate the work processes in which they are engaged.

Low-quality relationships have the opposite effect, undermining communication and hindering participants' ability to effectively coordinate their work. For example, when participants do not respect or feel respected by others who are engaged in the same work process, they tend to avoid communication, and even eye contact, with each other. Participants who do not share a set of superordinate goals for the work process are more likely to engage in blaming rather than problem-solving with each other when problems occur. Finally, participants who are not connected to each other through shared knowledge of the work process are less able to engage in timely communication with each other—they do not understand what others are doing well enough to anticipate the urgency of communicating particular information to them.

See Exhibit 2.1 for the mutual reinforcement that is expected to occur between the communication and relationship dimensions of relational coordination, illustrating how this cycle can occur in either a positive or negative direction.

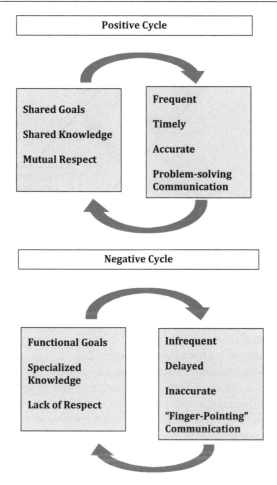

Exhibit 2.1 Mutually Reinforcing Cycles of Relational Coordination, Positive and Negative.

How Relational Coordination Drives Quality and Efficiency Outcomes

So how does relational coordination drive quality and efficiency outcomes? Any production process can be understood in terms of a production possibilities frontier, representing the optimal outcomes that can be achieved at different levels of quality and efficiency. On a given production possibilities frontier, quality and efficiency are in opposition to each other, such that one must be "traded off" in order to improve the other (Lapré & Scudder, 2009; Pagell, Klassen, Johnston, Shevchenko, & Sharma, 2015; Schmenner &

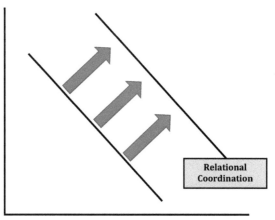

Exhibit 2.2 Impact of Relational Coordination on Production Possibilities Frontier

Swink, 1998). By increasing inputs per output, the quality of the outputs can be improved, but at the expense of efficiency. Conversely, by decreasing inputs per output, efficiency can be improved, but often at the expense of quality. This tradeoff is illustrated in Exhibit 2.2.

The production possibilities frontier can be shifted out to a more favorable position with the introduction of a fundamental process improvement. Total quality management and continuous quality improvement have both focused on achieving fundamental process improvements that enable the simultaneous achievement of both higher quality and greater efficiency, as outlined by James Womack, Daniel Jones, and Daniel Roos in their analysis of the auto industry and its transformation by Toyota (Womack, Jones, & Roos, 1991). The underlying argument, which Juran and Godfrey labeled the "cost of quality," or more accurately, the cost of poor quality, is that work processes that generate poor quality also tend to be inefficient, and that the same process improvements that lead to better quality outcomes often waste fewer resources as well (Juran & Godfrey, 2000).

Relational coordination is an example of a fundamental process improvement that enables participants to shift out their production possibilities frontier to a more favorable position by minimizing tradeoffs, for example achieving higher levels of quality while simultaneously achieving greater efficiencies, or achieving higher levels of safety while simultaneously achieving greater operational effectiveness (Caldwell, Roehrich, & George, 2017; Pagell et al., 2015). In sum, relational coordination enables employees to more effectively coordinate their work with each other, thus pushing out the production possibilities frontier to achieve higher quality outcomes while using resources more efficiently—for example, enabling hospital workers to achieve higher patient-perceived quality of care along with shorter patient lengths of stay. Relational coordination is therefore particularly relevant in industries that must maintain or improve quality outcomes while responding to cost pressures. In an increasingly competitive economy, nearly all industries are likely to face these paradoxical challenges.

How Relational Coordination Supports Client Engagement

At the same time, relational coordination is expected to increase client engagement, an increasingly important outcome for organizations due to the benefits of engaging clients as co-producers rather than passive recipients of outcomes (Aristidou & Barrett, 2018; Gittell & Douglass, 2012). By increasing the accuracy and consistency of the information clients receive, relational coordination among providers increases client trust and confidence, thus increasing both their willingness and their ability to engage with service providers (Weinberg, Lusenhop, Gittell, & Kautz, 2007). Finally, relational coordination is theorized to produce positive outcomes for the workers who engage in it and who experience it from others (Gittell, Weinberg, Pfefferle, & Bishop, 2008).

How Relational Coordination Drives Worker Well-Being

We know that having the necessary resources to accomplish one's work is an important source of well-being for workers (Hallowell, Schlesinger, & Zornitsky, 1996). Relational coordination is a form of organizational social capital, an asset that makes it easier to access resources needed to accomplish one's work (Adler & Kwon, 2002; Baker, 2000; Nahapiet & Ghoshal, 1998). Because of this instrumental benefit of relational coordination, we expect that relational coordination will be positively associated with job satisfaction.

There is a second way in which relational coordination is expected to increase worker well-being. We know from organizational psychology that high-quality relationships are a source of well-being for people at work (Dutton, 2003; Dutton & Heaphy, 2003; Dutton & Ragins, 2007; Kahn, 1998; Roger & Birute, 2000; Williams & Dutton, 1999). Dutton and Heaphy define a high-quality connection as one that is life giving and a low-quality connection as one that is life depleting. High-quality connections take many forms, but they have in common a keen awareness of and attunement to the needs of the other, and thus are energizing to the individuals involved in them. The energizing nature of high-quality connections comes from the recognition and validation of one's self by others. These high-quality connections tend to create a positive cycle that is generative of other high-quality connections, just as low-quality connections tend to create a negative cycle that is generative of other low-quality connections. Based on these intrinsic benefits, we therefore expect that the positive relationships that underpin relational coordination (shared goals, shared knowledge, mutual respect) will lead to higher levels of job satisfaction.

There is a third way that relational coordination provides both instrumental and intrinsic benefits to workers. There is a large and growing literature on the importance of positive connections for achieving worker resilience under stressful conditions (Ong, Bergeman, Bisconti, & Wallace, 2006; Powley, 2009; Stephens, Heaphy, Carmeli, Spreitzer, & Dutton, 2013; Sutcliffe & Vogus, 2003). The positive connections in relational coordination are expected to serve as a source of resilience by providing social support that increases workers' ability to cope with stress, thus reducing burnout (Gittell, 2008). At the same time, resilience provides instrumental benefits by enabling workers to maintain positive adjustment under highly disruptive conditions (Gittell, Cameron, Lim & Rivas, 2006).

How Relational Coordination Drives Learning and Innovation

Finally, relational coordination is theorized to support learning and innovation, thus providing organizations with adaptive capacity in addition to operational capacity (Noël, Lanham, Palmer, Leykum, & Parchman, 2013). Many innovations cut across organizational boundaries such that when participants become aware of what other parts of the organization do and understand the interdependencies between these parts, they can more easily see opportunities for innovation (Carlile, 2004; Dougherty, 1992). When participants are engaged in timely, problem-solving communication with their colleagues across organizational boundaries, they can more easily implement the opportunities they identify. Moreover, the high-quality relationships found in relational coordination are expected to boost psychological safety among participants (Carmeli & Gittell, 2009) thus reducing identity threat and loss of face when learning new skills or new role relationships, further increasing the potential for learning and innovation (Edmondson, 2004).

When Relational Coordination Matters Most—Contingency Effects

Relational coordination is expected to be particularly important for achieving high performance under high levels of task interdependence, uncertainty, and time constraints.

Task Interdependence

Given that coordination is the management of task interdependence, as argued by coordination scholars Malone and Crowston, coordination is only needed for work processes that are characterized by task interdependence (Malone & Crowston, 1994). But there are different types of task interdependence. According to James Thompson's classic typology, task interdependence can be pooled, sequential, or reciprocal (Thompson, 1967). Pooled interdependence exists between tasks that are dependent on a common pool of resources, or between tasks that produce intermediate outputs that must then be "pooled together" to achieve the desired output. Sequential interdependence exists between any two tasks where one depends on completion of the previous one in order to be completed. Reciprocal interdependence exists between any two tasks where each depends on completion of the other in order to be completed. Reciprocal interdependence is considered to be the most challenging of these three forms, from a coordination standpoint. According to Thompson's theory, reciprocal interdependence is the only type of interdependence that requires "mutual adjustment" in order to be effectively managed. See Exhibit 2.3 for an illustration of all three types of task interdependence.

Relational coordination is a form of coordination that enables workers to "mutually adjust" in the sense intended by Thompson, enabling them to coordinate their work "on the fly." Relational coordination is therefore expected to have a greater impact on the performance of work processes that have reciprocal task interdependencies, relative to those that have only pooled or sequential task interdependencies.

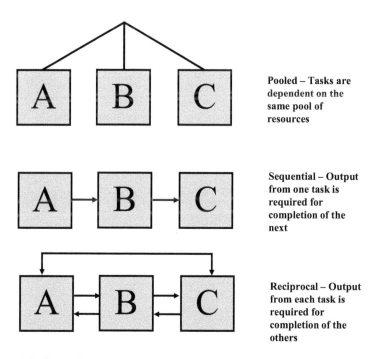

Pooled – Tasks are dependent on the same pool of resources

Sequential – Output from one task is required for completion of the next

Reciprocal – Output from each task required for completion of the others

Exhibit 2.3 Three Types of Task Interdependence

Uncertainty

According to information processing theories developed by scholars such as Jay Galbraith, Andrew Van de Ven et al. and Linda Argote, any form of uncertainty increases information-processing requirements, which increases the need for information-processing capacity (Argote, 1982; Galbraith, 1974; Ven et al., 1976). Coordinating mechanisms have differing levels of information-processing capacity. Programmed mechanisms such as protocols, routines, and information systems have lower levels of information processing capacity and thus are expected to be less useful under conditions of uncertainty. Nonprogrammed or feedback mechanisms have higher levels of information-processing capacity and thus are expected to be more useful under conditions of uncertainty. The communication and relationship ties that comprise relational coordination generate a high level of information-processing capability through relationship and communication connections among workers. Relational coordination is therefore expected to have a greater impact on the performance of work processes that are characterized by high levels of uncertainty, than for those characterized by low levels of uncertainty.

Time Constraints

Time constraints exacerbate the effects of both task interdependence and uncertainty, leaving little slack in the system and placing a premium on responsiveness as illustrated by Paul Adler in the automobile industry. Relational coordination is therefore expected to have a greater impact on the performance of work processes that are characterized by high levels of time constraints, relative to those with few time constraints (Adler, 1995).

Investments in relational coordination should therefore yield greater returns, the greater the levels of task interdependence, uncertainty, and time constraints in the target work process. Relational coordination may still improve performance of work processes with lower levels of task interdependence, uncertainty, or time constraints. But other things equal, the performance effects will be smaller.

Expanding Relational Coordination to Include More of the Relevant Stakeholders

Relational coordination theory has expanded more recently to reflect a broader understanding of who is involved in relational coordination networks, well beyond the core workers who were originally considered.

Coordinating with "Invisible Workers"

Like organizational theory more broadly, relational coordination theory sometimes has a blind spot towards workers who play supporting roles in the work process in a way that is invisible to top managers and even to supervisors and fellow workers. Bolinger, Klotz, and Leavitt have recently expanded relational coordination theory to address this challenge. They have drawn upon social identity theory to understand the role of "non-core" workers, their motivations to play these supporting roles, and the importance of ensuring relational coordination between core and noncore workers by making the work of the latter visible to the former (Bolinger et al., 2018).

Coordinating with Your Customers

Relational coordination theory was originally focused on achieving outcomes for customers, failing to recognize the value of coordinating directly with those customers and their families. Gittell and Douglass expanded relational coordination theory in a crucial way to consider the role of customers themselves in the process of coordination, arguing that the same dynamics of relational coordination could be extended to include customers in a process of *relational co-production* (Gittell & Douglass, 2012). Given the critical role that customers play in achieving many organizations' desired performance outcomes, we recommend continued theory development in this area. In our review of the evidence in Chapter 3, we will see that about 14 percent of findings thus far involve relational co-production with customers, with many research contributions from Jane Murray Cramm and Anna Nieboer in the context of chronic care and community-based care.

Coordinating with Others in Your Supply Network or Ecosystem

Others have explored relational coordination with supply partners, starting with Gittell and Weiss on patient care networks within and between organizations, and followed by Medlin and colleagues' work on cross-organizational supply networks in the software industry (Gittell & Weiss, 2004; Medlin, Aurifeille, & Quester, 2005). Caldwell, Roehrich, and George have built on this theory by exploring the role of relational coordination in social value creation by multiple firms engaged in cooperative efforts (Caldwell et al., 2017). Park and colleagues explored what happens when these multi-firm cooperative efforts fail, drawing upon the shared goals, problem-solving communication, and shared accountability elements of relational coordination (Park, Park, & Ramanujam, 2018). These authors are in effect innovating theories of the firm by combining relational coordination theory with strategic management and economic theories. In our review of the evidence in Chapter 3, we will see that around 36 percent of findings thus far involve relational coordination between organizations.

How Organizational Structures Support Relational Coordination—or Not

The achievement of relational coordination is not guaranteed, however. Rather its strength is expected to depend on the adoption of organizational structures that support and sustain it over time. Follett observed that coordination between departments often depends on personal connections, and that it is far more reliable when opportunities for coordination are built into organizational structures. And in the context of flight departures (Gittell, 1995), we found that:

> Lean resources in the form of less ground time and leaner staffing could inspire teamwork across roles to "get the job done," or the added stress could simply engender unproductive conflict and a deterioration of service. Other research suggests that Southwest [Airlines] has developed a set of organizational practices that build cohesion and common goals across groups, allowing the stress to be used in a productive way.

What do these organizational structures look like? Traditionally designed human resource practices tend to divide workers who carry out different functions, and therefore fail to support the development of relational coordination (Evans & Davis, 2005). Human resource practices like selection, training, accountability, and rewards can be designed instead to increase attention to the whole and help stakeholders to manage their interdependence, thus building relational coordination and producing improved outcomes (Gittell et al., 2010). Coordinating mechanisms, both programmed (e.g. shared information systems and shared protocols) and nonprogrammed (e.g. boundary spanners and shared meetings), are also expected to strengthen relational coordination and outcomes to the extent that they are designed to connect across all stakeholders whose work is in need of coordination, helping stakeholders to more easily see the whole and thus better manage their interdependence (Argote, 1982; Faraj & Xiao, 2006; Gittell, 2002).

These organizational structures can also be *combined* to form high-performance work systems in which each practice helps to reinforce a collaborative culture, over and above what one organizational structure can accomplish on its own (Gittell et al., 2010). In contrast to high-performance work systems that foster the development of individual knowledge and skills, or individual motivation and commitment, this type of high-performance work system fosters the development of connections among workers within and between organizations. The effects of these high-performance work systems on outcomes occur *through* their effects on relational coordination, as illustrated in Exhibit 2.4, and they have been explored systematically in the airline industry (Gittell, 2005), the healthcare industry

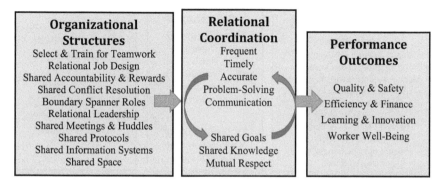

Exhibit 2.4 A High-Performance Work System that Supports Relational Coordination

(Gittell et al., 2010; McDermott, Conway, Cafferkey, Bosak, & Flood, 2017), and the banking industry (Siddique, Procter, & Gittell, 2019).

By offering a model that links organizational structures and relational networks to a wide range of desired performance outcomes, relational coordination provides a solid theoretical foundation for relational analytics.

The Relational Model of Organizational Change

When relational coordination is too weak for achieving desired performance outcomes, how can change agents intervene? To answer this question, relational coordination has evolved from a theory of performance into a theory of change, in partnership with Professor Amy Edmondson and Professor Ed Schein, with organizational leaders and change agents, and informed by other relational theories of change (Bartunek, 1984; Feldman & Rafaeli, 2002; Fletcher, Bailyn, & Beard, 2009; Kellogg, 2009). The result has been a more dynamic, iterative model called the Relational Model of Organizational Change shown in Exhibit 2.5. According to this model, two kinds of interventions can be used to jumpstart relational coordination, in addition to the structural interventions described above (Gittell, 2016; Gittell, Godfrey, & Thistlethwaite, 2012). *Relational interventions* are coaching and feedback strategies designed to start new conversations, thus shifting the culture toward higher relational coordination and enabling the implementation of new structures that further support the process. *Work process interventions* such as lean and plan-do-study-act cycles are also expected to strengthen relational coordination by providing participatory methods to identify the current state, envision a future state, and work systematically toward closing the gap.

Other authors have built further on the Relational Model of Organizational Change to make it useful for organizational leaders and change agents,

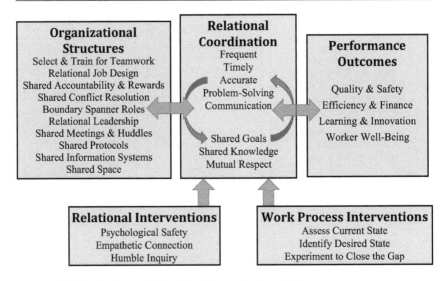

Exhibit 2.5 The Relational Model of Organizational Change

exploring how change occurs successfully and unsuccessfully when relationships are central to performance (Claggett & Karahanna, 2018; Gebo & Bond, 2020; Thomas, Sugiyama, Rochford, Stephens, & Kanov, 2018). We will review early evidence for this model of change in Chapter 3, then return to it in Chapter 10 when we describe how relational analytics can support your efforts to create positive change.

Summing Up

Relational coordination theory has several key attributes that provide a solid foundation for relational analytics. First, the theory understands coordination as occurring through a network of communication and relationship ties between roles. Second, the theory proposes specific dimensions of communicating and relating that matter for effective coordination. Third, relational coordination theory offers analytical tools to actually measure coordination as a network of ties. Fourth, the theory predicts that relational coordination drives a wide array of desired outcomes for multiple stakeholders and predicts that this influence will be strongest when work is highly interdependent, uncertain, and time constrained. Fifth, the theory explains how organizational structures can be designed to support relational coordination, and how other types of interventions—relational interventions and work process interventions—can be used to jumpstart the process of creating positive change. Finally, the theory has already been widely tested through empirical research. In the next chapter, we will assess the evidence thus far based on a systematic review of the empirical research.

References

Adler, P. S. (1995). Interdepartmental interdependence and coordination: The case of the design/manufacturing interface. *Organization Science*, 6(2), 147–167. doi:10.1287/orsc.6.2.147

Adler, P. S., & Heckscher, C. C. (2005). *The Firm as a Collaborative Community: Reconstructing Trust in the Knowledge Economy*. Oxford: Oxford University Press.

Adler, P. S., & Kwon, S.-W. (2002). Social capital: Prospects for a new concept. *Academy of Management Review*, 27(1), 17–40. doi:10.5465/amr.2002.5922314

Ancona, D. G., & Caldwell, D. F. (1992). Bridging the boundary: External activity and performance in organizational teams. *Administrative Science Quarterly*, 37(4), 634–665. doi:10.2307/2393475

Argote, L. (1982). Input uncertainty and organizational coordination in hospital emergency units. *Administrative Science Quarterly*, 27(3), 420–434. doi:10.2307/2392320

Aristidou, A., & Barrett, M. (2018). Coordinating service provision in dynamic service settings: A position-practice relations perspective. *Academy of Management Journal*, 61(2), 685–714. doi:10.5465/amj.2015.0310

Baker, W. E. (2000). *Achieving Success Through Social Capital: Tapping the Hidden Resources in Your Personal and Business Networks*. New York, NY: John Wiley & Sons.

Bartunek, J. M. (1984). Changing interpretive schemes and organizational restructuring: The example of a religious order. *Administrative Science Quarterly*, 29(3), 355. doi:10.2307/2393029

Bechky, B. A. (2006). Gaffers, gofers, and grips: Role-based coordination in temporary organizations. *Organization Science*, 17(1), 3–21. doi:10.1287/orsc.1050.0149

Bolinger, A. R., Klotz, A. C., & Leavitt, K. (2018). Contributing from inside the outer circle: The identity-based effects of noncore role incumbents on relational coordination and organizational climate. *Academy of Management Review*, 43(4), 680–703. doi:10.5465/amr.2016.0333

Caldwell, N. D., Roehrich, J. K., & George, G. (2017). Social value creation and relational coordination in public-private collaborations. *Journal of Management Studies*, 54(6), 906–928. doi:10.1111/joms.12268

Carlile, P. R. (2004). Transferring, translating, and transforming: An integrative framework for managing knowledge across boundaries. *Organization Science*, 15(5), 555–568. doi:10.1287/orsc.1040.0094

Carmeli, A., & Gittell, J. H. (2009). High-quality relationships, psychological safety, and learning from failures in work organizations. *Journal of Organizational Behavior*, 30(6), 709–729. doi:10.1002/job.565

Claggett, J. L., & Karahanna, E. (2018). Unpacking the structure of coordination mechanisms and the role of relational coordination in an era of digitally mediated work processes. *Academy of Management Review*, 43(4), 704–722. doi:10.5465/amr.2016.0325

Deming, W. E. (2000). *Out of the Crisis*. Cambridge, Mass.: MIT Press.

Dougherty, D. (1992). Interpretive barriers to successful product innovation in large firms. *Organization Science*, 3(2), 179–202. doi:10.1287/orsc.3.2.179

Dutton, J. E. (2003). *Energize Your Workplace: How to Create and Sustain High-Quality Connections at Work*. San Francisco, CA: Jossey-Bass.

Dutton, J. E., & Heaphy, E. D. (2003). Coming to life: The power of high quality connections at work. In K. S. Cameron, J. E. Dutton, & R. E. Quinn (Eds.), *Positive Organizational Scholarship: Foundations of a New Discipline*. San Francisco, CA: Berrett-Koehler.

Dutton, J. E., & Ragins, B. R. (2007). *Exploring Positive Relationships at Work: Building a Theoretical and Research Foundation)*. Mahwah, NJ; London: Lawrence Erlbaum Associates.

Edmondson, A. C. (2004). Learning from mistakes is easier said than done. *The Journal of Applied Behavioral Science*, 40(1), 66–90. doi:10.1177/00218863 04263849

Eisenberg, E. M. (1990). Jamming: Transcendence through organizing. *Communication Research*, 17(2), 139–164. doi:10.1177/009365090017002001

Evans, W. R., & Davis, W. D. (2005). High-performance work systems and organizational performance: The mediating role of internal social structure. *Journal of Management*, 31(5), 758–775. doi:10.1177/0149206305279370

Faraj, S., & Sproull, L. (2000). Coordinating expertise in software development teams. *Management Science*, 46(12), 1554–1568. doi:10.1287/mnsc.46.12.1554.12072

Faraj, S., & Xiao, Y. (2006). Coordination in fast-response organizations. *Management Science*, 52(8), 1155–1169. doi:10.1287/mnsc.1060.0526

Feldman, M. S., & Rafaeli, A. (2002). Organizational routines as sources of connections and understandings. *Journal of Management Studies*, 39(3), 309–331. doi:10.1111/1467-6486.00294

Fletcher, J. K., Bailyn, L., & Beard, S. B. (2009). Practical pushing: Creating discursive space in organizational narratives. In *Critical Management Studies at Work*. Edward Elgar Publishing.

Follett, M. P. (1949). *Freedom & Co-ordination: Lectures in Business Organisation*. London: Management Publications Trust.

Frey, L. (1996). Remembering and "re-membering": A history of theory and research on communication and group decision making. In R. Y. Hirokawa & M. S. Poole (Eds.), *Communication and Group Decision Making*. Thousand Oaks, CA; London: Sage Publications.

Galbraith, J. R. (1974). Organization design: An information processing view. *Interfaces*, 4(3), 28–36. doi:10.1287/inte.4.3.28

Gebo, E., & Bond, B. J. (2020). Improving interorganizational collaborations: An application in a violence reduction context. *The Social Science Journal*, 1–12. doi:10.1016/j.soscij.2019.09.008

Gittell, J. (1995). Cost/quality trade-offs in the departure process? Evidence from the major U.S. airlines. *Transportation Research Record*, 1480: 25–36.

Gittell, J. H. (2002a). Coordinating mechanisms in care provider groups: Relational coordination as a mediator and input uncertainty as a moderator of performance effects. *Management Science*, 48(11), 1408–1426. doi:10.1287/mnsc.48.11.1408.268

Gittell, J. H. (2002b). Relationships between service providers and their impact on customers. *Journal of Service Research*, 4(4), 299–311. doi:10.1177/10946705 02004004007

Gittell, J. H. (2005). *The Southwest Airlines Way: Using the Power of Relationships to Achieve High Performance*. New York: McGraw-Hill.

Gittell, J. H. (2006). Relational coordination: Coordinating work through relationships of shared goals, shared knowledge and mutual respect. In O. Kyriakidou & M. Özbilgin (Eds.), *Relational Perspectives in Organizational Studies: A Research Companion*. Cheltenham, UK; Northampton, MA: Edward Elgar Publishing.

Gittell, J. H. (2008). Relationships and resilience: Care provider responses to pressures from managed care. *The Journal of Applied Behavioral Science*, 44(1), 25–47. doi:10.1177/0021886307311469

Gittell, J. H. (2016). *Transforming Relationships for High Performance: The Power of Relational Coordination*. Palo Alto, CA: Stanford University Press.

Gittell, J. H., Cameron, K., Lim, S., & Rivas, V. (2006). Relationships, layoffs, and organizational resilience: Airline industry responses to September 11. *The Journal of Applied Behavioral Science*, 42(3), 300–329.

Gittell, J. H., & Douglass, A. (2012). Relational bureaucracy: Structuring reciprocal relationships into roles. *Academy of Management Review*, 37(4), 709–733. doi:10.5465/amr.2010.0438

Gittell, J. H., Godfrey, M., & Thistlethwaite, J. (2012). Interprofessional collaborative practice and relational coordination: Improving healthcare through relationships. *Journal of Interprofessional Care*, 27(3), 210–213. doi:10.3109/13561820.2012.730564

Gittell, J. H., Seidner, R., & Wimbush, J. (2010). A relational model of how high-performance work systems work. *Organization Science*, 21(2), 490–506. doi:10.1287/orsc.1090.0446

Gittell, J. H., Weinberg, D., Pfefferle, S., & Bishop, C. (2008). Impact of relational coordination on job satisfaction and quality outcomes: A study of nursing homes. *Human Resource Management Journal*, 18(2), 154–170. doi:10.1111/j.1748-8583.2007.00063.x

Gittell, J. H., & Weiss, L. (2004). Coordination networks within and across organizations: A multi-level framework. *Journal of Management Studies*, 41(1), 127–153. doi:10.1111/j.1467-6486.2004.00424.x

Gladstein, D. L. (1984). Groups in context: A model of task group effectiveness. *Administrative Science Quarterly*, 29(4), 499. doi:10.2307/2392936

Granovetter, M. S. (1973). The strength of weak ties. *The American Journal of Sociology*, 78(6), 1360–1380. doi:10.1086/225469

Hallowell, R., Schlesinger, L. A., & Zornitsky, J. (1996). Internal service quality, customer and job satisfaction: Linkages and implications for management. *Human Resource Planning*, 19(2), 20.

Havens, D. S., Vasey, J., Gittell, J. H., & Lin, W.-T. (2010). Relational coordination among nurses and other providers: Impact on the quality of patient care. *Journal of Nursing Management*, 18(8), 926–937. doi:10.1111/j.1365-2834.2010.01138.x

Heckscher, C. C., & Donnellon, A. (1994). *The Post-bureaucratic Organization: New Perspectives on Organizational Change*. Thousand Oaks, CA: Sage Publications.

Juran, J. M., & Godfrey, A. B. (2000). *Juran's Quality Handbook*. New York: McGraw Hill.

Kahn, W. (1998). Relational systems at work. In B. M. Staw & L. L. Cummings (Eds.), *Research in Organizational Behavior: An Annual Series of Analytical Essays and Critical Reviews*, Vol. 20 (pp. 39–76). Greenwich, CT; London: JAI Press.

Katz, R., & Tushman, M. (1979). Communication patterns, project performance, and task characteristics: An empirical evaluation and integration in an R &D setting. *Organizational Behavior and Human Performance*, 23(2), 139–162. doi:10.1016/0030-5073(79)90053-9

Kellogg, K. C. (2009). Operating room: Relational spaces and microinstitutional change in surgery. *American Journal of Sociology*, 115(3), 657–711. doi:10.1086/603535

Kogut, B., & Zander, U. (1996). What firms do? Coordination, identity, and learning. *Organization Science*, 7(5), 502–518. doi:10.1287/orsc.7.5.502

Lapré, M. A., & Scudder, G. D. (2009). Performance improvement paths in the U.S. airline industry: Linking trade-offs to asset frontiers. *Production and Operations Management*, 13(2), 123–134. doi:10.1111/j.1937-5956.2004.tb00149.x

Levin, D. Z., & Cross, R. (2004). The strength of weak ties you can trust: The mediating role of trust in effective knowledge transfer. *Management Science*, 50(11), 1477–1490. doi:10.1287/mnsc.1030.0136

Liang, D. W., Moreland, R., & Argote, L. (1995). Group versus individual training and group performance: The mediating role of transactive memory. *Personality and Social Psychology Bulletin*, 21(4), 384–393. doi:10.1177/0146167295214009

Malone, T. W., & Crowston, K. (1994). The interdisciplinary study of coordination. *ACM Computing Surveys*, 26(1), 87–119. doi:10.1145/174666.174668

March, J. G., & Simon, H. A. (1958). *Organizations*. New York; London: Wiley; Chapman & Hall.

McDermott, A. M., Conway, E., Cafferkey, K., Bosak, J., & Flood, P. C. (2017). Performance management in context: Formative cross-functional performance monitoring for improvement and the mediating role of relational coordination in hospitals. *The International Journal of Human Resource Management*, 30(3), 436–456. doi:10.1080/09585192.2017.1278714

Medlin, C. J., Aurifeille, J.-M., & Quester, P. G. (2005). A collaborative interest model of relational coordination and empirical results. *Journal of Business Research*, 58(2), 214–222. doi:10.1016/s0148-2963(02)00496-4

Nahapiet, J., & Ghoshal, S. (1998). Social capital, intellectual capital, and the organizational advantage. *Academy of Management Review*, 23(2), 242–266. doi:10.5465/amr.1998.533225

Newcomb, T. M. (1956). The prediction of interpersonal attraction. *American Psychologist*, 11(11), 575–586. doi:10.1037/h0046141

Noël, P. H., Lanham, H. J., Palmer, R. F., Leykum, L. K., & Parchman, M. L. (2013). The importance of relational coordination and reciprocal learning for chronic illness care within primary care teams. *Health Care Management Review*, 38(1), 20–28. doi:10.1097/HMR.0b013e3182497262

O'Reilly, C. A., & Roberts, K. H. (1977). Task group structure, communication, and effectiveness in three organizations. *Journal of Applied Psychology*, 62(6), 674–681. doi:10.1037/0021-9010.62.6.674

Ong, A. D., Bergeman, C. S., Bisconti, T. L., & Wallace, K. A. (2006). Psychological resilience, positive emotions, and successful adaptation to stress in later life. *Journal of Personality and Social Psychology*, 91(4), 730–749. doi:10.1037/0022-3514.91.4.730

Orlikowski, W. J., & Yates, J. (1994). Genre repertoire: The structuring of communicative practices in organizations. *Administrative Science Quarterly*, 39(4), 541. doi:10.2307/2393771

Pagell, M., Klassen, R., Johnston, D., Shevchenko, A., & Sharma, S. (2015). Are safety and operational effectiveness contradictory requirements: The roles of routines and relational coordination. *Journal of Operations Management*, 36(1), 1–14. doi:10.1016/j.jom.2015.02.002

Park, B. S., Park, H., & Ramanujam, R. (2018). Tua culpa: When an organization blames its partner for failure in a shared task. *Academy of Management Review*, 43(4), 792–811. doi:10.5465/amr.2016.0305

Pondy, L. R. (1967). Organizational conflict: Concepts and models. *Administrative Science Quarterly*, 12(2), 296–320. doi:10.2307/2391553

Powley, E. H. (2009). Reclaiming resilience and safety: Resilience activation in the critical period of crisis. *Human Relations*, 62(9), 1289–1326. doi:10.1177/001 8726709334881

Roger, L., & Birute, R. (2000). The soul at work: Human capital with a human face. *Rural Telecommunications*, 19(5), 44.

Saavedra, R., Earley, P. C., & Van Dyne, L. (1993). Complex interdependence in task-performing groups. *Journal of Applied Psychology*, 78(1), 61–72. doi:10.1037/0021-9010.78.1.61

Schmenner, R. W., & Swink, M. L. (1998). On theory in operations management. *Journal of Operations Management*, 17(1), 97–113. doi:10.1016/s0272-6963(98)00028-x

Siddique, M., Procter, S., & Gittell, J. H. (2019). The role of relational coordination in the relationship between high-performance work systems (HPWS) and organizational performance. *Journal of Organizational Effectiveness: People and Performance*, 6(4), 246–266. doi:10.1108/joepp-04-2018-0029

Stephens, J. P. (2020). How the show goes on: Using the aesthetic experience of collective performance to adapt while coordinating. *Administrative Science Quarterly*, 000183922091105. doi:10.1177/0001839220911056

Stephens, J. P., Heaphy, E. D., Carmeli, A., Spreitzer, G. M., & Dutton, J. E. (2013). Relationship quality and virtuousness: Emotional carrying capacity as a source of individual and team resilience. *The Journal of Applied Behavioral Science*, 49(1), 13–41. doi:10.1177/0021886312471193

Stevenson, W. B., & Gilly, M. C. (1993). Problem-solving networks in organizations: Intentional design and emergent structure. *Social Science Research*, 22(1), 92–113. doi:10.1006/ssre.1993.1005

Sutcliffe, K., & Vogus, T. (2003). Organizing for resilience. In K. S. Cameron, J. E. Dutton, & R. E. Quinn (Eds.), *Positive Organizational Scholarship: Foundations of a new discipline* (pp. 94–110). San Francisco, CA: Berrett-Koehler.

Thomas, N. K., Sugiyama, K., Rochford, K. C., Stephens, J. P., & Kanov, J. (2018). Experiential organizing: Pursuing relational and bureaucratic goals through symbolically and experientially oriented work. *Academy of Management Review*, 43(4), 749–771. doi:10.5465/amr.2016.0348

Thompson, J. D. (1967). *Organizations in Action: Social Science Bases of Administrative Theory*. New York: McGraw-Hill.

Tushman, M. L., & Nadler, D. A. (1978). Information processing as an integrating concept in organizational design. *Academy of Management Review*, 3(3), 613. doi:10.2307/257550

Van Maanen, J., & Barley, S. R. (1984). Occupational communities: Culture and control in organizations. *Research in Organizational Behaviour*, 6, 287–365.

Van de Ven, A. H., Delbecq, A. L., & Koenig, R. (1976). Determinants of coordination modes within organizations. *American Sociological Review*, 41(2), 322. doi:10.2307/2094477

Wageman, R. (1995). Interdependence and group effectiveness. *Administrative Science Quarterly*, 40(1), 145–180. doi:10.2307/2393703

Waller, M. J. (1999). The timing of adaptive group responses to nonroutine events. *Academy of Management Journal*, 42(2), 127–137. doi:10.5465/257088

Weick, K. E. (1993). The collapse of sensemaking in organizations: The Mann Gulch disaster. *Administrative Science Quarterly*, 38(4), 628–652. doi:10.2307/2393339

Weick, K. E., & Roberts, K. H. (1993). Collective mind in organizations: Heedful interrelating on flight decks. *Administrative Science Quarterly*, 38(3), 357–381. doi:10.2307/2393372

Weinberg, D. B., Lusenhop, R. W., Gittell, J. H., & Kautz, C. M. (2007). Coordination between formal providers and informal caregivers. *Health Care Management Review*, 32(2), 140–149. doi:10.1097/01.hmr.0000267790.24933.4c

Williams, M., & Dutton, J. E. (1999). Corrosive political climates: The heavy toll of negative political behavior in organizations. In R. E. Quinn, R. M. O'Neill, & L. St. Clair (Eds.), *Pressing Problems in Modern Organizations (That Keep Us Up at Night): Transforming Agendas for Research and Practice* (pp. 3–30). New York: Amacom.

Womack, J. P., Jones, D. T., & Roos, D. (1991). *The Machine That Changed the World: The Story of Lean Production*. New York: Harper Perennial.

Chapter 3

Evidence About the Outcomes and Predictors of Relational Coordination

Relational coordination theory has been tested in dozens of industries and dozens of countries around the world. In this chapter, we summarize the empirical evidence for the theory thus far, drawing extensively from a systematic review of the research conducted by Bolton, Logan, and Gittell (Bolton, Logan & Gittell, 2021).

Methods for This Systematic Review

To assess the empirical research supporting relational coordination theory to date and recommend a future research and practice agenda, we conducted a systematic review following Preferred Reporting Items for Systematic Reviews and Meta-Analyses (PRISMA) guidelines. The first step involved a search for peer-reviewed literature, published dissertations, and conference proceedings included in Google Scholar. We selected Google Scholar as our primary search engine due to the breadth of relational coordination literature across industries and contexts and a desire to capture the grey literature (for example dissertations and working papers), which would not be included in publication indexes alone. We searched for all items using the term relational coordination, appearing between January 1, 1991 and December 31, 2019, producing 3484 unique results. We chose January 1, 1991 as the starting point given that the term relational coordination was first found in the scholarly literature that year. In the second stage, we removed 81 duplicate citations. In the third stage, we systematically screened the abstracts of all remaining 3403 citations, eliminating 2487 works that did not meet our inclusion criteria (empirical, available in English, tested the relationship between relational coordination and its predictors or its outcomes). In the fourth stage, we reviewed the full texts of all 880 remaining studies, eliminating 647 any that did not meet our inclusion criteria or adequately operationalize relational coordination—either qualitatively or through a survey—or clearly describe their methodology. This process resulted in the identification of 233 empirical studies of sufficient rigor for inclusion in our review, the first of which was published in 2000, nine years after the term relational coordination first appeared in the scholarly literature. The review was carried out iteratively by Caroline Logan and Rendelle Bolton, facilitated by the Covidence systematic review online software. Inclusion and exclusion decisions at all steps were discussed to develop consensus between the two reviewers, with consultation by Jody Hoffer Gittell when a consensus decision could not be reached. A searchable database describing each individual finding included in the systematic review – as well as more recent findings - can be found at rcsurveyhelp.info.

The primary limitation of this systematic review, and all systematic reviews, is that null findings are less likely to be published than significant findings, due to the "file drawer effect." We have sought to reduce this bias created by the file drawer effect by broadening our review to include findings from dissertations and working papers, in addition to findings published in peer-reviewed journals.

Descriptive Data

Studies of relational coordination that qualified for inclusion in this review were carried out in 36 countries, located in North America, South America, Europe, Africa, Middle East, Asia, and South Pacific, and in 73 industry contexts within the commercial, education, healthcare, and human service sectors (see Exhibit 3.1).

In these studies, relational coordination was assessed in multiple ways. The majority of findings were based on the 7-item validated Relational Coordination Survey, while 21 percent were based on alternative survey measures of relational coordination including the original 6-item Relational Coordination Survey. In addition, 21 percent of findings were based on qualitative assessments of relational coordination. While relational coordination is typically measured across roles in the same organization, we found that 14 percent of findings were based on relational coordination with clients, and 36 percent were based on relational coordination between organizations. Many of these studies tested multiple hypotheses regarding the performance outcomes of relational coordination and/or the cross-cutting structures that support relational coordination, resulting in a total of 518 findings. Of these findings, 337 were reflected outcomes, and 181 involved predictors of relational coordination. All findings identified by the review are available in a searchable database at rcsurveyhelp.info and summarized in Exhibit 3.2.

Findings About the Outcomes of Relational Coordination

Findings regarding the outcomes of relational coordination were grouped into four categories based on the theory, including quality outcomes, efficiency outcomes, worker outcomes, and learning and innovation.

Exhibit 3.1 Industry and Country Contexts for Studies of Relational Coordination

Industry contexts (n = 73)		Country contexts (n = 36)
Commercial Sector	**Education Sector**	**North America**
• Accounting	• Early child education	• Canada
• Airlines	• E-learning	• United States
• Asset management	• Elementary education	**South America**
• Auditing	• Higher education	
• Banking	• Medical school	• Argentina
• Consulting	• Nursing school	• Ecuador
• Construction	• Primary education	
• Electronics	• Secondary education	**Europe**
• Engineering	• Translational research	• Austria
• Finance		• Belgium
• Fishing	**Healthcare Sector**	• Denmark
• Information	• Cardiology	• England
technology	• Care continuum	• France
• Machine suppliers	• Chronic care	• Germany
• Manufacturing	• Community based care	• Iceland
• Multinationals	• Diagnostics	• Ireland
• Pharmaceuticals	• Elder care	• Italy
• Pharmacy	• Emergency care	• Netherlands
• Private equity	• Gynecological care	• Norway
• Renewable energy	• Health systems	• Portugal
• Road infrastructure	• Hepatology	• Scotland
• Software	• Home care	• Spain
• Telecommunications	• Intensive care	• Sweden
• Venture investing	• Long term care	• Switzerland
	• Medical care	**Africa**
Human Services Sector	• Mental health care	
• Autism care	• Neonatal intensive care	• Egypt
• Child services	• Obstetric care	• Nigeria
• Community	• Oncology	• South Africa
collaboration	• Palliative care	**Middle East**
• Criminal justice	• Perioperative care	
• Disability care	• Primary care	• Israel
• Early child	• Psychiatric care	• Lebanon
intervention	• Public health	• Saudi Arabia
• Intellectual disability	• Rehabilitation care	**Asia**
care	• Specialty care	
• Social movements	• Surgical care	• China
• Sports	• Telehealth	• India
• Substance use	• Transplant care	• Japan
treatment	• Trauma care	• Malaysia
• Youth services	• Veterinary care	• Pakistan
		• Singapore
		• South Korea
		• Australia
		• New Zealand

Exhibit 3.2 Findings about Outcomes and Predictors of Relational
            Coordination

(1) Findings about Outcomes of Relational Coordination

Outcomes of relational coordination	Total findings about outcomes	Percent of findings consistent with the theory
Quality outcomes	222	80%
Efficiency outcomes	31	68%
Worker outcomes	63	87%
Learning and innovation outcomes	21	90%
Total findings about outcomes	**337**	**81%**

(2) Findings about Predictors of Relational Coordination

Predictors of relational coordination	Total findings about predictors	Percent of findings consistent with the theory
Structural interventions		
Relational job design	18	89%
Select and train for teamwork	18	72%
Shared accountability and rewards	22	95%
Shared conflict resolution	5	100%
Relational leadership roles	22	81%
Boundary spanner roles	14	71%
Shared meetings and huddles	25	92%
Shared space	9	89%
Shared protocols and routines	22	82%
Shared information systems	18	89%
Relational or work process interventions	10	80%
Total findings about predictors	**181**	**85%**

Quality Outcomes

In the airline industry, relational coordination across 12 care providers was associated with quality outcomes such as fewer passenger complaints, fewer late arrivals, and fewer baggage handling errors (Gittell, 2001). Subsequent studies in healthcare found relational coordination among interdisciplinary staff was positively associated with quality outcomes such as postoperative functional status, patient-reported quality of care and quality of life, family satisfaction with care, patient trust and confidence in their providers, and patient psychological well-being (Azar et al., 2017; Bae, Mark, & Fried, 2010; Cramm & Nieboer, 2012b, 2014, 2015; Gittell, et al, 2000; Gittell, 2002a; Gittell, 2008; Havens, Vasey, Gittell, & Lin, 2010; Noël, Lanham, Palmer, Leykum, & Parchman, 2013; Romanow, Rai, & Keil, 2018; Sakai, Naruse, & Nagata, 2015, 2016; Weinberg, Lusenhop, Gittell, & Kautz, 2007) as well as staff-reported quality of care (McDermott, Conway,

Cafferkey, Bosak, & Flood, 2017; McIntosh et al., 2014). These findings were further replicated in studies that were conducted in the pharmacy, professional services, higher education, and elder care industries (Alvarez, 2014; Drewery, Nevison, Pretti, & Pennaforte, 2016; Gittell, Weinberg, Pfefferle, & Bishop, 2008; Lenz, Sarens, & Hoos, 2017; Margalina, De-Pablos-Heredero, & Montes-Botella, 2015; Skakon, 2014).

Several studies assessed relational coordination between staff and their clients, including work that spanned across multiple organizations in the healthcare industry. For example, relational coordination between patients' family members and care providers across the continuum was positively associated with high-quality postsurgical outcomes (Weinberg et al., 2007). Similarly, relational coordination between workers and chronic care patients was associated with greater patient well-being and patient-perceived quality of care (Cramm & Nieboer, 2014, 2016). In sum, relational coordination predicted higher quality outcomes both within organizations (DeJesus, 2015; Havens et al., 2010; Noël et al., 2013) and between organizations (Hagigi, 2012). In the commercial sector, the lack of relational coordination between community stakeholders was associated with poor functioning of marine protected areas (Miles, Perea Muñoz, & Bayle-Sempere, 2020).

Relational coordination is also associated with client engagement. For example in healthcare, relational coordination between family members and care providers across the continuum of care was positively associated with family members' preparation for caregiving (Weinberg et al., 2007) and the implementation of shared decision making with patients (Tietbohl et al., 2015). Relational coordination between hospital employees and early intervention agencies was positively associated with family engagement, enrollment, and retention of drug-exposed infants in treatment (Derrington, 2012). In education, relational coordination among early childhood teaching staff was associated with greater parent engagement regarding their child's education (Douglass & Gittell, 2012), while relational coordination between care providers and families receiving services for children with autism was associated with lower parenting stress, greater parent ability to cope, and greater parent ability to care for their child (Warfield, Chiri, Leutz, & Timberlake, 2013).

Nearly 20 percent of findings regarding quality and safety outcomes have run counter to the theory. For example, in a multicity study of community-based efforts to reduce offender recidivism, relational coordination between agencies was associated with increased rather than reduced recidivism by criminal offenders (Bond & Gittell, 2010). Four studies of relational coordination among providers in outpatient healthcare settings reported null or negative findings regarding patient quality measures or patient satisfaction (Flieger, 2017; Hagigi, 2012; Lundstrøm et al., 2014; Shortell et al., 2017).

Efficiency Outcomes

In early studies conducted in the airline industry, relational coordination was associated with higher staff productivity and faster aircraft turnaround times (Gittell, 2001). In healthcare, relational coordination was associated with shorter risk-adjusted hospital length of stay for both medical and surgical patients, a measure of efficient resource utilization in the delivery of patient care (Gittell, et al, 2000; Gittell, et al, 2008). As expected, this association was strongest under conditions of greater uncertainty (Gittell, 2002b). Relational coordination was also associated with lower patient costs in healthcare in both inpatient (Gittell, et al, 2008; Hagigi, 2012) and outpatient settings (Hagigi, 2012), with improved cost outcomes in the pharmacy sector (Alvarez, 2014), with growth in deposits, advances and profitability in banking (Siddique, Procter, & Gittell, 2019), with market share gains in software (Medlin, Aurifeille, & Quester, 2005), with productivity, operational effectiveness, higher net profits and firm competitiveness in manufacturing (H. W. Lee & Kim, 2019).

About 32 percent of findings about efficiency outcomes have been mixed or have run counter to the theory. For example, two studies found relational coordination was associated with longer rather than shorter hospital lengths of stay (Brewer, 2006), one of them found this association only in the presence of higher nursing workloads (Lin, 2010). Hagigi found relational coordination was associated with higher rates of emergency department use for highly complex patients but lower rates of hospitalization for those same patients (Hagigi, 2012). A study of primary care practices found that relational coordination was associated with higher productivity as measured by face-to-face patient consultations per staff member, though not associated with consultations per physician, suggesting that relational coordination impacted team productivity but not individual productivity (Lundstrøm et al., 2014). Beyond healthcare, a study of accounting firms found that while relational coordination was not associated with employee productivity, it was positively associated with the relative market performance of firms (Fu, 2014). In footwear manufacturing, relational coordination between manufacturers, suppliers, and customers was associated with greater trust, commitment, and satisfaction but not with lower costs (Margalina, Benítez Gaibor, Martínez Mesias, & Zurita Mesa, 2018).

Worker Outcomes

In addition to quality and efficiency outcomes, relational coordination is expected to increase employee well-being and engagement. Findings thus far have been highly consistent with the theory. In healthcare relational coordination between nurses and their colleagues has been positively associated with job satisfaction, professional efficacy, motivation, identification with organizational values, and reduced burnout (Cramm,

Hoeijmakers, & Nieboer, 2013; Havens, Gittell, & Vasey, 2018; Havens, Warshawsky, & Vasey, 2013), while relational coordination between nurse managers and their colleagues has been positively associated with their work engagement and proactive work behaviors (Naruse, Yamamoto, Sugimoto, Fujisaki-Sakai, & Nagata, 2017; Warshawsky, Havens, & Knafl, 2012). Relational coordination across roles and between providers and patients has been positively associated with job involvement, satisfaction, use of one's competence on the job, confidence in collaboration, and social support (Albertsen, Wiegman, Limborg, Thörnfeldt, & Bjørner, 2014; Havens et al., 2018; Naruse, Sakai, & Nagata, 2014). In other studies, relational coordination among hospital employees was associated with an index of positive employee outcomes (McDermott et al., 2017), reduced turnover (Falatah & Conway, 2019), workplace spirituality (Faro Albuquerque, Campos Cunha, Dias Martins, & Brito Sá, 2014), and reduced conflicts and strikes (Ekwueme, 2018). Relational coordination was also associated with positive worker outcomes in sectors such as disability services (van der Meer, Nieboer, Finkenflügel, & Cramm, 2017) and higher education (Margalina et al., 2015). These findings have been replicated in settings as diverse as Europe, Africa, South Pacific, and Asia, suggesting that workers across cultural contexts have similar relational needs.

One reason for such consistent findings may be that relational coordination serves as a protective factor and as a source of resilience in the face of stress (Gittell, Weinberg et al., 2008). For example, in healthcare relational coordination reduced the adverse effects of time pressures on primary care clinic workers (McDonald, Rodriguez, & Shortell, 2018), and reduced the negative effects of time pressures on emotional exhaustion for nursing home workers (Cao & Naruse, 2018). Relational coordination may also support the specific behaviors and routines that have been found to promote a positive work environment (Cameron, Mora, Leutscher, & Calarco, 2011; Geue, 2018).

Learning and Innovation

Many innovations cut across organizational boundaries so that when participants become aware of what other parts of the organization do and understand the interdependence between these parts, they can more easily identify and implement opportunities for organizational change (Carlile, 2004; Deming, 2000). The first study of relational coordination and learning found that relationships of shared goals, shared knowledge and mutual respect were positively associated with the ability to learn from failures in software, electronics, and finance firms (Carmeli & Gittell, 2009). Relational coordination was positively associated with reciprocal learning in rural primary care clinics (Noël et al., 2013) and collaborative knowledge creation in the pharmacy sector (Alvarez, 2014). Relational coordination between employees offering different services (online vs. in person) was associated with successful service redesign in banking (Plé & Clegg, 2013). In addition, relational coordination was positively associated with the ability to innovate in the accounting industry (Fu, 2014), and with creative problem solving among information systems professionals (Bozan, 2017).

Other studies have explored the connection between relational coordination and psychological safety, widely acknowledged as a precondition for learning and change (Edmondson, 2004). For example, Stühlinger et al. (2019) found that relational coordination was associated with job satisfaction through its effect on psychological safety, while Carmeli and Gittell (2009) found that relational coordination was associated with learning from failure through its impact on psychological safety. Looking in the opposite direction, psychological safety in obstetric units was positively associated with the communication dimensions of relational coordination through its impact on the relational dimensions of relational coordination (Henrichs, 2013). These findings together provide support for the hypothesis that relational coordination strengthens learning and innovation, and that psychological safety plays a role in this process.

Findings About Predictors of Relational Coordination

Given that relational coordination drives many outcomes of interest to organization, how might organizations strengthen relational coordination? According to the original linear theory, shown in Exhibit 3.3, relational coordination can be strengthened by cross-cutting structures such as selection and training for teamwork, relational job design, relational leadership

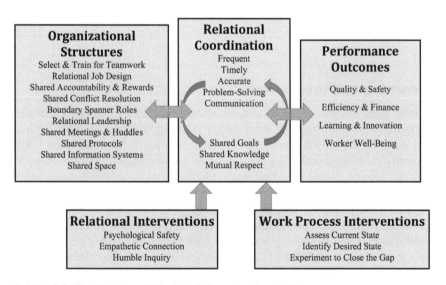

Exhibit 3.3 The Relational Model of Organizational Change

roles, boundary spanner roles, shared accountability and rewards, conflict resolution, shared meetings, shared space, shared protocols and routines, and shared information systems. According to the dynamic theory of relational coordination—the relational model of organizational change—alternative interventions provide direct support for relational coordination as well as indirect support by enabling the implementation of cross-cutting organizational structures. All findings identified by the review about predictors of relational coordination are available in a searchable database at rcsurveyhelp.info. These findings are summarized in Exhibit 3.2 and described below.

Selection and Training for Teamwork

Selection and training for teamwork are expected to set the stage for relational coordination by creating shared knowledge of the situation. Selection for teamwork was studied only twice thus far and was positively associated with relational coordination in both the airline industry (Gittell, 2000) and the healthcare industry (Gittell, Seidner, & Wimbush, 2010). Training for teamwork has been studied multiple times, in the form of interprofessional team training in healthcare (Abu-Rish Blakeney et al., 2019; Brazil, Purdy, Alexander, & Matulich, 2019; Ross, 2015) and in medical education (Warde, Vermillion, & Uijtdehaage, 2014). Most reported positive results of team training while some reported null results (Raghav, 2018; Trojan, Suter, Arthur, & Taylor, 2009). Beyond healthcare, studies in banking (Siddique et al., 2019) and pharmaceuticals (Koulikoff-Souviron & Harrison, 2010) found positive effects of team training on relational coordination, while a study of team training in the youth service sector found no effect (Jankowski, Schifferdecker, Butcher, Foster-Johnson, & Barnett, 2018).

Relational Job Design

Relational job design, defined as clear roles with flexible boundaries, is expected to strengthen relational coordination by creating role clarity including expectations of cross-role coordination. While clear roles and fluidity across role boundaries could be seen as opposing qualities of job design, both are characteristics of relational job design and both are expected to be positively associated with relational coordination. In the airline industry, flexible boundaries between well-defined jobs were positively associated with relational coordination (Gittell, 2000). This hypothesis was further supported by two qualitative studies that found flexible responsibility supported relational coordination between health professionals (Manski-Nankervis et al., 2014; Solberg, Hansen, & Bjørk, 2014). In banks, role clarity was positively associated with relational coordination (Siddique et al., 2019) and in primary care, explicit standardized job roles were positively associated with relational coordination (Cromp et al., 2015).

A baseline level of relational coordination may be needed to effectively implement relational job designs. Accordingly, one study found that relational coordination between workers and supervisors enabled a collaborative redesign of jobs (Kossek & Ollier-Malaterre, 2020), while another found that low levels of relational coordination were associated with the inability to change role boundaries (Bergman et al., 2015). Taken together, these findings are consistent with the dynamic theory of relational coordination in which job redesign promotes relational coordination, while relational coordination promotes job redesign (Gittell, 2016).

Relational Leadership Roles

Relational leadership is a way of leading that is attentive to building high-quality relationships with colleagues and supervisees. Smaller supervisory spans of control were found to enable a more relational approach to leadership and were associated with stronger relational coordination across functions in the study of flight departures (Gittell, 2001). This finding was replicated in a study of relational coordination between hospitals and early intervention agencies in the care of drug-addicted newborns (Derrington, 2012), and a study of outpatient care found that transformational leadership, defined as leading through shared vision, was positively associated with relational coordination (Bright, 2012). In addition, nurse representation in top leadership roles was positively associated with relational coordination across healthcare professions (Mark et al., 2008).

Similarly, relational approaches to leadership were positively associated with relational coordination in childcare (Douglass & Gittell, 2012), elder care (Jakobsen, Albertsen, Jorgensen, Greiner, & Rugulies, 2018), education (Kitching & van Rooyen, 2019), and construction (Hellenes & Thrap-Meyer, 2017). In a dynamic context, leadership facilitation of change through rewarding creativity, soliciting input, and providing a supportive context was positively associated with relational coordination (Huber, Rodriguez, & Shortell, 2020).

Boundary Spanner Roles

Boundary spanners or cross-functional liaisons are people whose role is to coordinate the work of others (Galbraith, 1974). Boundary spanners in the form of operations agents were associated with higher levels of relational coordination across roles in airlines (Gittell, 2000), a finding that was replicated for case managers in surgical care (Gittell, 2002) and education (Parsons, 2012; Skakon, 2014). Parsons carried out a qualitative study of elementary schools and found that a well-defined boundary spanner role was positively associated with relational coordination between school staff and external mental health providers. In a community collaborative to reduce youth violence, strengthening the cross-organizational boundary spanner role was associated with an increase in relational coordination across organizations (Gebo & Bond, 2020).

Several other findings have not supported the theory. The presence of a boundary spanner role was not associated with relational coordination between hospital employees and early intervention agencies in the care of drug-addicted newborns (Derrington, 2012), and in primary care clinics the presence of a care coordinator role was negatively associated with relational coordination among staff (Flieger, 2013). Another study found that a newly implemented boundary spanner role did not predict higher relational coordination overall, though it did predict higher relational coordination as experienced by physicians (Di Capua et al., 2017). A qualitative study found boundary spanners were more effective when other organizational practices such as clearly defined relational workspaces and opportunities for interaction with co-participants were in place (McEvoy, Escott, & Bee, 2010), while another found that boundary spanner roles were more effective in achieving desired outcomes when implemented in settings that already had relatively high levels of relational coordination (S. Lee, 2014). These findings are consistent with the dynamic model in which low levels of relational coordination reduce readiness to implement structures that focus attention on the whole (Gittell, 2016). In contexts with low relational coordination, stakeholders are locked into siloed thinking and have a hard time seeing the purpose of the cross-cutting structures. Even when they do see the purpose of these structures, they lack the relationships required to implement them effectively.

Shared Accountability and Rewards

Shared accountability across groups within an organization is theorized to support relational coordination by focusing worker attention on a shared goal (March & Simon, 1958). Nearly all findings thus far have been consistent with this proposition. Shared accountability was associated with relational coordination across diverse roles in airlines (Gittell, 2000), healthcare (Ghaffari, Wells, Creel, & Siañez, 2020; Gittell, 2008; Gittell et al., 2010), and banking (Siddique et al., 2019). Similarly, shared accountability in the form of multisource feedback was associated with relational coordination in manufacturing firms (H. W. Lee & Kim, 2019). Shared rewards were positively associated with relational coordination in both healthcare and banking (Gittell et al., 2010) (Siddique et al., 2019). McDermott et al. (2017) further found that formative performance monitoring with proactive feedback was positively associated with relational coordination in a study of the healthcare sector. Systems of shared accountability across organizations helped to strengthen relational coordination among key stakeholders in community-based schools (Van Rooyen, 2018) and in public/private partnerships (Sambaza, 2019). Taken together, these findings support the proposition that shared accountability and rewards help to strengthen relational coordination.

Conflict Resolution

Proactive horizontal conflict resolution is expected to support relational coordination by using conflicts to build relationships rather than allowing conflicts to fester, potentially causing lasting divides. Conflict resolution can be embedded into formal systems or be carried out as a regular function of frontline managers (Gittell, 2000). While only a few studies have been conducted thus far, the findings have been consistent. In airlines (Gittell, 2000), surgical care (Gittell et al., 2010), and eldercare (Jakobsen et al., 2018), proactive horizontal conflict resolution was found to be positively associated with relational coordination across roles. Exploring the reverse causal path, a study of hospital care found that relational coordination was associated with fewer conflicts between employees and managers and strikes (Ekwueme, 2018).

Shared Meetings

By providing opportunities for information and idea exchange, regular meetings between interdependent roles can provide structured opportunities to foster teamwork and strengthen relational coordination. In healthcare, the inclusiveness of interdisciplinary rounds was positively associated with relational coordination (Gittell, 2002). Schölmerich et al. (2014) supported this finding in a study of collaboration between hospital-based and community-based midwives and Solberg et al (2014, 2015) identified the absence of inclusive meetings as a barrier to improving relational coordination. Huddles with structured agendas likewise strengthened relational coordination in primary care (Cromp et al., 2015), while shared meetings were positively associated with relational coordination among elder care workers (Jakobsen et al., 2018), and structured interprofessional bedside rounds were associated with sustained positive changes in relational coordination (Abu-Rish Blakeney et al., 2019). Lastly, Derrington found that open houses and community events held by hospitals for early intervention agencies were associated with higher levels of relational coordination between the two types of organizations (Derrington, 2012).

Recent studies of shared meetings have gone beyond healthcare. Implementation of a collaborative interaction phase with meetings between contractors and subcontractors was found to strengthen relational coordination in the construction sector (Hellenes & Thrap-Meyer, 2017). Weekly coordination meetings, quarterly workshops, and retrospective meetings (but not board meetings) contributed to relational coordination as part of a lean initiative in software development (Berntzen, Moe, & Stray, 2019). Shared meetings in public–private partnerships were associated with higher relational coordination and social value creation (Sambaza, 2019). While the great majority of findings regarding this organizational structure have been positive, some have not. For example, an intervention involving regular cross-disciplinary meetings in a university research context did not produce an increase in relational coordination (Perloff et al., 2017). In supply chain dyads, meetings only increased relational coordination when meeting facilitators were able to create a relational space (Stjerne, Söderlund, & Minbaeva, 2019).

Shared Space

By creating proximity and greater opportunities for face-to-face communication, shared space is expected to strengthen relational coordination (McEvoy et al., 2010). Only a few findings about shared space were identified through our systematic review, and all were consistent with the hypothesis. In community-based care, relational workspaces supported relational coordination between case managers and their co-workers (McEvoy et al., 2010). In primary care, shared spaces were conducive to developing relational coordination among providers (Bergman et al., 2015; Cromp et al., 2015; Faruquee, Khera, & Guirguis, 2019). Similar findings were reported in community-based care (Bligaard Madsen & Burau, 2020; Williams, Johnson, Armaignac, Nemeth, & Magwood, 2019). However, a study of venture investing found that spatial proximity was not necessary for relational coordination; the author theorized that relational coordination is a form of proximity that does not depend on spatial proximity (Kuebart, 2019). These findings suggest that the importance of physical proximity for relational coordination may depend on the nature of the work.

Shared Protocols and Routines

Shared protocols are expected to strengthen relational coordination by providing visibility into the work process and illustrating interdependencies between the tasks to be carried out by the different stakeholders involved, consistent with relational coordination theory. This hypothesis was first developed and tested empirically in the context of surgical care, where Gittell (2002) found more inclusive interdisciplinary clinical pathways predicted stronger relational coordination among care providers, with stronger effects under conditions of greater uncertainty. Since then this relationship has been well tested with 22 reported findings. Shared protocols were associated with higher levels of relational coordination among members of healthcare provider teams (Aeyels et al., 2018; Hustoft et al., 2018), between teachers and parents (Douglass & Gittell, 2012), between educators and mental health providers (Parsons, 2012), and among participants in accounting firms (Manski-Nankervis, Furler, Young, Patterson, & Blackberry, 2015). In the context of neonatal intensive care units, shared protocols were reported by staff as a way to improve relational coordination (Solberg, Hansen, & Bjørk, 2015). Likewise, in the context of elder-care, the use of interdisciplinary care plans was positively associated with relational coordination (Jakobsen et al., 2018). The lack of standardized data reporting platforms was associated with weaker relational coordination between public managers and nonprofit managers in the contracting process (Carnochan, McBeath, Chuang, & Austin, 2018). However, other large-scale studies found no association between clinical pathways and relational coordination (Deneckere et al., 2012; Seys et al., 2019), and a study of primary care transformation found that standardized workflows did not strengthen relational coordination (Cromp et al., 2015).

The reverse relationship was explored as well. Patients in practices with higher levels of relational coordination were more likely to receive care aligned with clinical guidelines, protocols, and process recommendations (Cramm & Nieboer, 2012b; Hartgerink et al., 2014; Hartgerink et al., 2012). Taken together, this evidence suggests a mutually reinforcing cycle in which the use of shared protocols supports stronger relational coordination, while relational coordination supports the willingness to use shared protocols (Cramm & Nieboer, 2012a, 2012b), consistent with the dynamic model of relational coordination.

Shared Information Systems

Information systems are expected to strengthen relational coordination when they are accessible by stakeholders who have a need to coordinate and when they are implemented in a relational way, e.g. to supplement rather than replace other forms of communication and to provide visibility into the overall work process (Claggett & Karahanna, 2018). An early study of flight departures found using information systems to replace direct contact rather than complement it was negatively associated with relational coordination (Gittell, 2000). A study of community-based care found, the use of shared clinical information systems, decision support, and self-management support, were each positively associated with relational coordination among care providers (Cramm & Nieboer, 2012a). In addition, media richness and information usefulness were positively associated with relational coordination and the effectiveness of interorganizational patient transfers (Saryeddine, 2011) and the "deep use" of electronic order entry systems was positively associated with relational coordination (Romanow et al., 2018).

Sebastien found that the association between shared information systems and relational coordination depended on the relational context in which the information systems were used, helping to inspire the dynamic model of relational coordination by suggesting that some baseline relational coordination is required to successfully implement structural interventions to further relational coordination (Sebastien, 2014). Tang et al. (2019) further contributed to this dynamic model of change when they found that an IT intervention in the form of a care planner and patient-centered messaging was associated with increased relational coordination in one hospital unit but not another in the same hospital. They found that the clinic without increased relational coordination had no supporting structures. Otte-Trojel et al. (2017) found that relational coordination can mitigate challenges caused by lack of proximity among participants in a patient portal network, while Williams et al. (2019) found that telehealth was used more effectively in the presence of relational coordination.

Relational and Work Process Interventions

If structures cannot be changed to support relational coordination when the baseline level of relational coordination is too weak, how can change agents intervene to disrupt a culture stuck in a low-level equilibrium? The Relational Model of Organizational Change shown in Exhibit 3.3 proposes two kinds of interventions (Gittell, 2016). *Relational interventions* are coaching and feedback strategies designed to start new conversations to create new ways of thinking and relating, thus shifting the culture toward higher relational coordination and enabling the implementation of new structures that further support and strengthen the process, as described in the relational model of change (Torring et al., 2019). *Work process interventions* such as lean and plan-do-study-act cycles are expected to strengthen relational coordination by providing participatory methods to identify the current state, envision a future state, and work toward closing the gap (McMackin & Flood, 2019).

Nearly all reported findings about relational interventions thus far have been consistent with the theory. Relational interventions have been associated with increased relational coordination (Abu-Rish Blakeney et al., 2019; Brazil et al., 2019; Cramm & Nieboer, 2014; Purdy et al., 2020; Ross, 2015), and with increased efficiency (Bitter, 2017), and with improved quality (Goldstein, Gosik, Heisey, Filoromo, & Armen, 2014) in the healthcare industry. Often these relational interventions have been implemented in tandem with structural interventions such as cross-functional training programs (Cromp et al., 2015) and cross-functional meeting structures (Abu-Rish Blakeney et al., 2019). For example, in trauma care, relational and structural interventions implemented in tandem increased relational coordination (Brazil et al., 2019). However, in another setting a relational intervention of coaching and feedback had no measurable impact on relational coordination, despite being implemented in tandem with a new cross-functional meeting structure (Perloff et al., 2017). Some studies found that the same relational interventions worked for some teams but not others without being able to explain why, for example when seeking to create a relational space in meetings between supply chain partners in the context of a manufacturing supply chain intervention (Stjerne et al., 2019).

Three studies identified by our review tested the impact of work process interventions on relational coordination. In the first, no effects were found even though other outcomes improved (Lundstrøm et al., 2014). In the second study, lean adoption was associated with higher relational coordination as expected (Griend, 2019), and in the third study, relational and work process interventions increased relational coordination over time in two sites but increases were only sustained in the site that carried out structural interventions as well (Gebo & Bond, 2020).

Summing Up

In sum, of the 518 findings about the outcomes and predictors of relational coordination identified through our systematic review, 82 percent were supportive of relational coordination theory as it currently exists (81 percent of findings were supportive of outcomes and 85 percent were supportive of predictors). Findings did not differ notably across the 36 countries and 73 industry contexts, suggesting that relational coordination theory is broadly generalizable. Our systematic review has therefore identified a moderately strong base of support for the theory, and also suggests multiple opportunities to develop it further. So far we know a great deal about relational coordination in the US and in the health and human services sectors, for example, with a fairly large body of research in Scandinavia as well. We would benefit from more research in other areas of the world and in other sectors of the economy. We would also benefit greatly from more research that includes clients in measurement of relational coordination (currently represents 14 percent of findings), and the continued trend toward exploring how relational coordination works across organizational boundaries (currently represents 36 percent of findings).

So far we know much more about quality outcomes than we know about the impact of relational coordination on efficiency, worker well-being, or learning and innovation. Future research should explore these critically important outcomes, as well as exploring under what conditions relational coordination contributes to desired outcomes, and under what conditions it does not. Finally, we know much more about structural interventions than we know about relational or work process interventions. Given emerging evidence that structural interventions do not work by themselves to create positive change, we would like to see more research on relational and work process interventions. This research would be impactful indeed!

References

Abu-Rish Blakeney, E., Lavallee, D. C., Baik, D., Pambianco, S., O'Brien, K. D., & Zierler, B. K. (2019). Purposeful interprofessional team intervention improves relational coordination among advanced heart failure care teams. *Journal of Interprofessional Care*, 33(5), 481–489. doi:10.1080/13561820.2018.1560248

Aeyels, D., Bruyneel, L., Seys, D., Sinnaeve, P. R., Sermeus, W., Panella, M., & Vanhaecht, K. (2018). Better hospital context increases success of care pathway implementation on achieving greater teamwork: A multicenter study on STEMI care. *International Journal for Quality in Health Care*, 31(6), 442–448. doi:10.1093/intqhc/mzy197

Albertsen, K., Wiegman, I. M., Limborg, H. J., Thörnfeldt, C. & Bjørner, J. (2014). Quality of everyday rehabilitation in home care: A question of relational coordination?. In O. Broberg, N. Fallentin, P. Hasle, P. L. Jensen, A. Kabel, M. E. Larsen, & T. Weller (Eds.), *Human Factors in Organizational Design and Management –XI*, (pp. 499–505). IEA Press.

Alvarez, H. (2014). *The Role of Relational Coordination In Collaborative Knowledge Creation*. Maastricht University, PhD Dissertation.

Azar, J. M., Johnson, C. S., Frame, A. M., Perkins, S. M., Cottingham, A. H., & Litzelman, D. K. (2017). Evaluation of interprofessional relational coordination and patients' perception of care in outpatient oncology teams. *Journal of Interprofessional Care*, 31(2), 273–276. doi:10.1080/13561820.2016.1248815

Bae, S.-H., Mark, B., & Fried, B. (2010). Impact of nursing unit turnover on patient outcomes in hospitals. *Journal of Nursing Scholarship*, 42(1), 40–49. doi:10.1111/j.1547-5069.2009.01319.x

Bergman, A. A., Jaynes, H. A., Gonzalvo, J. D., Hudmon, K. S., Frankel, R. M., Kobylinski, A. L., & Zillich, A. J. (2015). Pharmaceutical role expansion and developments in pharmacist-physician communication. *Health Communication*, 31(2), 161–170. doi:10.1080/10410236.2014.940672

Berntzen, M., Moe, N. B., & Stray, V. (2019). *The Product Owner in Large-scale Agile: An Empirical Study through the Lens of Relational Coordination Theory*. In *International Conference on Agile Software Development*: 121–136. Springer.

Bitter, J. (2017). *Improving Multidisciplinary Teamwork in Preoperative Scheduling*. Radboud University Medical Center, PhD Dissertation.

Bligaard Madsen, S., & Burau, V. (2020). Relational coordination in inter-organizational settings. How does lack of proximity affect coordination between hospital-based and community-based healthcare providers? *Journal of Interprofessional Care*, 1–4. doi:10.1080/13561820.2020.1712332

Bolton, R., Logan, C.K., & Gittell, J.H. (2021). Revisiting relational coordination: A systematic review. *The Journal of Applied Behavioral Science*.

Bond, B. J., & Gittell, J. H. (2010). Cross-agency coordination of offender reentry: Testing collaboration outcomes. *Journal of Criminal Justice*, 38(2), 118–129. doi:10.1016/j.jcrimjus.2010.02.003

Bozan, K. (2017). *The Perceived Level of Collaborative Work Environments Effect on Creative Group Problem Solving in a Virtual and Distributed Team Environment*. Paper presented at the *Proceedings of the 50th Hawaii International Conference on System Sciences*. doi: 10.24251/hicss.2017.058

Brazil, V., Purdy, E., Alexander, C., & Matulich, J. (2019). Improving the relational aspects of trauma care through translational simulation. *Advances in Simulation*, 4, 10. doi:10.1186/s41077-019-0100-2

Brewer, B. B. (2006). Relationships among teams, culture, safety, and cost outcomes. *Western Journal of Nursing Research*, 28(6), 641–653. doi:10.1177/01939 45905282303

Bright, D. (2012). *Leadership for Quality Improvement in Disease Management*. Brandeis University, PhD Dissertation.

Cameron, K., Mora, C., Leutscher, T., & Calarco, M. (2011). Effects of positive practices on organizational effectiveness. *The Journal of Applied Behavioral Science*, 47(3), 266–308. doi:10.1177/0021886310395514

Cao, X., & Naruse, T. (2018). Effect of time pressure on the burnout of home-visiting nurses: The moderating role of relational coordination with nursing managers. *Japan Journal of Nursing Science*, 16(2), 221–231. doi:10.1111/jjns.12233

Carlile, P. R. (2004). Transferring, translating, and transforming: An integrative framework for managing knowledge across boundaries. *Organization Science*, 15(5), 555–568. doi:10.1287/orsc.1040.0094

Carmeli, A., & Gittell, J. H. (2009). High-quality relationships, psychological safety, and learning from failures in work organizations. *Journal of Organizational Behavior*, 30(6), 709–729. doi:10.1002/job.565

Carnochan, S., McBeath, B., Chuang, E., & Austin, M. J. (2018). Perspectives of public and nonprofit managers on communications in human services contracting. *Public Performance & Management Review*, 42(3), 657–684. doi:10.1080/1 5309576.2018.1495085

Claggett, J. L., & Karahanna, E. (2018). Unpacking the structure of coordination mechanisms and the role of relational coordination in an era of digitally mediated work processes. *Academy of Management Review*, 43(4), 704–722. doi:10.5465/ amr.2016.0325

Cramm, J. M., Hoeijmakers, M., & Nieboer, A. P. (2013). Relational coordination between community health nurses and other professionals in delivering care to community-dwelling frail people. *Journal of Nursing Management*, 22(2), 170–176. doi:10.1111/jonm.12041

Cramm, J. M., & Nieboer, A. P. (2012a). In the Netherlands, rich interaction among professionals conducting disease management led to better chronic care. *Health Affairs*, 31(11), 2493–2500. doi:10.1377/hlthaff.2011.1304

Cramm, J. M., & Nieboer, A. P. (2012b). Relational coordination promotes quality of chronic care delivery in Dutch disease-management programs. *Health Care Management Review*, 37(4), 301–309. doi:10.1097/hmr.0b013e3182355ea4

Cramm, J. M., & Nieboer, A. P. (2014). A longitudinal study to identify the influence of quality of chronic care delivery on productive interactions between patients and (teams of) healthcare professionals within disease management programmes. *BMJ Open*, 4(9), e005914–e005914. doi:10.1136/bmjopen-2014-005914

Cramm, J. M., & Nieboer, A. P. (2015). The importance of productive patient-professional interaction for the well-being of chronically ill patients. *Quality of Life Research: An International Journal of Quality of Life Aspects of Treatment, Care and Rehabilitation*, 24(4), 897–903. doi:10.1007/s11136-014-0813-6

Cramm, J. M., & Nieboer, A. P. (2016). The changing nature of chronic care and coproduction of care between primary care professionals and patients with COPD and their informal caregivers. *International Journal of Chronic Obstructive Pulmonary Disease*, 11, 175–182. doi:10.2147/COPD.S94409

Cromp, D., Hsu, C., Coleman, K., Fishman, P. A., Liss, D. T., Ehrlich, K., ... Reid, R. J. (2015). Barriers and facilitators to team-based care in the context of primary care transformation. *Journal of Ambulatory Care Management*, 38(2), 125–133. doi:10.1097/jac.0000000000000056

DeJesus, F. (2015). *The Impact of Relational Coordination and the Nurse on Patient Outcomes*. University of Central Florida, PhD Dissertation.

Deming, W. E. (2000). *Out of the Crisis*. Cambridge, MA: MIT Press.

Deneckere, S., Euwema, M., Van Herck, P., Lodewijckx, C., Panella, M., Sermeus, W., & Vanhaecht, K. (2012). Care pathways lead to better teamwork: Results of a systematic review. *Social Science & Medicine*, 75(2), 264–268. doi:10.1016/j.socscimed.2012.02.060

Derrington, T. (2012). *Engaging Drug-exposed Infants in Early Intervention Services: What Influences Service Engagement?* Brandeis University, PhD Dissertation.

Di Capua, P., Clarke, R., Tseng, C.-H., Wilhalme, H., Sednew, R., McDonald, K. M., ... Wenger, N. (2017). The effect of implementing a care coordination program on team dynamics and the patient experience. *The American Journal of Managed Care*, 23(8), 494.

Douglass, A., & Gittell, J. H. (2012). Transforming professionalism: Relational bureaucracy and parent–teacher partnerships in child care settings. *Journal of Early Childhood Research*, 10(3), 267–281. doi:10.1177/1476718x12442067

Drewery, D., Nevison, C., Pretti, T. J., & Pennaforte, A. (2016). Lifelong learning characteristics, adjustment and extra-role performance in cooperative education. *Journal of Education and Work*, 30(3), 299–313. doi:10.1080/13639080.2016.1181728

Edmondson, A. C. (2004). Learning from mistakes is easier said than done. *The Journal of Applied Behavioral Science*, 40(1), 66–90. doi:10.1177/0021886304263849

Ekwueme, O. (2018). *Nigerian Hospital-based Interprofessional Collaborative Patterns and Organizational Implications*. Walden University, PhD Dissertation.

Falatah, R., & Conway, E. (2019). Linking relational coordination to nurses' job satisfaction, affective commitment and turnover intention in Saudi Arabia. *Journal of Nursing Management*, 27(4), 715–721. doi:10.1111/jonm.12735

Faro Albuquerque, I., Campos Cunha, R., Dias Martins, L., & Brito Sá, A. (2014). Primary health care services: Workplace spirituality and organizational performance. *Journal of Organizational Change Management*, 27(1), 59–82. doi:10.1108/jocm-11-2012-0186

Faruquee, C. F., Khera, A. S., & Guirguis, L. M. (2019). Family physicians' perceptions of pharmacists prescribing in Alberta. *Journal of Interprofessional Care*, 34(1), 87–96. doi:10.1080/13561820.2019.1609432

Flieger, S. P. (2013). *Evaluation of a Patient-centered Medical Home Pilot: The Impact of Medical Homeness and Relational Coordination on Utilization, Costs and Quality*. Brandeis University, PhD Dissertation.

Flieger, S. P. (2017). Impact of a patient-centered medical home pilot on utilization, quality, and costs and variation in medical homeness. *The Journal of Ambulatory Care Management*, 40(3), 228–237. doi:10.1097/JAC.0000000000000162

Fu, N. (2014). The role of relational resources in the knowledge management capability and innovation of professional service firms. *Human Relations*, 68(5), 731–764. doi:10.1177/0018726714543479

Galbraith, J. R. (1974). Organization design: An information processing view. *Interfaces*, 4(3), 28–36. doi:10.1287/inte.4.3.28

Gebo, E., & Bond, B. J. (2020). Improving interorganizational collaborations: An application in a violence reduction context. *The Social Science Journal*, 1–12. doi:10.1016/j.soscij.2019.09.008

Geue, P. E. (2018). Positive practices in the workplace: Impact on team climate, work engagement, and task performance. *The Journal of Applied Behavioral Science*, 54(3), 272–301. doi:10.1177/0021886318773459

Ghaffari, A., Wells, R., Creel, L., & Siañez, M. (2020). A relational perspective on care coordination. *Health Care Management Review*, 45(2), 96–105. doi:10.1097/hmr.0000000000000208

Gittell, J. H. (2000). Organizing work to support relational co-ordination. *The International Journal of Human Resource Management*, 11(3), 517–539. doi:10.1080/095851900339747

Gittell, J. H. (2001). Supervisory span, relational coordination and flight departure performance: A reassessment of postbureaucracy theory. *Organization Science*, 12(4), 468–483. doi:10.1287/orsc.12.4.468.10636

Gittell, J. H. (2002a). Coordinating mechanisms in care provider groups: Relational coordination as a mediator and input uncertainty as a moderator of performance effects. *Management Science*, 48(11), 1408–1426. doi:10.1287/mnsc.48.11.1408.268

Gittell, J. H. (2002b). Relationships between service providers and their impact on customers. *Journal of Service Research*, 4(4), 299–311. doi:10.1177/1094670502004004007

Gittell, J. H. (2008). Relationships and resilience. *The Journal of Applied Behavioral Science*, 44(1), 25–47. doi:10.1177/0021886307311469

Gittell, J. H. (2016). *Transforming Relationships for High Performance: The Power of Relational Coordination*. Palo Alto, CA: Stanford University Press.

Gittell, J. H., Logan, C., Cronenwett, J., Foster, T. C., Freeman, R., Godfrey, M., & Vidal, D. C. (2020). Impact of relational coordination on staff and patient outcomes in outpatient surgical clinics. *Health Care Management Review*, 45(1), 12–20. doi:10.1097/hmr.0000000000000192

Gittell, J. H., Seidner, R., & Wimbush, J. (2010). A relational model of how high-performance work systems work. *Organization Science*, 21(2), 490–506. doi:10.1287/orsc.1090.0446

Gittell, J. H., Weinberg, D., Pfefferle, S., & Bishop, C. (2008). Impact of relational coordination on job satisfaction and quality outcomes: A study of nursing homes. *Human Resource Management Journal*, 18(2), 154–170. doi:10.1111/j.1748-8583.2007.00063.x

Goldstein, J., Gosik, K., Heisey, A., Filoromo, C., & Armen, S. (2014). *Critical Care Medicine*, 42, A1570. doi:10.1097/01.ccm.0000458368.20726.0d

Griend, D. C. (2019). *Lean and Employee Well-being*. University of Twente, Master's Thesis.

Hagigi, F. (2012). *Relational Coordination as a Driver of Cost and Quality Performance in Chronic Care*. Brandeis University, PhD Dissertation.

Hartgerink, J., Cramm, J., De Vos, A., Bakker, T., Steyerberg, E., Mackenbach, J., & Nieboer, A. (2014). Situational awareness, relational coordination and integrated care delivery to hospitalized elderly in the Netherlands: A comparison between hospitals. *BMC Geriatrics*, 14, 3. doi:10.1186/1471-2318-14-3

Hartgerink, J. M., Cramm, J. M., Bakker, T. J. E. M., van Eijsden, R. A. M., Mackenbach, J. P., & Nieboer, A. P. (2012). The importance of relational coordination for integrated care delivery to older patients in the hospital. *Journal of Nursing Management*, 22(2), 248–256. doi:10.1111/j.1365-2834.2012.01481.x

Havens, D. S., Gittell, J. H., & Vasey, J. (2018). Impact of relational coordination on nurse job satisfaction, work Engagement and burnout. *The Journal of Nursing Administration*, 48(3), 132–140. doi:10.1097/nna.0000000000000587

Havens, D. S., Vasey, J., Gittell, J. H., & Lin, W.-T. (2010). Relational coordination among nurses and other providers: Impact on the quality of patient care. *Journal of Nursing Management*, 18(8), 926–937. doi:10.1111/j.1365-2834.2010.01138.x

Havens, D. S., Warshawsky, N. E., & Vasey, J. (2013). RN work engagement in generational cohorts: The view from rural US hospitals. *Journal of Nursing Management*, 21(7), 927–940. doi:10.1111/jonm.12171

Hellenes, T., & Thrap-Meyer, R. (2017). *Fostering High-quality Relationships in Interorganizational Projects: A Case Study of Relational Coordination in the Norwegian Construction Industry*. BI Norwegian Business School, Master's Thesis.

Henrichs, B. C. (2013). *Psychological Safety as a Mediator of Relational Coordination in Interdisciplinary Hospital Care Units*. Marquette University, PhD Dissertation.

Huber, T. P., Rodriguez, H. P., & Shortell, S. M. (2020). The influence of leadership facilitation on relational coordination among primary care team members of accountable care organizations. *Health Care Management Review*, 45(4), 302–310. doi:10.1097/HMR.0000000000000241

Hustoft, M., Hetlevik, Ø., Aßmus, J., Størkson, S., Gjesdal, S., & Biringer, E. (2018). Communication and relational ties in inter-professional teams in Norwegian specialized health care: A multicentre study of relational coordination. *International Journal of Integrated Care*, 18(2), 9–9. doi:10.5334/ijic.3432

Jakobsen, L. M., Albertsen, K., Jorgensen, A. F. B., Greiner, B. A., & Rugulies, R. (2018). Collaboration among eldercare workers: Barriers, facilitators and supporting processes. *Scandinavian Journal of Caring Sciences*, 32(3), 1127–1137. doi:10.1111/scs.12558

Jankowski, M. K., Schifferdecker, K. E., Butcher, R. L., Foster-Johnson, L., & Barnett, E. R. (2018). Effectiveness of a trauma-informed care initiative in a state child welfare system: A randomized study. *Child Maltreatment*, 24(1), 86–97. doi:10.1177/1077559518796336

Kitching, A. E., & van Rooyen, B. (2019). Key aspects for the sustainable coordination of a process to facilitate holistic well-being in South African schools. *Health Promotion International*, 35(4), 692–701. doi:10.1093/heapro/daz060

Kossek, E. E., & Ollier-Malaterre, A. (2020). Desperately seeking sustainable careers: Redesigning professional jobs for the collaborative crafting of reduced-load work. *Journal of Vocational Behavior*, 117, 103315. doi:10.1016/j.jvb.2019.06.003

Koulikoff-Souviron, M., & Harrison, A. (2010). Evolving HR practices in a strategic intra-firm supply chain. *Human Resource Management*, 49(5), 913–938. doi:10.1002/hrm.20388

Kuebart, A. (2019). Geographies of relational coordination in venture capital firms. *European Planning Studies*, 27(11), 2206–2226. doi:10.1080/09654313.2019.1620696

Lee, H. W., & Kim, E. (2019). Workforce diversity and firm performance: Relational coordination as a mediator and structural empowerment and multisource feedback as moderators. *Human Resource Management*, 59(1), 5–23. doi:10.1002/hrm.21970

Lee, S. (2014). *Coordinating Care: A Relational Systems Approach*. University of Minnesota School of Public Health, PhD Dissertation.

Lenz, R., Sarens, G., & Hoos, F. (2017). Internal audit effectiveness: Multiple case study research involving chief audit executives and senior management. *EDPACS*, 55(1), 1–17. doi:10.1080/07366981.2017.1278980

Lin, W. T. (2010). *Relationships between Nursing Unit Contextual-structural Fit and Unit-level Patient Outcomes*. University of North Carolina Chapel Hill, PhD Dissertation.

Lundstrøm, S. L., Edwards, K., Knudsen, T. B., Larsen, P. V., Reventlow, S., & Søndergaard, J. (2014). Relational coordination and organisational social capital association with characteristics of general practice. *International Journal of Family Medicine*, 2014, 618435–618435. doi:10.1155/2014/618435

Manski-Nankervis, J.-A., Furler, J., Blackberry, I., Young, D., O'Neal, D., & Patterson, E. (2014). Roles and relationships between health professionals involved in insulin initiation for people with type 2 diabetes in the general practice setting: A qualitative study drawing on relational coordination theory. *BMC Family Practice*, 15, 20–20. doi:10.1186/1471-2296-15-20

Manski-Nankervis, J.-A., Furler, J., Young, D., Patterson, E., & Blackberry, I. (2015). Factors associated with relational coordination between health professionals involved in insulin initiation in the general practice setting for people with type 2 diabetes. *Journal of Advanced Nursing*, 71(9), 2176–2188. doi:10.1111/jan.12681

March, J. G., & Simon, H. A. (1958). *Organizations*. New York; London: Wiley; Chapman & Hall.

Margalina, V. M., Benítez Gaibor, M. K., Martínez Mesias, J. P., & Zurita Mesa, E. D.L. M.. (2018). Relational coordination in the footwear manufacturing value chain of the province of Tungurahua, Ecuador. In *Advances in Intelligent Systems and Computing* (pp. 370–379): Springer International Publishing.

Margalina, V. M., De-Pablos-Heredero, C., & Montes-Botella, J. L. (2015). Achieving quality in e-learning through relational coordination. *Studies in Higher Education*, 42(9), 1655–1670. doi:10.1080/03075079.2015.1113953

Mark, B. A., Hughes, L. C., Belyea, M., Bacon, C. T., Chang, Y., & Jones, C. A. (2008). Exploring organizational context and structure as predictors of medication errors and patient falls. *Journal of Patient Safety*, 4(2), 66–77. doi:10.1097/PTS.0b013e3181695671

McDermott, A. M., Conway, E., Cafferkey, K., Bosak, J., & Flood, P. C. (2017). Performance management in context: Formative cross-functional performance monitoring for improvement and the mediating role of relational coordination in hospitals. *The International Journal of Human Resource Management*, 30(3), 436–456. doi:10.1080/09585192.2017.1278714

McDonald, K. M., Rodriguez, H. P., & Shortell, S. M. (2018). Organizational influences on time pressure stressors and potential patient consequences in primary care. *Medical Care*, 56(10), 822–830. doi:10.1097/MLR.0000000000000974

McEvoy, P., Escott, D., & Bee, P. (2010). Case management for high-intensity service users: Towards a relational approach to care co-ordination. *Health & Social Care in the Community*, 19(1), 60–69. doi:10.1111/j.1365-2524.2010.00949.x

McIntosh, N., Burgess, J. F., Meterko, M., Restuccia, J. D., Alt-White, A. C., Kaboli, P., & Charns, M. (2014). Impact of provider coordination on nurse and physician perceptions of patient care quality. *Journal of Nursing Care Quality*, 29(3), 269–279. doi:10.1097/ncq.0000000000000055

McMackin, J., & Flood, P. (2019). A theoretical framework for the social pillar of lean. *Journal of Organizational Effectiveness: People and Performance*, 6(1), 39–55. doi:10.1108/joepp-06-2018-0039

Medlin, C. J., Aurifeille, J. M., & Quester, P. G. (2005). A collaborative interest model of relational coordination and empirical results. *Journal of Business Research*, 58(2), 214–222. doi:10.1016/s0148-2963(02)00496-4

Miles, A., Perea Muñoz, J. M., & Bayle-Sempere, J. T. (2020). Low satisfaction and failed relational coordination among relevant stakeholders in Spanish Mediterranean marine protected areas. *Journal of Environmental Management*, 272, 111003. doi:10.1016/j.jenvman.2020.111003

Naruse, T., Sakai, M., & Nagata, S. (2014). Reliability and validity of the Japanese version of the Relational Coordination Scale. *Japanese Journal of Public Health*, 61, 563–573. Retrieved from http://www.scopus.com/inward/record.url?scp=849 53343143&partnerID=8YFLogxK

Naruse, T., Yamamoto, N., Sugimoto, T., Fujisaki-Sakai, M., & Nagata, S. (2017). The association between nurses' coordination with physicians and clients' place of death. *International Journal of Palliative Nursing*, 23(3), 136–142. doi:10.12968/ijpn.2017.23.3.136

Noël, P. H., Lanham, H. J., Palmer, R. F., Leykum, L. K., & Parchman, M. L. (2013). The importance of relational coordination and reciprocal learning for chronic illness care within primary care teams. *Health Care Management Review*, 38(1), 20–28. doi:10.1097/HMR.0b013e3182497262

Otte-Trojel, T., Rundall, T. G., de Bont, A., & van de Klundert, J. (2017). Can relational coordination help inter-organizational networks overcome challenges to coordination in patient portals? *International Journal of Healthcare Management*, 10(2), 75–83. doi:10.1080/20479700.2015.1101911

Parsons, D. (2012). *Connecting Public School Students with Community-based Mental Health Services*. Brandeis University, PhD Dissertation.

Perloff, J., Rushforth, A., Welch, L. C., Daudelin, D., Suchman, A. L., Hoffer Gittell, J., … Selker, H. P. (2017). Intervening to enhance collaboration in translational research: A relational coordination approach. *Journal of Clinical and Translational Science*, 1(4), 218–225. doi:10.1017/cts.2017.10

Plé, L., & Clegg, S. (2013). How does the customer fit in relational coordination? An empirical study in multichannel retail banking. *Management (France)*, 16, 1. doi:10.3917/mana.161.0001

Purdy, E. I., McLean, D., Alexander, C., Scott, M., Donohue, A., Campbell, D., … Brazil, V. (2020). Doing our work better, together: A relationship-based approach to defining the quality improvement agenda in trauma care. *BMJ Open Quality*, 9(1), e000749. doi:10.1136/bmjoq-2019-000749

Raghav, S. (2018). *Multiple Identity Interactions: Implications for Work Outcomes*. Western Australia University, PhD Dissertation.

Romanow, D., Rai, A., & Keil, M. (2018). CPOE-enabled coordination: Appropriation for deep structure use and impacts on patient outcomes. *MIS Quarterly*, 42(1), 189–212. doi:10.25300/misq/2018/13275

Ross, D. (2015). *In Pursuit of High Performing Health Care Teams: A Test of Teamstepps as a Model to Improve Relational Coordination in Ambulatory Care Teams*. California School of Professional Psychology, PhD Dissertation.

Sakai, M., Naruse, T., & Nagata, S. (2015). Relational coordination between professionals predicts satisfaction with home visit nursing care. *Clinical Nursing Studies*, 4(1). doi:10.5430/cns.v4n1p1

Sakai, M., Naruse, T., & Nagata, S. (2016). Relational coordination among home healthcare professions and goal attainment in nursing care. *Japan Journal of Nursing Science*, 13(3), 402–410. doi:10.1111/jjns.12117

Sambaza, J. R. (2019). *Relational Coordination towards Social Value Creation in Public-private Partnerships in the Private Equity Sector*. University of Pretoria, PhD Dissertation.

Saryeddine, T. (2011). *Moving Patients across Organizations: Exploring the Antecedents of Effective and Efficient Referral Processes*. University of Toronto, PhD Dissertation.

Schölmerich, V. L. N., Posthumus, A. G., Ghorashi, H., Waelput, A. J. M., Groenewegen, P., & Denktaş, S. (2014). Improving interprofessional coordination in Dutch midwifery and obstetrics: A qualitative study. *BMC Pregnancy and Childbirth*, 14, 145–145. doi:10.1186/1471-2393-14-145

Sebastien, I. (2014). *The Influence of Information Systems Affordances on Work Practices in High Velocity, High Reliability Organizations: A Relational Coordination Approach*. University of Hawaii, PhD Dissertation.

Seys, D., Deneckere, S., Lodewijckx, C., Bruyneel, L., Sermeus, W., Boto, P., ... Vanhaecht, K. (2019). Impact of care pathway implementation on interprofessional teamwork: An international cluster randomized controlled trial. *Journal of Interprofessional Care*, 1–9. doi:10.1080/13561820.2019.1634016

Shortell, S. M., Poon, B. Y., Ramsay, P. P., Rodriguez, H. P., Ivey, S. L., Huber, T., ... Summerfelt, T. (2017). A multilevel analysis of patient engagement and patient-reported outcomes in primary care practices of accountable care organizations. *Journal of General Internal Medicine*, 32(6), 640–647. doi:10.1007/s11606-016-3980-z

Siddique, M., Procter, S., & Gittell, J. H. (2019). The role of relational coordination in the relationship between high-performance work systems (HPWS) and organizational performance. *Journal of Organizational Effectiveness: People and Performance*, 6(4), 246–266. doi:10.1108/joepp-04-2018-0029

Skakon, J. (2014). Relational and course coordination at the university: Can the principles of relational coordination incorporated into the course coordinator role strengthen constructive alignment?. In O. Broberg, N. Fallentin, P. Hasle, P. L. Jensen, A. Kabel, M. E. Larsen, & T. Weller (Eds.), *Human Factors in Organizational Design and Management–XI* (pp. 625–630). IEA Press.

Solberg, M. T., Hansen, T. W. R., & Bjørk, I. T. (2014). Oxygen and ventilator treatment: Perspectives on interprofessional collaboration in a neonatal intensive care unit. *Journal of Research in Interprofessional Practice and Education*, 4(1). doi:10.22230/jripe.2014v4n1a172

Solberg, M. T., Hansen, T. W. R., & Bjørk, I. T. (2015). The need for predictability in coordination of ventilator treatment of newborn infants – A qualitative study. *Intensive and Critical Care Nursing*, 31(4), 205–212. doi:10.1016/j.iccn.2014.12.003

Stjerne, I. S., Söderlund, J., & Minbaeva, D. (2019). Crossing times: Temporal boundary-spanning practices in interorganizational projects. *International Journal of Project Management*, 37(2), 347–365. doi:10.1016/j.ijproman.2018.09.004

Stühlinger, M., Schmutz, J. B., & Grote, G. (2019). I hear you, but do I understand? The relationship of a shared professional language with quality of care and job satisfaction. *Frontiers in Psychology*, 10, 1310–1310. doi:10.3389/fpsyg.2019.01310

Tang, T., Heidebrecht, C., Coburn, A., Mansfield, E., Roberto, E., Lucez, E., ... Quan, S. D. (2019). Using an electronic tool to improve teamwork and interprofessional communication to meet the needs of complex hospitalized patients: A mixed methods study. *International Journal of Medical Informatics*, 127, 35–42. doi:10.1016/j.ijmedinf.2019.04.010

Tietbohl, C. K., Rendle, K. A. S., Halley, M. C., May, S. G., Lin, G. A., & Frosch, D. L. (2015). Implementation of patient decision support interventions in primary care. *Medical Decision Making*, 35(8), 987–998. doi:10.1177/0272989x15602886

Tørring, B., Gittell, J. H., Laursen, M., Rasmussen, B. S., & Sørensen, E. E. (2019). Communication and relationship dynamics in surgical teams in the operating room: An ethnographic study. *BMC Health Services Research*, 19(1), 1–16

Trojan, L., Suter, E., Arthur, N., & Taylor, E. (2009). Evaluation framework for a multi-site practice-based interprofessional education intervention. *Journal of Interprofessional Care*, 23(4), 380–389. doi:10.1080/13561820902744106

van der Meer, L., Nieboer, A. P., Finkenflügel, H., & Cramm, J. M. (2017). The importance of person-centred care and co-creation of care for the well-being and job satisfaction of professionals working with people with intellectual disabilities. *Scandinavian Journal of Caring Sciences*, 32(1), 76–81. doi:10.1111/scs.12431

Van Rooyen, B. (2018). *The Sustainable Coordination of an Integrated Multi-level Process to Facilitate Holistic Well-being in South African School Communities*. North-West University, PhD Dissertation.

Warde, C. M., Vermillion, M., & Uijtdehaage, S. (2014). A medical student leadership course led to teamwork, advocacy and mindfulness. *Family Medicine*, 46(6), 459–462.

Warfield, M. E., Chiri, G., Leutz, W. N., & Timberlake, M. (2013). Family well-being in a participant-directed autism waiver program: The role of relational coordination. *Journal of Intellectual Disability Research*, 58(12), 1091–1104. doi:10.1111/jir.12102

Warshawsky, N. E., Havens, D. S., & Knafl, G. (2012). The influence of interpersonal relationships on nurse managers' work engagement and proactive work behavior. *The Journal of Nursing Administration*, 42(9), 418–425. doi:10.1097/NNA.0b013e3182668129

Weinberg, D. B., Lusenhop, R. W., Gittell, J. H., & Kautz, C. M. (2007). Coordination between formal providers and informal caregivers. *Health Care Management Review*, 32(2), 140–149. doi:10.1097/01.hmr.0000267790.24933.4c

Williams, L.-M. S., Johnson, E., Armaignac, D. L., Nemeth, L. S., & Magwood, G. S. (2019). A mixed methods study of tele-ICU nursing interventions to prevent failure to rescue of patients in critical care. *Telemedicine and e-Health*, 25(5), 369–379. doi:10.1089/tmj.2018.0086.

Chapter 4

Choosing a Research/Evaluation Design to Answer Your Questions

Now that we have reviewed hundreds of findings about how relational coordination drives outcomes and how organizations strengthen it, it is time to ask your own questions. You may want to know how strong relational coordination is in your organization, or how it varies across different parts of your organization, or how it varies across different organizations in your industry, as in the study of flight departures in *The Southwest Airlines Way* and the study of hospitals in *High-Performance Healthcare*. To get even more practical, you may want to know whether and how strongly relational coordination influences the outcomes that matter for succeeding in your industry given your organization's strategy. And if relational coordination does influence outcomes that matter in your industry given your organization's strategy, you may want to assess which interventions succeed in strengthening it.

Regardless of your question, you will need a research/evaluation design to answer it. In this chapter we help you to think through the questions you are trying to answer, then help you to create a design that can answer those questions.

What is Research/Evaluation Design?

Research design is a set of strategies and tools that help us to answer very practical questions, particularly questions about cause and effect. The gold standard for testing causal relationships is experimentation when we vary the cause randomly and follow up after a period of time to discover the occurrence of the expected outcome. We learned a great deal in Chapter 2 about the theorized predictors (causes) and outcomes (effects) of relational coordination, and in Chapter 3 we learned about the findings thus far. For example, we might want to test a new type of payment method (reward structure) that we believe will strengthen relational coordination between key stakeholders. To assess the impact of this new payment method on relational coordination, we would randomly choose which networks will be given the new payment method, and which networks will not. We would assess relational coordination before the intervention, and then again after the intervention, to assess whether there is an increase in relational coordination in the networks that used the new payment method relative to those who did not. We might assess in addition whether there was a change in outcomes for the clients served by these networks.

This is called an experimental design, or specifically a randomized control trial, and it is considered to be the best way to test for causality. Creating experiments that account for multiple factors can be difficult, however. As an alternative, we can create a quasi-experimental design to answer our questions without creating an experiment where the intervention is randomly assigned to some and not to others. Quasi-experiments depend on finding real-world comparisons that allow us to simulate key elements of an experiment while adjusting for the absence of random assignment.

Research vs. Evaluation Design

Research design is typically used by researchers in universities or think tanks to create new knowledge about what works. Evaluation design is typically used by practitioners in consulting firms or funding organizations to assess whether desired outcomes have been achieved by a particular intervention designed to achieve those outcomes. There is significant crossover between research and practice, however, and many of the underlying design principles for research and evaluation design are the same. From here on out, we will use the term "research design" to refer to both research design and evaluation design.

How to Strengthen Your Research Design

To strengthen your research design, consider four elements that are common to all research designs: (1) assignment to experimental conditions, (2) comparison groups, (3) measurement, and (4) treatment/intervention. We briefly explain these four elements and provide examples of how you can design your study to minimize threats to validity.

Assignment

In an experimental design, we randomly assign our subjects who could be individuals, teams, organizations, networks, or even countries into control (nonexperimental) and intervention (experimental) groups. If we are testing a new drug, we would randomly choose which individuals will receive the new drug and which individuals will not. In quasi-experimental studies, we lack the ability to randomly assign our subjects into control and intervention groups, either because we want to observe what they are doing naturally, without assigning them, or because they may refuse to be assigned. They may refuse to be randomly assigned because they do not want to be involved in the intervention, or because they do want to be involved in the intervention and may end up instead in the control group. We are not referring here to the consenting process to participate in the research, where eligible subjects have the ability to opt-in or out of the study. Instead, assignment refers to which subjects will be involved in the intervention and which subjects will serve as the control group. Assignment to intervention and control groups can involve significant commitments to engage in certain behaviors—or not to engage in certain behaviors—and these commitments may not be easy to achieve.

To overcome this limitation, one strategy is to establish a cutoff based approach to boost the strength of nonrandom assignment. A cutoff based assignment entails that early in the study design, the researcher sets a threshold for a specific characteristic of eligible subjects to determine their assignment into one group versus another. For example, a teacher who works with one or more students with learning or health disabilities is anticipated to have a more complex network which might include a psychologist, social worker, and treating physician. Thus, in the research design, we can compare their network to that of other teachers, where the characteristic used for cutoff is teaching a student with a disability. It is preferable to acknowledge these cutoff characteristics early in the study design, so researchers can promote equal or higher recruitment in each of study groups. If researchers decide to assign participants based on a specific cutoff characteristic later, after data collection, the assignment in the study groups would be called stratification instead.

If this is not practical given your research question, you can also skip assignment altogether and simply measure natural variations in relational coordination that are found between units, between organizations, or between different patients, students, or clients.

Comparison Groups

Randomization is considered the golden component in study design for one simple fact- its ability to create equal comparable groups so it is clear that it is only the intervention that has changed the studied outcome. Achieving this goal requires quasi-experimental studies to maximize the comparability of the control group. Nonrandom comparison groups can be internally or externally selected. Internal selection of control groups is choosing a sample from within the same site or institution, who ideally are not exposed or enrolled in the studied intervention. For example, to review the effectiveness of a training program, the researcher can pretest all eligible participants then observe the studied outcome among those who completed the program – the treatment group – and compare it to those on the waitlist – the control group.

Case Study 4.1:   Is the Doctor In? A Relational Approach to Job Design and The Coordination of Work

(Gittell, Weinberg, Bennett, & Miller, 2008)

Why we chose this study. This study used a quasi-experimental design, where the researchers took advantage of a natural experiment in one hospital's medical units to assess the impact of physician job design on relational coordination and desired quality and efficiency outcomes. The researchers collected patient-level data on relational coordination in order to compare patients who had physicians with one type of job design, to patients on the same unit who had physicians with a different job design. They then used the hospital's own patient-level data to measure quality and efficiency outcomes, adjusted for differences in patient characteristics. This study illustrates:

- A quasi-experimental design, where the researchers took advantage of a natural experiment
- The use of patient-level data on relational coordination where each patient's network of relational coordination was measured
- A control group that included patients in the same units treated by physicians with a different job design
- Both primary and secondary data sources—relational coordination was collected directly by the researchers while quality and efficiency outcome data were obtained from patient records.

Background. The design of jobs encompasses more than setting tasks; it involves determining the degree of specialization. In other words, in the process of designing a job, the proportion of the total work process assigned to this job should be taken into account.

As healthcare in the United States grew and branched into a giant complex system, the provision of healthcare turned into a segmented work process, with health care professionals undertaking a high level of job specialization. Authors in this study discussed three types of specialization that can be used to classify the jobs of healthcare professionals: functional, stage-based, and site-based specialization. *Functional specialization* is the division of the work process into recurring limited tasks, hence raising both the efficiency and expertise level of the workers. For example, a pulmonary patient may visit in the course of his or her treatment all of the following providers: pulmonologist, asthma clinician, cough therapist, interventional pulmonary surgeon. *Stage-based specialization* is another level of specialization that breaks down care into primary care, acute care,

(*Continued*)

Case Study 4.1 (Continued)

rehabilitative care, and so on. Finally, *site-based specialization* is classifying the job by its location: hospital, clinic, community center.

With multiple levels of specialization, coordination becomes a real challenge. Leaders of a Massachusetts hospital noticed the challenge for doctors to provide care for their patients while coordinating with hospital personnel. These doctors worked in their own private care practices in the community, only coming to the hospital when one of their patients became hospitalized. These leaders implemented a new job design called a hospitalist, which is a physician based in the hospital leading a hospital (site-based) team to care for admitted patients. As a result of the new job design, patients admitted to the hospital had the option to either continue under the care of their own doctor who is based in the community or to be treated by the hospitalist and his or her care team.

Research aim. To understand the effect of stage and site-based specialization on relational coordination and its further impact on efficiency performance measured by total costs and excess length of hospital stay, and quality performance measured by patient mortality, and readmission within 7 and 30 days.

Design and methods. This quasi-experimental study recruited two groups; an intervention or treatment group where admitted patients opted to use the hospitalists and their care team during the period of study, and a control group, or "status quo," where admitted patients kept their private doctors to lead their hospital-based care team. To avoid recall bias, immediately after patient discharge, all those who provided care for that patient were invited to complete the Relational Coordination Survey about their experience of coordinating care for that patient. Hence the unit of analysis of this study was the patient and that patient's specific care team. Then using medical records, researchers collected other variables such as treatment costs, length of stay, readmission, and mortality as quality performance outcomes. To account for the impact on these outcomes of variability in patients' characteristics and needs, the researchers included control variables such as illness severity, age, gender, length of stay in the intensive care unit, and propensity scores for opting-in to be treated by a hospitalist.

Results. Modeling the effect of job design on performance showed that patients treated by a hospitalist have significantly shorter hospital stays and lower treatment costs. While mortality rate as quality performance was not significantly different according to whether the patient was treated by a hospitalist or their original private doctor,

(*Continued*)

Case Study 4.1 (Continued)

both readmission at 7 days and 30 days were significantly lower for patients cared for by a hospitalist. Modeling the effect of job design on relational coordination showed that patients treated by a hospitalist have significantly stronger networks of relational coordination among members of their care team, particularly between the physician and nonphysician members of that care team. Thus, the study concluded that having a hospitalist with a hospital-based care team produces better quality and efficiency performance, due to stronger relational coordination. To learn more about the study, please check the full paper here.

Takeaway lessons for research design. This study took advantage of a natural experiment, where hospital management recognized and addressed collaboration challenges by creating the hospitalist job design. As the intervention was not planned by researchers, there was no pretest data collected. To neutralize the variability between patients and underlying medical causes led to hospitalist selection, study researchers used internal controls as a comparison group. Additionally, a propensity score that measured the probability of being treated by a hospitalist was calculated and added to the statistical models so that any additional differences in efficiency and quality performance could be attributed to the physician rather than to differences in the patients they treated.

This study design illustrates that a thoughtful selection of the control group is essential to ensure its comparability to the intervention group when we do not have full control over the implementation of natural experiments. In this study, researchers calculated propensity scores for all participants—intervention and control—and used these scores to adjust efficiency and quality performance outcome models.

This design also illustrates that secondary data can provide a powerful and cost-effective means to expand a study's scope of analysis. In this study, the researchers were able to model the impact of the intervention on performance outcomes such as treatment costs, excess length of stay, readmission, and mortality for the following 6 months after primary data collection without additional cost through usage of an already available patient record database.

External controls are selected from relatively different settings, for example, using employees from a business in another field as controls. Though internal controls are believed to be superior to external controls, having multiple externally selected comparison groups detects clearer associations and produces stronger inferences.

Measurement

One of the key elements of causality is that the cause happens before the effect. To determine temporality, measurement of both the cause (predictor) and the effect (outcome) should be implemented twice. The initial pretest determines the extent of characteristics in the sample and establishes a baseline point to assess the success of future interventions or treatments. Sometimes, your research design might require multiple pretests. If your outcome is changing over time due to maturation, testing, or instrumentation, then multiple pretests will help to provide a baseline trend. This is particularly true when studying social relationships or work relationships. For example, a study on work relationships among teams in a startup company might report weak communication and collaboration skills if the pretest is implemented early. But another pretest a few months later might reveal stronger collaboration, as teams work together and their experience of work and each other expands, even before any intervention is made. This change can then be attributed to maturation due to the experience of working together. Otherwise the effect of any team building or relational intervention would have a biased overestimated impact.

A posttest is the measurement that assesses changes in the outcome after an intervention has been implemented. The timing of the posttest measurement needs to consider potential lagged effects of the intervention on the outcome. If an intervention such as a training or a new protocol takes time to impact subject behavior, or takes even longer to impact the customer experience, you will want to delay your posttest accordingly, or conduct multiple posttests to observe these lagged effects. Likewise, multiple posttests may be vital to measure a possible waning of the intervention's effect.

Intervention

An intervention is a key element in designing both experimental and quasi-experimental studies. Whether it is naturally occurring or manipulated by the researcher, only a well-defined intervention can be assessed and replicated. Training programs, interprofessional rounds, and standardized work processes are examples of interventions that can be tested through quasi-experimental studies before being widely adopted and implemented.

Examples of Research Designs Investigating Relational Coordination

There is no ideal research design. Rather the best design depends on the questions you are trying to answer and the sources of variation that are available to learn from (Shadish, 2002). In order to help you design your

Case Study 4.2:   The Role of Relational Coordination in the Relationship Between High-Performance Work Systems and Organizational Performance

(Siddique, Procter, & Gittell, 2019)

Why we chose this study. This study uses a cross-sectional descriptive research design to examine the impact of a system of management practices on both relational coordination and desired performance outcomes. One of its strengths of this study is the number of sites (1300 branches of a national bank), each with its own measures of management practices, relational coordination, and desired performance outcomes. Thus, it provides a great example of how to study the impact of management practices on relational coordination and desired performance outcomes in a large multisite organization, or even in a large multisite study where the sites belong to separate organizations.

Background. High-performance work systems are made up of complementary management practices that are designed to enhance employee effectiveness. While former research has focused on skill and motivation enhancing, this study mainly explores opportunity-enhancing human resources practices through the mediation effect of relational coordination. Researchers investigated one of the largest banks in Pakistan (the State Bank of Pakistan) and mapped high-performance work systems based on three components of the ability–motivation–opportunity model. Researchers assessed employee training as a proxy for ability-enhancing practices, while employment security, contingent compensation, and appraisal were assessed as proxies for motivation-enhancing practices. Finally, employee participation, job description, and information sharing were thought to be indicative of opportunity-enhancing practices. The studied bank has more than 1,300 branches across Pakistan and deals with more than 3,000 banking institutions worldwide. Each of its branches is relatively similar in size and structure, facilitating comparison for the purpose of this study.

Research aim. This research study pursued one precise aim, to determine the mediation effect of workplace relationships, measured as relational coordination, between high-performance work systems and desired performance outcomes, building upon an earlier study

(*Continued*)

Case Study 4.2 (Continued)

that established this relationship in healthcare (Gittell, Seidner, & Wimbush, 2010).

Methods and design. Due to the large, branched nature of the organization under study, researchers sampled branches through a two-step stratified proportionate random sample. In the first stage, three regions were selected to survey, which comprise more than 50 percent of all 1,300 branches. Secondly, a sample of 45 percent was randomly selected from all branches in the three selected regions (755 branches). Then the researchers mailed a survey to all employees working in the sampled 340 branches, which included the Relational Coordination Survey as well as questions assessing the management practices in the high-performance work system based on the ability–motivation–opportunity model. Branch-level performance outcomes included total deposits, advances, and profits and were collected longitudinally for 8 months following survey distribution.

Results. Researchers used mediation models to test whether high-performance work systems positively impacted performance outcomes through their impact on relational coordination. Statistical analysis affirmed the hypothesis that relational coordination acts as a partial mediator between high-performance work systems and desired performance outcomes including banking deposits, advances, and profits, meaning that high-performance work systems impact performance through their impact on relational coordination. Analyses also showed all three parts of this high-performance work system—opportunity, skill, and motivation-enhancing HR practices—impacted desired performance outcomes through their impact on relational coordination.

Takeaway lessons for research design. As with the previous study of hospitalist job design, this study explores the impact of management practices on desired performance outcomes, mediated by relational coordination. But it does so by focusing on a system of management practices rather than just a single one, and it does so by exploring variations across many sites, rather than variations across individual patients in the same site, as in the previous study.

research or evaluation, we provide examples of how others have investigated relational coordination. Each of these studies used a distinctive design that was well aligned with the questions it was trying to answer and the sources of variation that were available to learn from.

Case Study 4.3:   Using an Electronic Tool to Improve Teamwork and Interprofessional Communication to Meet the Needs of Complex Hospitalized Patients: A Mixed Methods Study

(Tang et al., 2019)

Why we chose this study. The study provides a great example of a rolling intervention using participants who were waiting to receive the intervention as internal controls. Additionally, researchers adopted multiple tools to monitor changes, electronic survey, face-to-face communication analysis through video recordings, in addition to secondary data.

Background. The increasing complexity needed to treat medical patients due to multi-morbidity has created the need for innovative interventions to share skills and expertise among professionals who are involved in patient care. Implementing care through interprofessional teams represents both an advantage and a challenge, however. In this new era of highly specialized medical professionals, highly complex medical cases require the contribution of various experts to be properly managed. Yet the real challenge remains for interprofessional team members to efficiently cooperate, even with technology such as pagers, short messaging service, and email exchanges. Researchers approached frontline clinicians to participate in the design of an electronic interprofessional communication platform to overcome existing technology limitations such as workflow interruptions, potential privacy and security breaches, lack of context needed to prioritize, and poor care continuity with limited accessibility to some members of the care team. At a large community teaching hospital in Ontario, Canada with 63,962 inpatient admissions in 2017–2018, researchers studied their newly developed platform to enhance interprofessional communication and coordination on two of the five general internal medicine wards. The new platform was implemented as an addition to the current hospital's primary health information system. This new platform included two modules:

- Interprofessional care planner: A one-page summary for current medical, nursing, psychosocial, and functional information about the patient, that is accessible and updatable by any member of the care team regardless of discipline.
- Interprofessional care messaging: Nontime sensitive patient-related messages that are visible to all members of the care team.

(Continued)

Study 4.3 (Continued)

Research aim. This study aimed to investigate the effect of the newly implemented electronic platform on communication and coordination among the care team and its further impact on care outcomes.

Methods and design. A mixed-method study design was adopted by the researchers. Quantitative assessment included an electronic survey of the relational coordination tool that was sent to medical personnel, working in the selected two medical wards. The intervention was launched in two phases, one ward at a time with a 3-month interval between Ward A and Ward B. Therefore, the Relational Coordination Survey was conducted three times; first at baseline prior to the intervention, creating a "pretest data point." The second Relational Coordination Survey was conducted after launching the platform into Ward A, rendering this second data point a posttest for Ward A and a second pretest point for Ward B. Finally, the third RC survey was conducted after the launch in Ward B, which constituted the second posttest data point for Ward A and the first posttest data point for Ward B. To assess the impact on patient care, researchers collected from medical records the incidence of adverse events defined as "temporary or permanent harm that might require treatment or prolong hospitalization" in Wards A and B during the time of the study. Furthermore, to assess face-to-face communication, researchers videotaped four team rounds (meetings to coordinate patient care) from each ward over the course of 2 weeks, then noted any changes in the time spent discussing patient care and making plans. Semi-structured phone interviews with clinicians aided in understanding in greater depth the clinicians' perception of the new technology platform's impact on teamwork, communication, patient care, and workflow efficiency.

Results. The new technology platform improved relational coordination in Ward A despite no significant change in face-to-face communication time during rounds. However, there was no change in the incidence of adverse events during the time of the study. There was no change in relational coordination or the incidence of adverse events following implementation of the new technology platform in Ward B. Still, clinicians in both wards reported positive perceptions about the impact of the platform especially knowledge accessibility and safer shift duty handovers.

Takeaway lessons for research design. This study exemplifies an interventional design with internal controls, using a stepwise design. Secondly, this study shows that the length of time between pre- and postintervention assessments may be an important factor in verifying the impact of interventions on desired outcomes, for interventions that are expected to change behaviors over time.

Case Study 4.4:   Impact of Care Pathway Implementation on Interprofessional Teamwork: An International Cluster Randomized Controlled Trial

(Seys et al., 2019)

Why we chose this study. This research design shows how to develop randomized clinical trials to assess the impact of a bundle of interventions on relational coordination and desired performance outcomes. The intervention in this case included all three kinds of interventions that have been identified in the Relational Model of Organizational Change. The intervention was organized around a *structural intervention*—the adoption of shared protocols in the form of clinical pathways—shown in Gittell (2002) and in multiple subsequent studies to be a positive predictor of relational coordination. In addition, a *relational intervention* was included, with interprofessional teams reflecting together on baseline relational coordination data to understand how different groups were experiencing relational coordination. Finally, a *work process intervention* was included—the use of Plan-Do-Study-Act cycles of improvement by teams throughout the implementation process.

Background. Among the different interventions to boost teamwork in healthcare, some believe that care pathways are the most effective quality improvement intervention for low complexity and low uncertainty care processes. According to relational coordination theory, however, clinical pathways are a type of shared protocol, and are expected to be even more effective as work becomes more complex by providing each group involved in the care process with insights regarding how their tasks relate to the tasks of other groups (Adler & Borys, 1996; Gittell, 2002). The European Pathway Association defines a care pathway as "a complex intervention for the mutual decision making and organization of care for a well-defined group of patients during a well-defined period." In their approach, pathway development mainly focuses on behavior change through cross-training, self-correction, and team-building exercises. A care pathway has multiple active components; an evidence-based care approach to their assigned disease, enhanced coordination throughout the care process, improved communication with patients, improved teamwork, increased follow-up, and raised efficiency. This study included intervention and nonintervention teams from four countries: Belgium, Ireland, Italy, and Portugal.

Research aim. This research study aimed to evaluate the impact of care pathways on relational coordination, to provide further

(*Continued*)

Case Study 4.4 (Continued)

understanding on the different active components of care pathway interventions, and to compare the effectiveness of these different components.

Methods and design. This study was designed as a posttest only cluster randomized controlled trial. Researchers studied the impact of care pathways on interprofessional teamwork among teams responsible for treating Chronic Obstructive Pulmonary Disease (COPD) and teams responsible for treating Proximal Femur Fracture (PFF). Since interprofessional teamwork requires a holistic analysis of team dynamics, teams are unit of analysis for this study and relational coordination was chosen as the measure for interprofessional teamwork. Researchers randomly assigned treating teams to either implement the care pathway (intervention group) or to engage in the usual care without the care pathway (control group). Stratified randomization was used to balance teams in the control and treatment groups on a country level to ensure an equal number of teams across the four participating countries. The sample frame from each country listed hospitals that provided treatment to the target patient populations, then stratified them by hospital type (teaching versus nonteaching), size of hospitals (<600 and ≥600 beds), and annual volume of patients (<300 and ≥300 patients).

Each team "cluster" was assigned a random number by a third party not involved in the study, then another third-party researcher randomly allocated clusters into either intervention or control group, to ensure the randomization process isn't biased by study researchers' preference. Teams selected into the intervention group had 9 months to implement the care pathway, then an evaluation of team indicators was conducted simultaneously for the intervention and control groups. Additionally, researchers used some qualitative methods such as process evaluation to identify the extent of effectiveness of different

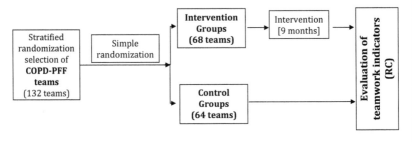

Exhibit 4.1 Illustration of Study Design.

Case Study 4.4 (Continued)

active components of care pathway intervention. See Exhibit 4.1 for an illustration of the study design.

From four countries, a total of 132 teams (65 COPD teams and 67 PFF teams) agreed to participate, where 68 teams were assigned to the intervention group (33 COPD teams and 35 PFF teams). Sixty-four teams were assigned to the control group (32 COPD teams and 32 PFF teams). Researchers used relational coordination scores as the main team process indicator and estimated a cutoff score of 4 on a 5-point scale from aggregated team scores as the indicative point of a successful outcome. Care pathway implementation for this study included three active components:

- Formative evaluation: Teams in the intervention cluster completed a baseline Relational Coordination Survey and an evaluation of patient process indicators for 20 consecutive patients. Both the relational coordination and patient results were discussed within each intervention team as a basis for reflection and learning.
- Evidence-based interventions: All teams in the intervention cluster attended a training workshop on evidence-based interventions for the target patient population, based on an extensive literature review, and carried out in-hospital interventions and information sharing for safe discharge.
- Training in pathway development: A care pathway implementation protocol, based on Deming's Plan-Do-Study-Act cycle and behavioral change strategies, was taught to the study coordinator in each team in the intervention cluster through one-day workshops. Study coordinators were responsible for teaching other team members and for coordinating the implementation of the care pathway.

Results

Results of the evaluation were not published at the time this manuscript was written. Please follow up at rcsurveyhelp.info for updated references and resources.

Takeaway Lessons for Research Design

This study illustrates that randomized clinical trials with random assignment can be used in social science, even to assess the impact of a complex intervention. This study also shows that structural and relational interventions can be replicated across multiple geographical sites using standardized methods, further enhancing external validity through detailed documentation. Finally, this study used a cutoff for high and low relational coordination scores to transform relational coordination from a continuous variable into a dichotomous variable. The resulting use of relational coordination as a yes/no variable is acceptable, especially for experimental designs where "yes/no" variables tend to be preferred. However, researchers have typically preferred to use relational coordination as a continuous variable in order to avoid unnecessary loss of information. Study 4.5 illustrates this approach in another example of an experimental design.

Case Study 4.5:   Improving Interorganizational Collaborations: An Application in a Violence Reduction Context

(Gebo & Bond, 2020)

Why we chose this study. This study introduces a broader scope for assessment and strengthening relational coordination across multiple organizations and multiple sectors. While the previous study used an intervention to strengthen relational coordination among professionals working within the same organization, and replicated the intervention across many organizations, this study used an intervention to strengthen relational coordination across multiple organizations that were working together in a city to serve the same population, and replicated the intervention across multiple cities. This study thus introduces cities as the unit of analysis and calculates a global relational coordination score for each city across multiple diverse entities. Furthermore, the study spanned two and a half years and featured an intervention that was carried out for 18 months. The length of the study enabled the researchers to assess the sustainability of the studied interventions.

  Background. Public problems like addiction, violence, criminal recidivism, and similar societal challenges have complex causes and therefore need to be tackled on multiple frontiers simultaneously. Addressing societal issues involves multiple entities and requires interorganizational collaboration. This study uses the Comprehensive Gang Model (CGM), a criminal justice initiative, as a testing ground for the impact of interorganizational collaboration through the lens of relational coordination. The CGM initiative includes multiple diverse organizations such as criminal justice, other government units, social services, faith-based, and grassroots organizations. The initiative aims

(*Continued*)

Case Study 4.5 (Continued)

to address the social, physical, and psychological needs of at-risk and gang-involved individuals as a pathway to reduce gang and youth violence. CGM proposes several strategies:

- Suppression, including arrest and prosecution.
- Provision of prosocial opportunities, including employment, training, and education for gang-involved individuals.
- Prevention services, such as after-school programming, to those most at-risk for gang membership.
- Organizational change that mainly focuses on interorganizational collaboration and communication, and finally,
- Community mobilization with communities participating in shaping and promoting the success of the initiative.

Research aim. The CGM initiative has two main goals: (1) to increase community capacity to work together on gang and youth violence problems; and (2) to reduce gang and youth violence. These goals are reached through a coordinated effort among the five strategies noted above. This study aimed to improve interorganizational collaborative capacity by adding relational coordination interventions to the existing CGM model.

Methods and design. Researchers adopted a mixed-method study with a quasi-experimental design. Cities are the unit of analysis in this study, to enable a holistic assessment of the intervention's impact. Four cities from one state in the Northeastern region of the United States have been chosen for this study. All four cities have been implementing the CGM model to reduce gang and youth violence. Two of them received support for relational coordination interventions while the other two acted as controls. Using an action research approach, intervention cities underwent interventions that included (1) a root cause inquiry and coaching around baseline Relational Coordination Survey results and (2) work process interventions. Researchers provided support for the intervention sites for a period of 18 months by providing constant feedback and suggestions based on their observation and interactions with key stakeholders. In intervention City A, the suggestions which mainly focused on organizational change mechanisms (e.g. shared meetings, protocols, and information systems) were incorporated in the city planning documents and the researchers' role expanded to include facilitation. In intervention City A, the researchers became boundary spanners across key stakeholders involved in the initiative and held small weekly planning meetings to

(*Continued*)

Case Study 4.5 (Continued)

follow up on the implementation of interorganizational collaborative protocols and to troubleshoot problems. In intervention City B, the structural change efforts included the development of a steering committee, but no one took on the role of a boundary spanner to coordinate across key stakeholders.

The Relational Coordination Survey was distributed to participating stakeholders in all four cities—intervention and control—at baseline, 6 months into the intervention, again at 18 months at the end of intervention and again 1-year postintervention, thus providing four data points for relational coordination. A global RC score was calculated for each city at each assessment round based on the reported RC scores from stakeholders in each participating city. Parallel to the Relational Coordination Survey data collected from all four cities, the researchers conducted face-to-face interviews. Both interviews and coaching sessions were analyzed and coded to provide qualitative insights into intervention implementation and challenges.

Exhibit 4.2 Global RC Results in Four Rounds of Assessment

Global RC Results[a]

Global RC Index	Round 1	Round 2	Round 3	Round 4
Intervention City A	3.12	3.38	3.77***	4.00**
Comparison City A	3.75	3.66	3.64	3.58
Intervention City B	3.39	3.83***	3.69	3.40
Comparison City B	3.44	3.33	3.31	3.37

[a] Results compared to baseline (Round 1); Two-tailed
** $p < 0.01$
*** $p < 0.001$

Results. As shown in Exhibit 4.2, there was no significant change in RC global scores for the control sites. Both intervention cities showed a significant statistical increase in RC scores. The increase was sustained for intervention City A, while intervention City B returned to near baseline RC scores at the last two assessment points. Qualitative results regarding differences in intervention implementation corresponded to the differences in quantitative results. In particular, in early meetings with City B stakeholders, there was a sense of support and strength in the already formalized structures and programs. Therefore, there was little desire to create a cross-organizational liaison to serve as a city-wide boundary spanner. The study concluded that structural interventions with a clear focus on outcomes are necessary for sustained relational change.

> **Takeaway Lessons for Research Design**
>
> In research design, the appropriate unit of analysis depends on the study objectives. In this study, cities rather than organizations were the unit of analysis given the focus on a city-wide multi-stakeholder collaborative effort. This study also illustrates the usefulness of multi-period follow-up data collection in an interventional study, to assess sustainability and to assess how nuances in implementation might contribute to sustainability.

Summing Up

In this chapter, we have provided a roadmap to consider when choosing a research design to study causal relationships between relational coordination and its outcomes; or between relational coordination and the interventions that are expected to strengthen it; or both, as in the study of high-performance work systems above by Siddique et al., (2019), where relational coordination was tested as a mediator between organizational structures and performance outcomes. Prior to measuring relational coordination, thoughtful consideration of research design is crucial. The best research design depends on the questions you are asking, and on the practicality of creating interventions, compared to learning from variations that already exist. Though randomized controlled trials are the gold standard for assessing causality, quasi-experimental or observational designs can provide strong suggestive evidence of causality, if they test a theoretically grounded hypothesis and take account of the design elements we introduced in this chapter.

Once you have identified a research design that works reasonably well to answer the questions you are asking, it is time to measure a key network construct—relational coordination.

References

Adler, P. S., & Borys, B. (1996). Two types of bureaucracy: Enabling and coercive. *Administrative Science Quarterly*, 41(1), 61–89. doi:10.2307/2393986

Gebo, E., & Bond, B. J. (2020). Improving interorganizational collaborations: An application in a violence reduction context. *The Social Science Journal*, 1–12. doi:10.1016/j.soscij.2019.09.008

Gittell, J. H. (2002). Relationships between service providers and their impact on customers. *Journal of Service Research*, 4(4), 299–311. doi:10.1177/109467 0502004004007

Gittell, J. H., Seidner, R., & Wimbush, J. (2010). A relational model of how high-performance work systems work. *Organization Science*, 21(2), 490–506. doi:10.1287/orsc.1090.0446

Gittell, J. H., Weinberg, D. B., Bennett, A. L., & Miller, J. A. (2008). Is the doctor in? A relational approach to job design and the coordination of work. *Human Resource Management*, 47(4), 729–755. doi:10.1002/hrm.20242

Seys, D., Deneckere, S., Lodewijckx, C., Bruyneel, L., Sermeus, W., Boto, P., ... Vanhaecht, K. (2019). Impact of care pathway implementation on interprofessional teamwork: An international cluster randomized controlled trial. *Journal of Interprofessional Care*, 1–9. doi:10.1080/13561820.2019.1634016

Shadish, W. R. (2002). *Experimental and Quasi-experimental Designs for Generalized Causal Inference*. Boston: Houghton Mifflin.

Siddique, M., Procter, S., & Gittell, J. H. (2019). The role of relational coordination in the relationship between high-performance work systems (HPWS) and organizational performance. *Journal of Organizational Effectiveness: People and Performance*, 6(4), 246–266. doi:10.1108/joepp-04-2018-0029

Tang, T., Heidebrecht, C., Coburn, A., Mansfield, E., Roberto, E., Lucez, E., ... Quan, S. D. (2019). Using an electronic tool to improve teamwork and interprofessional communication to meet the needs of complex hospitalized patients: A mixed methods study. *International Journal of Medical Informatics*, 127, 35–42. doi:10.1016/j.ijmedinf.2019.04.010

Chapter 5

Measuring Relational Coordination

In this chapter, we outline methods for measuring relational coordination, including the setup of your survey and the collection of your data. In addition to outlining the most common methods for measuring relational coordination, we also share some important variations—for example, measuring relational coordination around individual clients, measuring relational coordination in multistage work processes, and measuring relational coordination in cross-organizational work processes. We also show how to measure relational leadership between staff and their leaders, and how to measure relational coproduction between staff and their clients.

Before you measure relational coordination, permission must be obtained from Brandeis University through a brief process outlined at rcsurveyhelp. info. You may also work with survey providers licensed by Brandeis University; for an updated list please visit rcsurveyhelp.info. These providers offer support for setting up the Relational Coordination Survey, algorithms for conducting preliminary descriptive analyses of the data, and reports that include visualizations of the data for the purpose of sharing results with key stakeholders. Whether you use a survey vendor or measure relational coordination yourself, this book may be useful given that it offers advanced analytic methods with additional analytic support available through rcsurveyhelp.info.

Why the Network Approach to Measuring Relational Coordination?

Relational coordination is measured based on a network methodology in which each dyadic tie is measured separately. Wouldn't it be simpler to ask respondents to assess the quality of their communication and relationships with all roles globally, rather than assess it separately with each key role involved in the work? Certainly. Indeed, in a recent study in which researchers had access to only a few representatives from each organization, not nearly enough to enable a network measure of relational coordination, they asked instead a subset of the relational coordination questions about patterns of interaction in the organization as a whole. This study did find statistically significant relationships between the global measure of relational coordination and outcomes of interest (Carmeli & Gittell, 2009).

However, there are several powerful benefits of measuring relational coordination as a network of ties, rather than relying on a global assessment. First, there is an accuracy consideration: When respondents are asked to assess the quality of their communication and relationships with all roles globally, a particularly positive or negative connection with one of the other roles could disproportionately influence the overall assessment due to the so-called halo effect, or reverse halo effect. By asking respondents to evaluate separately their connections with each other role in the work process, the accuracy of measurement is enhanced.

The second reason to measure relational coordination as a network of ties is the ability to disaggregate the network into its component ties for the purpose of diagnosis and intervention. By measuring each cross-role tie separately, the researcher or practitioner creates the possibility of doing a sensitivity analysis to learn which of the ties has the greatest impact on which aspects of performance. For ensuring that diabetic patients receive a foot check when they arrive for an appointment, coordination between the front desk, the medical assistant, and the primary care physician may be most essential. For ensuring that diabetic patients control their HCa13 levels in between appointments, coordination between the patient, the informal care provider, the case manager, the school nurse, and family members may be the most essential. In other words, when coordinating work across multiple roles, each tie potentially has a different impact on different performance outcomes. Once we measure relational coordination as a network of ties, we have the opportunity to test for these differential effects, an opportunity that is lost with a global assessment of relational coordination.

Following the same logic, with a network assessment of relational coordination the researcher or practitioner can diagnose which ties are weakest in order to decide how to intervene, as is typical in a data-driven performance improvement process. That researcher or practitioner can then assess with a fair amount of granularity how a particular intervention impacts the strength of ties. For example, in the study called "Is the Doctor In?" the largest differences in relational coordination between the old and new physician job design were found in relational coordination between the physician and nonphysician members of the team, with the biggest difference in relational coordination between the physician and nurse. This type of assessment, drilling down to the level of the role dyad within the team, is only possible with a network measure. For these reasons, relational coordination is designed to be measured as a network of ties. We will return to this issue in Chapter 10 when we discuss the role of relational analytics for creating positive change.

Survey Items

In addition to being a network construct, relational coordination is typically measured using seven survey questions to reflect the seven dimensions of relational coordination, including four questions about communication (frequency, timeliness, accuracy, problem-solving) and three questions about relationships (shared goals, shared knowledge, mutual respect). Respondents from each of the roles believed to be most central to the focal work process are asked to answer each of the following questions about each of the other roles, with responses recorded on a 5-point Likert-type scale. For validated survey items and response categories, visit rcsurveyhelp.info. For a description of the qualitative data analysis used to develop the original Relational Coordination Survey, please read "Relational Coordination: Coordinating Work Through Shared Goals, Shared Knowledge and Mutual Respect" in *Relational Perspectives in Organizational Studies: A Research Companion* (Gittell, 2006). Note that the original Relational Coordination Survey had six items rather than seven—accurate communication was added later, as we explain below.

Relational Coordination Survey questions were designed to minimize the problem of self-report or social desirability bias, where respondents tend to overestimate their own socially desirable behavior. For example, respondents might overestimate the extent to which they communicate in a timely way with other employees, but be less inclined to overestimate the extent to which other employees communicate with them in a timely way. The Relational Coordination Survey was therefore designed to ask respondents to report the behaviors of *others* as opposed to being asked to report their own behaviors. For example, we ask: "Do people in these groups communicate with you in a timely way about [focal work process or client population]?" To learn more about socially desirable responses to survey questions, see Rosenthal and Rosnow (1991).

In addition, the Relational Coordination Survey questions were designed to elicit respondents' perceptions of typical patterns rather than specific incidents in order to minimize recall bias. To understand the rationale for measuring typical patterns of interaction rather than specific incidents, see Freeman, Romney, and Freeman (1987). Finally, in order to reduce the problem of retrospective response error, the questions do not ask for retrospective reports; rather they ask respondents to describe current working conditions. To learn more about reducing the problem of retrospective response error by asking about current conditions, see Marsden (1990).

Who to Survey, About Whom, and About What

So how do we measure relational coordination? Relational coordination is measured by surveying participants in a particular work process about their communication and relationships with other participants in that work process. Because coordination is the management of interdependencies between tasks, and because people are typically assigned to tasks through their roles, relational coordination is typically measured as coordination between roles rather than between unique individuals although we will also consider cases where it is better to measure relational coordination between unique individuals.

The first step in measuring relational coordination is to identify a work process that requires coordination—the focal work process—then to identify the roles that are involved in carrying out that focal work process. It is helpful to conduct informational interviews or relational mapping to identify all roles that are expected to impact the quality and efficiency outcomes of that focal work process. The set of roles involved in a patient care process, for example, may include *physicians, nurses, therapists, case managers,* and *social workers.* These groups are listed in the Relational Coordination Survey instrument below each of the seven relational coordination questions, enabling the survey respondent to answer each of the questions about their coordination with members of each of these roles. See rcsurveyhelp.info for samples of the Relational Coordination Survey.

The next step is to identify which of these roles you will be able to survey. If you are able to survey *all* of the roles you have identified as being central to the work process, you will end up with a complete or symmetric matrix of relational coordination ties as shown in Exhibit 5.1.

Perhaps you will have access to survey only a subset of the roles involved in the work process. Partial access is not unusual and is not insurmountable, so long as you sample the same subset of roles consistently throughout the study. If you are able to survey only a subset of the roles involved in the work process, you will end up with an asymmetric matrix of relational coordination ties as shown in Exhibit 5.2. In the case of an asymmetric matrix, you can still learn a great deal about relational coordination—you can learn about relational coordination between the roles that were surveyed, about relational coordination between them and the roles that were not surveyed, and about relational coordination *within* the roles that were surveyed. But you cannot learn about relational coordination between any

Exhibit 5.1 Symmetric Matrix of Relational Coordination Ties

Relational Coordination Reported by These Roles	Relational Coordination Reported with These Roles				
	Physicians	Nurses	Physical Therapists	Case Managers	Social Workers
Physicians	**3.82**	3.94	4.03	3.75	3.70
Nurses	3.81	**4.48**	4.27	4.03	3.92
Physical Therapists	3.85	4.25	**4.71**	4.06	3.94
Case Managers	3.83	4.36	4.43	**4.45**	4.37
Social Workers	3.93	4.01	4.03	4.17	**4.36**
All	3.85	4.21	4.29	4.09	4.06

Exhibit 5.2 Asymmetric Matrix of Relational Coordination Ties

	Relational Coordination Reported with These Roles				
Relational Coordination Reported by These Roles	Physicians	Residents	Nurses	Therapists	Case Managers
Nurses	3.77	3.93	**4.35**	3.86	4.05
Therapists	2.36	2.46	3.97	**4.28**	3.74
Case Managers	3.65	3.25	4.23	3.17	**4.52**
All	3.26	3.21	4.18	3.77	4.10

two roles that were not surveyed, or about coordination *within* any of the roles that were not surveyed. For example, consider the asymmetric matrix of relational coordination ties found in Study 1 described in Chapter 4—"Is the Doctor In?" In the asymmetric matrix in Exhibit 5.2 we can see that relational coordination with physicians and residents is consistently weaker than relational coordination with nurses, therapists, social workers, and case managers. We can also see that participants tend to have stronger relational coordination with those in the same role than with those in other roles. But we cannot assess relational coordination *among physicians, among residents,* or *between physicians and residents.*

The bottom line is as follows. If there are two roles that need to engage in coordination with each other due to task interdependence between them, you must include at least one of those roles in your survey in order to assess their *between-role* coordination. If there is a role for which within-role coordination may be essential for desired performance outcomes, you must include that role in your survey in order to assess *within-role coordination* among its members.

Including the "Not Applicable" (NA) Response Option—Or Not?

In addition to response options 1 through 5 on a Likert-type scale, the Relational Coordination Survey is sometimes constructed to include a "not applicable" option, to allow respondents to indicate that coordinating with a particular role is not relevant or necessary, from their perspective. When analyzing the data, there are then two possible ways to interpret the "not applicable" response: (1) coordination is in fact *not needed* between those two roles, so NA should be recoded as a missing value, and (2) that coordination *is needed* but not perceived to be needed in which case NA should be re-coded as a weak tie.

You can determine whether coordination is in fact needed by conducting expert interviews from multiple perspectives in advance about the interdependencies in the work process. When there is insufficient information about the work process to distinguish whether coordination is needed between two particular roles, it is advisable to analyze the data both ways: (1) recoding NA = missing or (2) recoding NA = 1 or 2, to determine how sensitive the results are to the interpretation of NA responses, then report the results of this sensitivity analysis along with other findings.

Systematic Approaches for Determining Which Ties are Relevant or "Applicable"

More systematic approaches to "not applicable" have been introduced recently. One approach has been to use the Relational Coordination Survey to measure both desired and actual relational coordination, treating desired relational coordination as an indicator of task interdependence and as a benchmark for assessing the adequacy of current tie strength. For example, the "relational coordination scale was administered to prison officers within the Norwegian prison system ... using an adaptation of the instrument in which actual and desired levels of relational coordination between employees are evaluated. This differentiates between prison officers' expectations of optimum levels of collaboration with other professional groups, dependent on the role function and codependence vs. actual levels of collaboration" (Hean, Ødegård, & Willumsen, 2017). This measurement innovation should be particularly useful in distributed networks where it cannot be presumed that all ties among all roles are relevant for achieving desired performance outcomes.

Another approach developed by Joint Action Analytics is to convene one expert from each of the roles in a given work process *before* the Relational Coordination Survey is launched to assess where coordination is needed. Using an interdependence matrix, one expert from each role is asked whether coordination is needed with each of the other roles, asking "who do you need to work with for success?" If experts from any two roles agree that their coordination is *not* needed for the work process being measured, then the survey will be set up to avoid measuring coordination for that dyad; otherwise respondents from both roles will be invited to assess coordination with each other. This innovation has the impact of shortening the survey and also reduces irritation for survey respondents who would have to indicate "not applicable" each time they are asked about coordination with a role they do not need to coordinate with.

Unit of Observation and Unit of Analysis

The unit of observation for relational coordination is the individual participant in the work process, represented by the individual survey respondent. These individual respondents are then aggregated into a larger unit of analysis in order to construct a measure of relational coordination. That unit of analysis will depend on the hypothesis you are exploring. If you are studying an intervention that is expected to improve relational coordination of a particular work process, and the performance of that work process, your unit of analysis will be different periods of time, i.e. before and after the intervention has been implemented. If you are doing a cross-sectional study in which multiple sites that independently carry out the same work process are expected to have different levels of relational coordination, which are expected to result in different levels of performance, your unit of analysis will be the site. If you are doing both – testing an intervention across multiple sites that independently carry out the same work process – your unit of analysis will be multiple sites over multiple periods of time.

Measuring Coordination Around a Focal Work Process or an Individual Client?

Instead of asking Relational Coordination Survey questions about a focal work process or about a focal client population served by that work process, the Relational Coordination Survey questions can be asked instead about relational coordination for individual clients. See rcsurveyhelp.info for an example of this alternative survey. With this alternative approach, one can construct a measure of relational coordination that is specific to individual clients, which is useful in organizations where different practices or interventions are being used for different clients. In this case, all questions in a particular survey are asked about the respondents' specific interactions with all other roles regarding a particular client. This approach allows greater specificity and allows you to capture variations in how coordination plays out from client to client. But it also introduces a greater potential for retrospective response error. To minimize that response error, it is desirable to survey participants as soon as possible after they have interacted with a particular client. The other challenge arises if the same participants are involved in providing service to multiple clients, thus requiring them to complete numerous surveys for the same study, one about each individual client, rather than a single survey about general patterns of interaction. Numerous surveys sent to a given participant about individual clients may be completed, but response rates are more challenging to achieve given the greater burden on the study participants.

One study that measured relational coordination for individual clients was "Is the Doctor In?," presented as Case Study 4.1 in Chapter 4. This was a one-hospital study in which some patients were cared for by physicians with the traditional job design, while other patients were cared for by physicians with a new "hospitalist" job design. It was hypothesized that the new physician job design would result in higher levels of relational coordination between physicians and other members of the care provider team, thus resulting in better risk-adjusted patient outcomes including shorter lengths of stay, lower total costs, fewer readmissions, and lower mortality. Measuring relational coordination for individual patients enabled the assessment of this new job design that had been adopted for some patients and not others. To address the challenge of asking survey respondents to complete multiple surveys about their coordination for individual patients, three strategies were used:

- A prominent physician leader invited respondents to participate;
- Each survey was accompanied by Hershey's Kiss candy to thank respondents in advance for survey completion;
- Physicians themselves were not asked to complete the surveys given the likelihood that they would not take the time to respond to multiple surveys, thus relational coordination was assessed using an asymmetric matrix as described above. Specifically, physicians did not rate coordination from other care providers or with each other, but other care providers rated coordination as they experienced it with each other, and with physicians.

Measuring Relational Coordination Among Individuals

Relational coordination is typically measured between roles rather than between individuals. But in some work processes, only one person plays a particular role, such as a case manager on a particular unit on a particular shift. In other work processes, each role is played by only one person, for example, in a top management team, with one CEO, one COO, one Vice President of Marketing, and so on. Even when the role is carried out by only one person, it is still possible to set up the Relational Coordination Survey to ask about coordination with the role rather than with the individual in it.

However there are times when you may want to measure coordination with particular individuals within a role either because you believe there are variations in their individual relational coordination that the organization can learn from, or to provide feedback to the participants themselves on their individual relational coordination ratings for developmental purposes. One example is the physician job design study mentioned above, where some patients on a unit had physicians with a new, innovative job design and other patients had physicians with the preexisting job design. Coordination was measured about specific patients in this study, so respondents were not asked about the quality of coordination with all physicians, or all nurses, but rather about the quality of coordination between the specific doctor, nurse, resident, case manager, and so on who were assigned to that specific patient. In this approach, the survey itself has the same number of questions as a survey based on roles—the survey has 7 questions * # roles. The only difference is that each role has in parentheses after it the name of the individual who was assigned to that particular client. But while the survey is no longer than the typical Relational Coordination

Survey, many more surveys are needed to assess relational coordination specifically as it occurred for specific individual clients. This measurement approach—measuring the network of relational coordination around individual clients—was also used in the study by Weinberg, Lusenhop, Gittell and Kautz called "Coordination Between Formal Providers and Informal Caregivers" to follow individual patients and their caregivers as they moved from surgery, to rehabilitation facilities to home care (Weinberg, Lusenhop, Gittell, & Kautz, 2007).

Another example is when you ask survey respondents to assess relational coordination with each individual member of a particular role for purposes of developmental feedback and learning. In the case of an intervention in the Billings Clinic intensive care unit, the change team decided that all roles involved in the intensive care unit would be measured at the role level, except physicians who would be measured as individuals. The change team believed there were important variations between the coordination behaviors of individual physicians that individual measurement would uncover, creating an opportunity for learning. As described in *Transforming Relationships for High Performance*, the Relational Coordination Survey in this case was set up to ask each respondent to assess coordination with each role involved in the work process, but for physicians, to assess coordination with each individual physician (Gittell, 2016). Results were shared back with everyone in the intensive care unit, showing variation among physicians but without identifying them by name. The highest performers were asked to self-identify, and Fish Bowl conversations were hosted to explore what they did differently.

This approach lengthens the survey considerably. Say there are, for example, 10 different roles involved in the focal work process, and 6 different physicians in the physician role. To simply measure coordination between roles, the survey would have 7 RC questions * 10 roles = 70 questions. But to measure coordination between all roles except for physicians, then measure coordination with and among physicians as individuals, the survey needed to have (7 RC questions * 9 roles) + (7 RC questions * 6 physicians) = 63+42 = 105 questions. While this approach requires a longer survey, however, respondents may only be asked to complete it a handful of times—at baseline and then for several follow-up time periods.

Including Both Core and Noncore Roles in Your Survey

As you identify the roles that are involved in the focal work process in need of coordination, you may find that some of the roles are far less visible than others and might easily be overlooked by participants if you don't probe more deeply. These roles might be carrying out "invisible work" due to their lower status, and may in fact be crucial for coordination given the coordination responsibilities that are often associated with these lower status roles

(Bolinger, Klotz, & Leavitt, 2018; Fletcher, 2001). Your challenge is to ensure that these roles are included in the survey. This can be done using a relational mapping process among experts in the organization, asking repeatedly—is there anyone else involved? One of the authors led a workshop with physicians and nurses and asked each team to create a relational map for their own improvement project. One team returned from its relational mapping process to report to the larger group: "We realized the patient care assistant spends more time with the patient than any of us, and we never think of them."

Once these invisible roles have been identified, preferably by the participants themselves, you will then be able to include them in the Relational Coordination Survey, and identify whether the participants who play those roles experience weak relational coordination from their colleagues in higher status roles. Based on recent studies, we expect that invisible low-status roles experience significantly weaker relational coordination than higher status roles, due primarily to their lack of visibility, status, and power. We anticipate that the weaker relational coordination they experience will put quality and safety at risk, and may also negatively impact their well-being (Olaleye, 2020).

The following case study investigates why patient care technicians in a large medical center experienced the lowest relational coordination both baseline and postintervention. Because this study was not yet complete, we present the findings only in a conceptual way. Findings and publication information are available at rcsurveyhelp.info.

Case Study 5.1:   The Nature of Invisible Work: Role Stratification and the Impact of Relational Coordination

(Olaleye, 2020)

Background. Noncore roles form a critical part of the healthcare workforce and play an important role in teams and organizations across industries because they engage in essential supporting work (Bolinger et al., 2018; Overbeck, Correll, & Park, 2005). They are defined as those roles that appear to be incidental to the strategic goals of an organization (Gittell, 2011; Humphrey, Morgeson, & Mannor, 2009).

A set of interventions that aimed to boost relational coordination between roles at a large academic medical center in Boston revealed that a particular role—Patient Care Technicians (PCTs)—reported the lowest relational coordination scores among all of the roles that were

---

(*Continued*)

Case Study 5.1 (Continued)

surveyed. Qualitative findings revealed that PCTs were excluded from important team activities and ironically, had been excluded from all aspects of the structural and relational interventions that were designed to strengthen relational coordination. It was revealed that PCTs were not considered to be important for decision making about patients and hence had been excluded from the process. However, it was also observed that PCTs interacted very closely with the patients and their families, and contributed significantly to patient and family experience in the inpatient wards.

Conceptual framework. Oftentimes, work that is important to the mission and vision of healthcare organizations is unrecognized, unappreciated, and undervalued. This has been described in the literature as "invisible work" (DeVault, 2014). Former research on invisible work tends to attribute the invisibility of the work to the demographic characteristics (e.g. race, gender, and/or socioeconomic status) of the individuals performing the work (DeVault, 2014; Fletcher, 2001). However, invisible work can also be linked to roles occupied by low to moderately skilled workers. These workers often do the "essential" supporting work that goes unseen, for example, cleaners and housekeepers, as was clearly demonstrated during the COVID-19 pandemic. These workers are likely to report low relational coordination from other roles, with potentially negative consequences for performance outcomes. Even when interventions are designed to strengthen relational coordination, these workers are less likely to be included, precisely because their work is perceived to be relatively unimportant.

Conclusion. The Relational Coordination Survey has the flexibility to include both core and noncore workers in the same survey, to assess and improve the coordination between them. If desired performance outcomes are likely to be influenced in your setting by the strength of relational coordination between core and noncore workers (Gittell, 2011), then you will want to be especially attentive to identifying and including noncore roles in your Relational Coordination Survey.

Administering the Survey

Sampling Participants

Once you have identified the roles you will survey, you will want to survey participants from each of these roles. The typical approach has been to survey every person in every role that has been selected for inclusion, but one could instead survey only full-time employees, for example. For roles with many participants, one could also use random sampling of participants within each role, which would be a form of stratified random sampling.

In Person, by Mail, and Online Options

As with any survey, there are multiple ways to get the Relational Coordination Survey into the hands of respondents. This survey can be administered in person, by mail, or by sending a unique link to individual participants to give them access to an electronic survey platform.

In the original study of relational coordination, carried out by one of the authors in the airline industry, a highly time-intensive approach was used. The researcher delivered the survey in person and was present to answer questions from respondents as they completed the study. At each of the nine participating sites, the researcher administered the survey in person on a single day to employees working the morning shift, distributing surveys in the break rooms. All surveys were conducted on weekdays between Tuesday and Thursday, to avoid disrupting the operations and to increase the number of surveys completed because passenger loads were typically lighter on these three days. Respondents typically required 20 minutes to complete the survey. The overall response rate for this survey was 89 percent.

The same researcher conducted the second study of relational coordination in the surgical care context when she was a busy junior faculty member with young children, and therefore chose a less time-intensive approach. At each of the nine participating sites, a key departmental administrator designated by the department chief was asked to identify all eligible care providers. The administrator was supplied with written guidelines as to whom should be included, in this case all care providers from the 5 particular roles who were directly or indirectly involved with providing care for joint replacement patients. Surveys were then mailed by the researcher to all identified care providers during the second month of the study period, with one repeat mailing during the study period for nonrespondents. The researcher received responses from 338 of 666 providers, for an overall response rate of 51 percent. Note that this mailed survey approach resulted in a response rate that was significantly lower than the response rate when the survey was administered in person.

In recent years, the Relational Coordination Survey has typically been administered using an online format, inviting participants through an email message from their own organization or a trusted third party. The data are collected electronically, avoiding the need for data entry, and thus are readily analyzed and shared back with participants. While this method carries the risk of "survey fatigue," current vendors of the Relational Coordination Survey have developed best practices for maximizing participation, including advice for engaging with participants in advance of the survey.

Measuring Relational Coordination with Leaders—Relational Leadership

One innovation in the measurement of relational coordination is to measure it not only among coworkers, but also between workers and their leaders. While the questions may be identical to the seven questions used for relational coordination, the construct when conceptualized and measured between workers and leaders, or among leaders themselves, is called relational leadership. Relational leadership is leading through relationships of shared goals, shared knowledge, and mutual respect, supported by communication that is sufficiently frequent, timely, accurate, and focused on problem-solving rather than blaming when problems emerge. Relational leaders are those who work to build these relationships *with* the people they lead— and *among* the people they lead (Gittell, 2016; Gittell & Douglass, 2012). While relational leadership has been associated with female leadership styles, this is not exclusively the case (see Lipman-Blumen, 2000; Fletcher, 2004). Relational leadership includes the willingness and ability to step away from the expert role to learn from others, a capability known as fluid expertise (Fletcher, 2004) or humble inquiry (Schein, 2013). This style of leadership appears to be gaining traction in organizations, though command and control leadership styles are still quite easy to find.

Relational leadership provides participants with a visible role model for relational coordination and thus is expected to strengthen relational coordination. Nearly all findings identified in the systematic review described above in Chapter 3 have thus far been supportive of this hypothesis (Arena et al., 2016; Bright, 2012; Derrington, 2012; Douglass & Gittell, 2012; Gittell, 2001; Hornstrup, 2015; Hornstrup, Storch, & Kølle, 2018). Anne Douglass' insights into relational leadership began in her work as a practitioner, as she noticed the critical role of leaders in setting a tone for relational coordination among staff, and relational coproduction with clients. All three dynamics seemed essential for achieving desired outcomes, and how leaders led seemed to set the stage for it all. Douglass went on to study this process and has made both academic and practical contributions to our understanding of relational leadership (Douglass, 2017).

Carsten Hornstrup's insights into relational leadership began as he was working with municipalities to support the delivery of high-quality services to citizens. Like Douglass, he noted certain kinds of leadership behaviors were conducive to supporting collaboration, then he went on to identify those behaviors more specifically through empirical study. In one study, carried out in close collaboration with leaders and employees from Danish welfare organizations, he created a new measure of relational leadership. The scale was developed with inspiration from prior research on relational coordination (Gittell, 2016), extreme teaming (Edmondson & Harvey, 2017), and relational leadership (Ospina & Uhl-Bien, 2012) and informed by interviews with employees and leaders. The methodology consisted of partnering with employees and managers in ten Danish municipalities through iterative development, testing, and validation of the concept. The scale was later presented to leaders and employees, and through interviews, focus groups, and discussions it was validated qualitatively, before it was tested and validated statistically. The Relational Leadership Scale developed through this work consists of three dimensions; Directional Leadership (shared goals, shared strategy, and clear expectations), Engaged Leadership (active support, conflict resolution, and insisting on involvement), and

Involving Leadership (active participation, involvement, and respect). Find out how to access it through rcsurveyhelp.info.

A common alternative has been to measure relational leadership between leaders and followers using the same seven dimensions as for relational coordination. One methodological contribution would be to compare findings from using the two distinct measures of relational leadership. Are the two measures correlated? Do workers who experience stronger relational leadership from their leaders tend to engage more strongly in relational coordination with their colleagues? Which measure is more consistently predictive of desired outcomes? Which measure is more useful to share back with participants for the purpose of creating positive change, or do they work better together?

Measuring Relational Coordination with Clients— Relational Coproduction

Another innovation has been to measure relational coordination between workers and their clients—also known as relational coproduction. Relational coproduction is defined as partnering with clients through reciprocal relationships of shared goals, shared knowledge, and mutual respect, supported by communication that is sufficiently frequent, timely, accurate, and focused on problem-solving rather than blaming when things go wrong (Gittell, 2016; Gittell & Douglass, 2012). There are well-developed theories of coproduction, starting decades ago in the public sector, then spreading to the for-profit and nonprofit sectors as organizations seek to engage their clients in doing some of the necessary work to achieve the desired outcomes (Batalden et al., 2016).

The measurement of relational coproduction between the service delivery team and the service recipient was first conducted in the postsurgical care context (Weinberg et al., 2007), and later in contexts as diverse as early childhood education (Douglass & Gittell, 2012), chronic care (Cramm & Nieboer, 2014, 2016), disability care (Warfield, Chiri, Leutz, & Timberlake, 2013), and commercial banking (Plé & Clegg, 2013). Measuring relational coordination with the client may be especially important for being able to predict desired outcomes when the client's own actions make a difference for outcomes, for example, when the work process extends over time or across organizations. We expect that when professionals have high levels of relational coordination with each other, they will be better able to engage in relational coproduction with their clients. There is some early evidence to support this hypothesis (Hornstrup et al., 2018).

Measuring Relational Coordination in a Multistage or Cross-Organizational Work Process

One measurement challenge for relational coordination is that in some work processes, the necessary roles change over time as the work progresses. This happens, for example, in project-based work, and also in long term work processes such as postoperative patient care, cancer care, mental health care, and so on. One way to address a multistage work process in which the roles change from stage to stage is to measure relational coordination distinctly at each stage of the work process. When there are also roles that remain fairly consistent across all the stages, for example, system integrators, you can include them across all stages. You can use this approach for any work process where roles change over time, whether in the construction sector or cancer care or anywhere else. Using the same approach, you can also measure relational coordination in a cross-organizational work process, within and between the organizations that are involved. Doing this does not require any major changes to the Relational Coordination Survey. You can cutomize the Relational Coordination Survey following examples available at rcsurveyhelp.info. In Chapter 7, we share an example of the data output from a multi-stage, cross-organizational analysis in matrix form.

Other Innovations in the Measurement of Relational Coordination

As the Relational Coordination Survey has spread to different industries and countries, people have introduced other innovations in measurement.

Accurate Communication Added as the Seventh Dimension

One early innovation was to expand relational coordination from a 6-item construct to a 7-item construct by adding accurate communication as a dimension of relational coordination (see Gittell et al. (2000). It became apparent when studying surgical care that accurate communication, along with frequent, timely, and problem-solving communication, was an important dimension of relational coordination. Accurate communication was also critically important in the airlines where the survey was first developed, but in the airlines, accuracy was already at such a high level given the emphasis on safety that it was not emphasized by interviewees with whom the original Relational Coordination Survey was developed. This was not the case in healthcare, where accuracy was a major challenge and remains an ongoing challenge when coordinating care among healthcare professionals.

Frequent Communication Question and Response Options Changed

The question about frequent communication was changed from "How frequently do you communicate with people in these groups about [focal work process]?" to "How frequently do people in these groups communicate with you about [focal work process]?" The rationale for this change in 2010 was to achieve consistency with the wording of the other questions on the survey. All other Relational Coordination Survey questions ask the respondent to evaluate the behavior of the other groups, rather than to evaluate the respondent's own behavior, to minimize social desirability bias. This logic had not been applied to the frequency question initially, given that frequency is less value-laden than the other questions and thus less likely to be vulnerable to social desirability bias. Ultimately however the frequency question was altered simply to achieve consistency of perspective with the other Relational Coordination Survey items.

Response categories for the frequency question were also altered in 2010 from a 5-point scale ranging from 1="Never" to 5= "Constantly," to a 5-point scale with the following response options: 1="Far Too Little," 2="Too Little," 3="Just Right," 4="Too Much," 5="Far Too Much." The motivation for this change was the recognition that more frequent communication does not indicate higher quality communication. The appropriate frequency of communication as judged from the perspective of the respondent is more relevant than the absolute amount of communication. To indicate that the right amount of communication is the best scenario and that too little communication is the worst scenario, responses for Frequent Communication are re-coded for the purpose of analysis in the following way: 1="Far Too Little," 2="Far Too Much," 3="Too Little," 4="Too Much," and 5="Just Right."

Short-form Survey Created

A short form of the Relational Coordination Survey has also been developed with fewer items and fewer response categories. This shorter Relational Coordination Survey was created for the purpose of surveying respondents who had less time to respond and/or lower levels of education. Results from this version of the survey were published in 2008 in an article called "Impact of Relational Coordination on Job Satisfaction and Quality Outcomes: A Study of Nursing Homes." The short-form survey has not yet undergone the same rigorous validation process as the full Relational Coordination Survey (Gittell, Weinberg, Pfefferle, & Bishop, 2008).

New Language Options Added

In addition, the Relational Coordination Survey has been translated into about multiple different languages thus far. Some of these language options have been validated, and some have not. Comparing relational coordination with other validated measures of teamwork.

How does relational coordination compare with other ways of measuring coordination or teamwork? First, relational coordination is not just a measure—it is part of a comprehensive theory for understanding how people contribute to performance through their coordination with each other, and how their organizations support or undermine that process. But for those who are looking primarily for a way to measure teamwork or coordination, relational coordination is one of many measures to consider. A systematic review of care coordination measurement tools was carried out by McDonald (2010) in the healthcare context, and can be referenced for the purpose of comparing relational coordination to other measurement tools (McDonald, 2010).

More recently, a systematic review of teamwork measures in healthcare was carried out by Valentine, Nembhard, and Edmondson (2015). Results are shown in Exhibit 5.3. Two of the 30 measures they considered were neither bounded nor unbounded and neither of these was validated; those 2 measures are therefore not shown on this table.

Exhibit 5.3 Comparing Relational Coordination Measure to Other Validated Measures of Teamwork in Healthcare (Valentine et al., 2015)

Bounded and Validated

1. Team Survey (Millward & Jeffries)
2. Team Effectiveness (Pearce & Sims)
3. Cross-functional Team Process (Alexander et al.)
4. Teamwork Quality Survey (Hoegl & Gemenden)
5. Team Emergency Assessment Measure (TEAM) (Cooper et al.)

Unbounded and Validated

1. Relational Coordination (Gittell)
2. Nursing Teamwork Survey (Kalisch et al.)

Bounded and Not Yet Validated

1. Team Process Scale (Brannick et al.)
2. Team Member Exchange (TMX) Quality Scale (Seers)
3. Collaboration Scale (Kahn & McDonough)
4. Team Climate Inventory (Anderson & West)
5. Team Process Quality (Hauptman & Hirji)
6. Team Functioning (Strasser et al.)
7. Teamwork Scale (Friesen et al.)
8. Team Organization (La Duckers et al.)
9. Primary Care Patient Safety Climate Measure (PC-SafeQuest)
10. Team Roleing Survey (Strasser et al.)
11. Collaborative Practice Assessment Tool (CPAT) Schroder et al.)

Unbounded and Not Yet Validated

1. ICU Nurse-Physician Collaboration (Shortell et al.)
2. Collaboration and Satisfaction about Care Decisions (Baggs)
3. Professional Working Relationships (Adams et al.)
4. Hospital Survey on Patient Safety (Sorra & Nieva)
5. Perceptions about Interdisciplinary Collaboration Scale (Copnell et al.)
6. Teamwork Scale (Hutchinson et al.)
7. Safety Attitudes Questionnaire (Sexton et al.)
8. Leiden Operating Theater and Intensive Care Safety (LOTICS) (Van Beuzekom et al.)
9. Collaboration Scale (Masse et al.)
10. Nurse-Physician Collaboration (Ushiro)

These results suggest that there were 7 fully validated measures of team-work in healthcare at the time of this review, and that the Relational Coordination Survey was one of them. These results also suggest that there were only 2 fully validated measures of teamwork in healthcare that were also "unbounded," meaning that they were capable of measuring teamwork across organizational boundaries as well as within organizational boundaries (Valentine et al., 2015). One is the Relational Coordination Survey and the other is the Nursing Teamwork Survey. See the upper right-hand quadrant of Exhibit 5.3.

Summing Up

In sum, relational coordination is distinguished from other methods for measuring teamwork due to its assessment of each dyadic tie in the network rather than the more common global assessment of a team's relationships. This network methodology provides greater specificity in measurement given that the roles you may be interested in can be specified exactly—whether within and/or across departmental and/or organizational boundaries. The network methodology underlying the relational coordination measurement approach provides greater accuracy and unique diagnostic capabilities.

As we have shown in this chapter, there are many options for measuring relational coordination based on a powerful network methodology that is readily customizable to the particular coordination challenge you want to address. You can collect your relational coordination data on your own with permission from Brandeis University, based on the information we have shared in this chapter, or with the help of a survey vendor; for an updated list please visit rcsurveyhelp.info. You will then be ready to create variables from your data.

References

Arena, M., Douglass, A., Gauthier, V., Hornstrup, C., Lichtenstein, B. B., & Stephens, J. P. (2016). Relational coordination and complexity leadership: Enabling the dynamics of adaptive systems. *Academy of Management Proceedings*, 2016(1), 14148. doi:10.5465/ambpp.2016.14148symposium

Batalden, M., Batalden, P., Margolis, P., Seid, M., Armstrong, G., Opipari-Arrigan, L., & Hartung, H. (2016). Coproduction of healthcare service. *BMJ Quality & Safety*, 25(7), 509–517. doi:10.1136/bmjqs-2015-004315

Bolinger, A. R., Klotz, A. C., & Leavitt, K. (2018). Contributing from inside the outer circle: The identity-based effects of noncore role incumbents on relational coordination and organizational climate. *Academy of Management Review*, 43(4), 680–703. doi:10.5465/amr.2016.0333

Bright, D. (2012). *Leadership for Quality Improvement in Disease Management*. Brandeis University, PhD Dissertation.

Carmeli, A., & Gittell, J. H. (2009). High-quality relationships, psychological safety, and learning from failures in work organizations. *Journal of Organizational Behavior*, 30(6), 709–729. doi:10.1002/job.565

Cramm, J. M., & Nieboer, A. P. (2014). A longitudinal study to identify the influence of quality of chronic care delivery on productive interactions between patients and (teams of) healthcare professionals within disease management programmes. *BMJ Open*, 4(9), e005914–e005914. doi:10.1136/bmjopen-2014-005914

Cramm, J. M., & Nieboer, A. P. (2016). The changing nature of chronic care and coproduction of care between primary care professionals and patients with COPD and their informal caregivers. *International Journal of Chronic Obstructive Pulmonary Disease*, 11, 175–182. doi:10.2147/COPD.S94409

Derrington, T. (2012). *Engaging Drug-exposed Infants in Early Intervention Services: What Influences Service Engagement?*. Brandeis University, PhD Dissertation.

DeVault, M. L. (2014). Mapping invisible work: Conceptual tools for social justice projects. *Sociological Forum*, 29(4), 775–790. doi:10.1111/socf.12119

Douglass, A. (2017). Redefining leadership: Lessons from an early education leadership development initiative. *Early Childhood Education Journal*, 46(4), 387–396. doi:10.1007/s10643-017-0871-9

Douglass, A., & Gittell, J. H. (2012). Transforming professionalism: Relational bureaucracy and parent–teacher partnerships in child care settings. *Journal of Early Childhood Research*, 10(3), 267–281. doi:10.1177/1476718x12442067

Edmondson, A. C., & Harvey, J. F. (2017). *Extreme Teaming: Lessons in Complex, Cross-sector Leadership*. Bingley: Emerald Publishing.

Fletcher, J. K. (2001). *Disappearing Acts: Gender, Power, and Relational Practice at Work*. Cambridge, MA: MIT Press.

Fletcher, J. K. (2004). The paradox of postheroic leadership: An essay on gender, power, and transformational change. *The Leadership Quarterly*, 15(5), 647–661. doi:10.1016/j.leaqua.2004.07.004

Freeman, L. C., Romney, A. K., & Freeman, S. C. (1987). Cognitive structure and informant accuracy. *American Anthropologist*, 89(2), 310–325. doi:10.1525/aa.1987.89.2.02a00020

Gittell, J. H. (2001). Supervisory span, relational coordination and flight departure performance: A reassessment of postbureaucracy theory. *Organization Science*, 12(4), 468–483. doi:10.1287/orsc.12.4.468.10636

Gittell, J. H. (2006). Relational coordination: Coordinating work through relationships of shared goals, shared knowledge and mutual respect. In O. Kyriakidou & M. Özbilgin (Eds.), *Relational Perspectives in Organizational Studies: A Research Companion*. Cheltenham, UK; Northampton, MA: Edward Elgar.

Gittell, J. H. (2011). New directions for relational coordination theory. In K.S. Cameron and G. Spreitzer (Eds.), *Oxford Handbook of Positive Organizational Scholarship*, pp. 74–94, Oxford, UK: Oxford University Press.

Gittell, J. H. (2016). *Transforming Relationships for High Performance: The Power of Relational Coordination*. Palo Alto, CA: Stanford University Press.

Gittell, J. H., & Douglass, A. (2012). Relational bureaucracy: Structuring reciprocal relationships into roles. *Academy of Management Review*, 37(4), 709–733. doi:10.5465/amr.2010.0438

Gittell, J. H., Fairfield, K. M., Bierbaum, B., Head, W., Jackson, R., Kelly, M., … Zuckerman, J. (2000). Impact of relational coordination on quality of care, postoperative pain and functioning, and length of stay. *Medical Care*, 38(8), 807–819. doi:10.1097/00005650-200008000-00005

Gittell, J. H., Weinberg, D., Pfefferle, S., & Bishop, C. (2008). Impact of relational coordination on job satisfaction and quality outcomes: A study of nursing homes. *Human Resource Management Journal*, 18(2), 154–170. doi:10.1111/j.1748-8583.2007.00063.x

Hean, S., Ødegård, A., & Willumsen, E. (2017). Improving collaboration between professionals supporting mentally ill offenders. *International Journal of Prisoner Health*, 13(2), 91–104. doi:10.1108/ijph-12-2016-0072

Hornstrup, C. (2015). *Strategic Relational Leadership: Building Organizational Capacity to Change*. Tilburg University, PhD Dissertation. Available from http://worldcat.org/z-wcorg/database.

Hornstrup, C., Storch, J., & Kølle, M. (2018). *Relational Capacity: Coherence of Public Organisations*: Forlaget Mindspace : [Sælges på internettet].

Humphrey, S. E., Morgeson, F. P., & Mannor, M. J. (2009). Developing a theory of the strategic core of teams: A role composition model of team performance. *Journal of Applied Psychology*, 94(1), 48–61. doi:10.1037/a0012997

Lipman-Blumen, J. (2000). *Connective Leadership: Managing in a Changing World*. New York, NY: Oxford University Press.

Marsden, P. V. (1990). Network data and measurement. *Annual Review of Sociology*, 16(1), 435–463. doi:10.1146/annurev.so.16.080190.002251

McDonald, K. M. (2010). Care coordination measures atlas. *Agency for Healthcare Research and Quality*. Retrieved from https://www.ahrq.gov/ncepcr/care/coordination/atlas.html

Olaleye, O. (2020). *The Nature of Invisible Work: Role Stratification and the Impact of Relational Coordination*. Heller School. Brandeis University. Working Paper.

Ospina, S., & Uhl-Bien, M. (2012). *Advancing Relational Leadership Research: A Dialogue among Perspectives (Leadership Horizons)*. Information Age Publishing Inc.

Overbeck, J., Correll, J., & Park, B. (2005). Internal status sorting in groups: The problem of too many stars. *Research on Managing Groups and Teams*, 7, 169–199. doi:10.1016/S1534-0856(05)07008-8

Plé, L., & Clegg, S. (2013). How does the customer fit in relational coordination? An empirical study in multichannel retail banking. *Management (France)*, 16, 1. doi:10.3917/mana.161.0001

Rosnow, R. L., & Rosenthal, R. (1991). If you're looking at the cell means, you're not looking at only the interaction (Unless All Main Effects Are Zero). *Psychological Bulletin*, 110(3), 574–576. doi:10.1037/0033-2909.110.3.574

Schein, E. H. (2013). *Humble inquiry: The Gentle Art of Asking Instead of Telling*. Oakland: Berrett-Koehler Publishers.

Valentine, M. A., Nembhard, I. M., & Edmondson, A. C. (2015). Measuring teamwork in health care settings: A review of survey instruments. *Medical Care*, 53(4), e16–e30. doi:10.1097/MLR.0b013e31827feef6

Warfield, M. E., Chiri, G., Leutz, W. N., & Timberlake, M. (2013). Family well-being in a participant-directed autism waiver program: The role of relational coordination. *Journal of Intellectual Disability Research*, 58(12), 1091–1104. doi:10.1111/jir.12102

Weinberg, D. B., Lusenhop, R. W., Gittell, J. H., & Kautz, C. M. (2007). Coordination between formal providers and informal caregivers. *Health Care Management Review*, 32(2), 140–149. doi:10.1097/01.hmr.0000267790.24933.4c

Chapter 6

Constructing Relational Coordination Variables

Once you've collected your relational coordination data, the next step is to create your variables. In this chapter, you will learn to create variables for each of the seven dimensions of relational coordination. You'll learn how to use factor analysis and Cronbach's alpha to assess whether those seven dimensions form a single construct called the RC Index, or two separate constructs called RC Relationships and RC Communication. Next you will learn how to separate out relational coordination within roles, from relational coordination between roles. You'll also learn how to use proportional weighting to account for missing data, and how to create relational coordination as a categorical variable instead of a continuous variable, if needed. The statistical codes and video tutorials that support this chapter are accessible through rcsurveyhelp.info.

Constructing the Seven Dimensions of Relational Coordination

The first step in constructing the RC Index is to create a variable for each of the seven dimensions: Frequent Communication, Timely Communication, Accurate Communication, Problem-Solving Communication, Shared Goals, Shared Knowledge, and Mutual Respect. For example, Timely Communication is the average of a respondent's ratings of all roles regarding the timeliness of each role's communication with the respondent. Let's say that the respondent number 13 has rated the timeliness of communication he or she experiences from each of the roles as follows:

Timely Communication

$$\left[\left(\text{Role}^1 = 5\right) + \left(\text{Role}^2 = 5\right) + \left(\text{Role}^3 = 4\right) + \left(\text{Role}^4 = 2\right) + \left(\text{Role}^5 = 1\right)\right] / $$
$$\text{N roles}(5) = 3.4$$

Using the same simple process, we can construct all seven dimensions of relational coordination. For Frequent Communication, however, re-coding is needed because response 3 signifies the ideal frequency of communica-tion, and so is re-coded to 5. The frequency dimension is re-coded as follows: Far Too Little= 1, Too Little= 3, Just Right=5, Too Much=4, Far Too Much=2.

The score for each dimension is a mean of the aggregated scores of the ratings provided by all respondents regarding all the roles on this specific dimension. For example, the frequency of communication score will be an average of the scores reported by all the respondents regarding all roles on the frequency of communication. See Exhibit 6.2 for the equations used to construct these variables. You will end up with seven variables for each survey respondent associated with each of the seven dimensions of relational coordination—one for the frequency of communication, one for the timeliness of communication, one for the accuracy of communication, and so on.

Exhibit 6.1 Survey Responses from Respondent 13 (from Site A, Role 4)

Frequent Communication	Far too little	Too little	Just right	Too much	Far too much
Role 1	1	2	3	4	5
Role 2	1	2	3	4	5
Role 3	1	2	3	4	5
Role 4	1	2	3	4	5
Role 5	1	2	3	4	5
Timely Communication	Never	Rarely	Occasionally	Often	Always
Role 1	1	2	3	4	5
Role 2	1	2	3	4	5
Role 3	1	2	3	4	5
Role 4	1	2	3	4	5
Role 5	1	2	3	4	5
Accurate Communication	Never	Rarely	Occasionally	Often	Always
Role 1	1	2	3	4	5
Role 2	1	2	3	4	5
Role 3	1	2	3	4	5
Role 4	1	2	3	4	5
Role 5	1	2	3	4	5
Problem-Solving Communication	Never	Rarely	Occasionally	Often	Always
Role 1	1	2	3	4	5
Role 2	1	2	3	4	5
Role 3	1	2	3	4	5
Role 4	1	2	3	4	5
Role 5	1	2	3	4	5

(Continued)

Exhibit 6.1   (Continued)

Frequent Communication	Far too little	Too little	Just right	Too much	Far too much
Shared Goals	Not at All	A Little	Somewhat	A Lot	Completely
Role 1	1	2	3	4	5
Role 2	1	2	3	4	5
Role 3	1	2	3	4	5
Role 4	1	2	3	4	5
Role 5	1	2	3	4	5
Shared Knowledge	Nothing	A Little	Some	A Lot	Everything
Role 1	1	2	3	4	5
Role 2	1	2	3	4	5
Role 3	1	2	3	4	5
Role 4	1	2	3	4	5
Role 5	1	2	3	4	5
Mutual Respect	Not at All	A Little	Somewhat	A Lot	Completely
Role 1	1	2	3	4	5
Role 2	1	2	3	4	5
Role 3	1	2	3	4	5
Role 4	1	2	3	4	5
Role 5	1	2	3	4	5

Exhibit 6.2   Equations to Construct the Seven Dimensions of Relational
Coordination

Variable Name	Equation
Freq	mean (FreqRole1 FreqRole2 FreqRole3 FreqRole4 FreqRole5)
Time	mean (TimeRole1 TimeRole2 TimeRole3 TimeRole4 TimeRole5)
Accu	mean (AccuRole1 AccuRole2 AccuRole3 AccuRole4 AccuRole5)
Prob	mean (ProbRole1 ProbRole2 ProbRole3 ProbRole4 ProbRole5)
Goal	mean (GoalRole1 GoalRole2 GoalRole3 GoalRole4 GoalRole5)
Know	mean (KnowRole1 KnowRole2 KnowRole3 KnowRole4 KnowRole5)
Resp	mean (RespRole1 RespRole2 RespRole3 RespRole4 RespRole5)

Using Factor Analysis and Cronbach's Alpha to Assess Construct Validity

Special attention to construct validity is needed in order to justify aggregating the seven dimensions into either a single construct, or multiple constructs. Therefore, you should test the validity of aggregating the seven dimensions of relational coordination into one or more constructs. This process begins with factor analysis.

Exhibit 6.3 Exploratory Factor Analysis and Cronbach's Alpha from the Two Original Studies of Relational Coordination (Gittell, 2010)

	Study 1: Flight Departures	*Study 2: Patient Care*
Frequent Communication	0.55	0.57
Timely Communication	0.71	0.78
Accurate Communication	NA [1]	0.80
Problem-Solving Communication	0.62	0.78
Shared Goals	0.54	0.63
Shared Knowledge	0.57	0.63
Mutual Respect	0.72	0.66
Eigenvalue for Factor 1	2.32	3.41
Cronbach's Alpha	0.80	0.86

[1] Accurate Communication is not shown in Study 1, given that it did not emerge as a dimension of relational coordination until Study 2

Factor analysis is a method to test patterns of correlation between actual data collected through a set of measured variables and the conceptual construct hypothesized behind those measures. In the original study of flight departures and the original study of patient care, exploratory factor analyses (EFAs) were conducted (see Exhibit 6.3). Note that Accurate Communication is not shown in Study 1, given that it did not emerge as a dimension of relational coordination until Study 2. As shown in Exhibit 6.3, eigenvalues for Factor 1 in each study were well above 1, and all factor loadings were greater than 0.40, with no cross-loadings greater than 0.40. No items were dropped, and it was concluded that relational coordination was a single factor inclusive of both the communication and relationship dimensions. Cronbach's alpha tests for both studies produced scores that were well above the 0.70 recommended for new constructs, and equal to or greater than 0.80, the recommended threshold for established constructs (Nunnally, 1978).

Principles of Factor Analysis

Now that we've reviewed the original EFAs conducted with relational coordination data, let's delve more deeply into factor analysis. Large sets of measures are hard to interpret individually, as their cross-correlations can proliferate into a large complex matrix. Factor analysis has the advantage of being a statistical analysis that identifies unique constructs which different measures correlate to or load into. These unique constructs are called common factors. Factor analysis estimates the strength and direction of influence of these conceptual constructs or factors on each of the measures. These estimates are called factor loadings.

Whether one uses EFA or confirmatory factor analysis (CFA) depends on how much the researcher knows or foresees regarding the underlying conceptual factors linked to the measures. When expectations about the underlying structure of correlations are unclear or incomplete, as in the original two studies of relational coordination described above, EFA or unrestricted factor analysis is better suited to explore the number and structure of correlated common factors. When there are clear predictions about the number of common factors and their specific influence on each of the measures, it is better to use CFA or restricted factor analysis procedures.

When to Use Exploratory or Confirmatory Factor Analysis

EFA is mainly used when the researcher has no expectations about the number of common factors influencing the measured variables. Hence EFA answers about the nature of correlations between the different measured variables, specifically in the early stages of the research. For any given set of measures, EFA helps identify the constructs "latent factors" that influence the measured variables empirically, instead of tuition and relying solely on theoretical reasoning. Furthermore, when researchers begin constructing new instruments, EFA is crucial in identifying scale dimensionality or potential subscales. On the other hand, if the theory clearly identifies the exact number of factors and which measured variables they influence, CFA is the preferred procedure (Fabrigar & Wegener, 2011).

Assessing Relational Coordination through Exploratory or Confirmatory Factor Analysis

From the beginning, relational coordination theory identified two latent constructs: communication and relationships. The dimensions of Frequent Communication, Timely Communication, Accurate Communication, and Problem-Solving Communication have been hypothesized as measures of the communication involved in high-quality coordination; while the dimensions of Shared Goals, Shared Knowledge and Mutual Respect have been hypothesized as measures of the relationships involved in high-quality coordination. The theory furthermore highlights the iterative connection between the communication and relationship dimensions, in that they are expected to influence each other over time, as described by Gittell in "Relational Coordination: Coordinating Work Through Relationships of Shared Goals, Shared Knowledge and Mutual Respect" (Gittell, 2006).

Employees who felt disrespected by members of another function avoided communication (and even eye contact) with members of that function. The absence of frequent dialogue in turn solidified the existence of distinct "thought worlds" for each functional area, undermining relationships of shared knowledge. Without relationships of shared knowledge, employees were less able to engage in timely communication when circumstances changed, not knowing with sufficient precision who needed to know what and with what urgency. The lack of timely communication undermined relationships of shared goals, reinforcing the belief that each function was looking out for itself. Without shared goals, the easiest response to problems was to blame others for having caused the problem rather than to engage in problem-solving communication. The focus of communication around blaming rather than problem-solving further undermined mutual respect. This negative cycle decreased the potential for effective coordination to occur.

Among well-established teams, the communication dimensions of the construct are expected to become closely correlated with the relational dimensions of the construct through this mutually reinforcing process. Accordingly, the airline study identified through EFA a single latent factor rather than two. Most of the other studies that have used the relational coordination scale have empirically tested structural validity by running EFA on the observed dimensions of relational coordination, and their analysis has typically indicated one main latent factor that influences all the dimensions. Thus, the RC Index has been the construct produced from the relational coordination scale, and many researchers have refrained from calculating separate communication and relationship subscales based on the output from their EFA.

Case Study 6.1:   Communication and Relationships: How Two Constructs of Relational Coordination Explain the Wellbeing of Family Caregivers

(Warfield & Naim Ali, 2020)

Background. Self-directed or participant-directed waiver programs represent a new service model to support people with disabilities who have opted to live in the community rather than living in specialized care institutions. These programs pay caregivers to provide care to a family member with a disability. In a cross-sectional study, 121 paid family caregivers who provide care services through this program were interviewed to assess the impact of relational coordination between themselves and waiver program personnel—state officials, financial consultants, and insurance care managers—on their life satisfaction, mental well-being and financial well-being. Statistical analysis revealed significantly different impacts of the communication and relationship dimensions of relational coordination on these outcomes of interest. For example, the Communication Subscale affected caregivers' mental well-being while the Relationships Subscale and the RC Index had no significant impact on this outcome. In order to create two separate subscales, researchers had to confirm the validity and reliability of a

(Continued)

Case Study 6.1 (Continued)

Exhibit 6.4 Statistical Output from Exploratory Factor Analysis

Factor	Eigenvalue	Difference	Proportion	Cumulative
Factor 1	3.04649	2.90011	1.0663	1.0663
Factor 2	0.14639	0.05723	0.0512	1.1175
Factor 3	0.08916	0.08326	0.0312	1.1487
Factor 4	0.0059	0.06267	0.0021	1.1508
Factor 5	−0.05677	0.11301	−0.0199	1.1309
Factor 6	−0.16978	0.03452	−0.0594	1.0715
Factor 7	−0.2043	0.0000	−0.0715	1
CHI^2	290.69***			

*** $p < 0.001$

Exhibit 6.5 Factor Loadings of Different Dimensions on the Main
Common Factor

Variable	Factor 1	Factor 2	Factor 3	Factor 4	Uniqueness
Frequency	0.12	0.21	0.19	0.01	0.90
Timeliness	0.68	0.17	−0.11	−0.03	0.50
Accuracy	0.67	0.00	−0.16	0.02	0.52
Problem-Solving	0.81	0.05	0.02	0.05	0.34
Shared Goals	0.77	−0.10	0.06	0.00	0.39
Shared Knowledge	0.58	−0.24	0.08	−0.01	0.60
Mutual Respect	0.74	0.05	0.06	−0.05	0.45

two-factor model. The following section compares the different outputs of exploratory and confirmatory factor analysis conducted on the same population.

EFA. EFA conducted on the seven dimensions identified a single construct, suggested by the observation that Factor 1 had by far the highest eigenvalue of 3.046 as shown in Exhibit 6.4. Exhibit 6.5 shows the factor loadings and uniqueness levels. Note that the factor loadings represent the correlation between each variable and each factor, while uniqueness indicates the proportion of the common variance of the variable that is not associated with the factors. The results in Exhibit 6.4 indicate that there is one factor underlying the seven dimensions.

CFA. CFA confirmed the two-factor model to be an excellent fit for the data. The dimensions of Timely Communication, Accurate Communication, and Problem-Solving Communication fully loaded onto one latent construct called Communication, while the dimensions of Shared Goals, Shared Knowledge, and Mutual Respect fully loaded onto a second construct called Relationships. Both constructs

(*Continued*)

Case Study 6.1 (Continued)

were found to be highly and positively correlated with a covariance of 0.93 (p<0.001). CFA model fit statistics showed the following:

Model chi-square "chi-square statistic we obtain from the maximum likelihood statistic" of 14.87 (p = 0.316) and statistically nonsignificant, which means there was no significant variation to reject the model or in our case the two constructs hypothesis (Pituch, 2015).

Confirmatory factor index "values can range between 0 and 1 (values greater than 0.90, conservatively 0.95 indicate good fit)" was 0.99 which indicates a good fit model (Schumacker & Lomax, 2016).

The root mean square error of approximation (RMSEA) was 0.035, with values less than 0.05 indicating excellent fit. Additionally the standardized root mean squared residual (SRMR) was 0.037, with values less than 0.08 deemed acceptable and values of 0 indicating perfect fit (Hooper, Coughlan, & Mullen, 2008).

After affirming the fitness of using the two-factor model, Structural Equation Modeling (SEM) was used to measure the factor loadings and their p-values. For more on this analysis and its statistical output, refer to rcsurveyhelp.info.

In some studies of relational coordination, however, researchers have conducted statistical analysis that used communication and relationship dimensions separately to model outcomes, based on observing different outcomes of the communication dimensions compared to the relationship dimensions (Romanow, Rai, & Keil, 2018). Other researchers have created the two subconstructs to more closely diagnose and evaluate networks between the studied roles (Hustoft et al., 2018). The following study of relational coordination in a community-based care model provides a detailed example of the latter.

Creating the Relational Coordination Index or the Communication and Relationships Subindices

The RC Index is a scale constructed for each respondent by averaging his or her aggregated scores of the seven dimensions (Frequency, Timeliness,

Exhibit 6.6 Creating the RC Index and Its Communication and Relationships Subindices

Variable Name	Equation
Total RC Index	Standardized Mean of All Seven Dimensions (Freq Time Accu Prob Goal Know Resp)
Communication Subindex	Standardized Mean of the Four Communication Dimensions (Freq Time Accu Prob)
Relationships Subindex	Standardized Mean of Three Relationship Dimensions (Goal Know Resp)

Accuracy, Problem-Solving, Shared Goals, Shared Knowledge, Mutual Respect) across all roles regardless of missing values. The RC Index for the site is then created by averaging the RC Index for all respondents in that site. We recommend an additive scaling method in which each item is standardized with a mean of zero and a standard deviation of one. If you have found a two-factor solution using CFA, this justifies creating the Communication and Relationships Subindices. Coding for both options is shown in Exhibit 6.6.

Computing Relational Coordination Within and Between Roles

The next step is to create distinct measures of within-role relational coordination and between-role relational coordination. Why? According to organizational theory, coordination challenges are typically greater *between* roles than *within roles*, given the silos created by organizational and professional structures (Dougherty, 1992; Gittell & Douglass, 2012).

If you think of a matrix diagram, between-role coordination is represented by the off-diagonal squares, and within-role coordination is represented by the on-diagonal squares. If you think of a network map, between-role coordination is represented by the lines between the nodes, while within-role coordination is represented by the nodes themselves. This will be further illustrated in Chapter 7. To create within and between-role measures of relational coordination, you simply refine your existing measures by adding a filter. For your between-role RC scores, you generate a new variable averaging the already created RC scores after using a filter to exclude respondents' ratings of their own role. For your within-role RC score, you generate a new variable using a filter to include only the respondents' ratings of their own role. See Exhibit 6.7 for statistics used to calculate within and between-role relational coordination.

While many studies do not report whether their findings are based on overall relational coordination or between-role relational coordination, many of the original published findings were based on between-role

Exhibit 6.7 Calculating Within and Between-Role Relational Coordination

Variable Name	Equation
Within-Role Relational Coordination	= RC_Role1 if Participant Role = Role1 & = RC_Role2 if Participant Role = Role2 & = RC_Role3 if Participant Role = Role3 & = RC_Role4 if Participant Role = Role4 & = RC_Role5 if Participant Role = Role5

Between-Role Relational Coordination	= mean (RC_Role2 RC_Role3 RC_Role4 RC_Role5)
	  if Participant Role = Role1
	& = mean (RC_Role1 RC_Role3 RC_Role4 RC_Role5)
	  if Participant Role = Role2
	& = mean (RC_Role1 RC_Role2 RC_Role4 RC_Role5)
	  if Participant Role = Role3
	& = mean (RC_Role1 RC_Role2 RC_Role3 RC_Role5)
	  if Participant Role = Role4
	& = mean (RC_Role1 RC_Role2 RC_Role3 RC_Role4)
	  if Participant Role = Role5

relational coordination. Depending on the nature of the work you are studying, you might find that between-role relational coordination matters most for quality and efficiency outcomes, for example, while within-role relational coordination may matter equally or more for worker well-being. After deciding which is appropriate to your study, you can simply state in your methods section that relational coordination is conceptualized and measured in your study as within-role coordination, between-role coordination, overall coordination, or all of the above.

Computing Relational Coordination Between Particular Roles

In addition to distinguishing between relational coordination within roles versus between roles, you may also want to assess relational coordination between *particular* roles at the dyadic level. Relational coordination with Role 1, for example, will be an average of the seven different scores reported by the respondent for their relational coordination with Role 1: RCRole1 = mean (FreqRole1 TimeRole1 AccuRole1 ProbRole1 GoalRole1 KnowRole1 RespRole1). If there are 5 roles in your study, for example, this will result in 5 new variables for each survey respondent—one for relational coordination with Role 1, another for relational coordination with Role 2, and so on. Equations and codes to construct each of these variables can be accessed online at rcsurveyhelp.info. As shown in Exhibit 6.8, these calculations enable you to produce the equivalent of a 360-degree evaluation of each role from the perspective of each of the other roles. This 360-degree evaluation of a particular role will be shown visually in Chapter 7 as an *ego view of the relational coordination network*.

Exhibit 6.8 360 Feedback—Calculating Relational Coordination as Experienced by All Roles with Each Other Role

Variable Name (Relational Coordination Reported with These Roles)	Equation (Relational Coordination Reported by These Roles)
RC_Role1	mean (FreqRole1 TimeRole1 AccuRole1 ProbRole1 GoalRole1 KnowRole1 RespRole1)
RC_Role2	mean (FreqRole2 TimeRole2 AccuRole2 ProbRole2 GoalRole2 KnowRole2 RespRole2)
RC_Role3	mean (FreqRole3 TimeRole3 AccuRole3 ProbRole3 GoalRole3 KnowRole3 RespRole3)
RC_Role4	mean (FreqRole4 TimeRole4 AccuRole4 ProbRole4 GoalRole4 KnowRole4 RespRole4)
RC_Role5	mean (FreqRole5 TimeRole5 AccuRole5 ProbRole5 GoalRole5 KnowRole5 RespRole5)

Accounting for Missing Values Using Proportional Weighting

All surveys are subject to missing values to some extent, as participants' responsiveness differs based on their motivation and commitment to data collection. Data cleaning and correcting for missingness for the Relational Coordination Survey will follow the same steps as for all other survey analyses. But we have reason to expect differences in the level of relational coordination reported depending on the role of the respondent, due to the organizational and professional structures that can differentially shape how each role experiences relational coordination. Therefore, to preserve the integrity of each role's contribution to your relational coordination measures, your measures should be corrected using proportional weights, particularly when missing values exceed 10 percent of the responses for any

Exhibit 6.9 Calculating Sampling or Proportional Weights

Roles	# Respondents from Invited Sample	# Invited in Selected Sample	Weights "Nominator"	Weights "Denominator"	Proportional Weights
Doctors	3	5	5/35 ≈ 0.14	3/25 ≈ 0.12	0.14/0.12 = **1.19**
Nurses	15	20	20/35 ≈ 0.57	15/25 ≈ 0.6	0.57/0.6 = **0.95**
Medical Assistants	7	10	10/35 ≈ 0.29	7/25 ≈ 0.28	0.29/0.28 = **1.02**
Total	**25**	**35**	—	—	—

given role. Here is an example of staff working in a clinic that shows how to correct relational coordination scores using proportional weights.

Equation for survey "proportional" weight calculation=

$$W_P = \frac{\text{percent of the Population}}{\text{percent of the Respondents}} = \frac{\dfrac{P_i}{P_{\text{total}}}}{\dfrac{R_i}{R_{\text{total}}}}$$

Following the above equation, we first calculate the nominator which is "percent of total target population within each role" by dividing total number of invited participants per role (P_i) over the total number of invited participants across all roles (P_{total}). Then to calculate the denominator which is "the percent of respondents within each role", we divide the number of respondents from each role (R_i) over the total number of respondents across all roles (R_{total}) (see above table).

Custom Weighting Note

Proportional weighting is the default weighting method to adjust for missingness in survey data. Yet in some instances, for conceptual and methodological reasons, researchers need to administer a customized weight to adjust the scores. Please refer to rcsurveyhelp.info for sample codes to create custom weights for your relational coordination measures.

Continuous Versus Nominal Reporting of the RC Index

Using the RC Index as a continuous variable yields a great advantage for predicting outcomes of interest and for comparing scores between sites and over time. Nonetheless, there may be reasons to create a noncontinuous score. For example in Chapter 4, Case Study 4.4 was a randomized control trial where researchers needed the outcomes—including relational coordination—to be binary to succinctly appraise the success or failure of their intervention. The RC Index can be categorized into three incremental terciles. Based on previous studies, strong between-role ties are usually represented with scores equal to or above 4.0, while moderate between-role ties are those with scores equal to or above 3.5 but below 4.0. Finally, weak between-role ties are often identified as ties with scores below 3.5. For within-role ties, the terciles differ given that within-role ties tend to be significantly stronger than between-role ties. Any changes in these terciles, based on updated data from a meta-analysis of completed studies, can be found at rcsurveyhelp.info.

We recommend using the RC Index as a continuous variable to benefit from the full range of variation, and to avoid losing valuable information. However, if necessary, categorical variables can be generated following the above-mentioned ranges, even creating dichotomous variables where ties are defined as either strong (above 4.0) or not.

Summing Up

Chapter 6 has shown you how to take your relational coordination data and transform it into variables—and then into validated constructs. We hope you have paused to visit the online materials—including video tutorials, coding, and sample data sets—to practice creating variables and validated constructs on your own. You will then be ready to begin visualizing your data through matrices and networks see to more clearly the relational patterns that people are experiencing, and to help them to see more clearly what they are experiencing as well.

References

Dougherty, D. (1992). Interpretive barriers to successful product innovation in large firms. *Organization Science*, 3(2), 179–202. doi:10.1287/orsc.3.2.179

Fabrigar, L. R., & Wegener, D. T. (2011) *Exploratory Factor Analysis*. Oxford, UK: Oxford University Press.

Gittell, J. H. (2006). Relational coordination: Coordinating work through relationships of shared goals, shared knowledge and mutual respect. In O. Kyriakidou & M. Özbilgin (Eds.), *Relational Perspectives in Organizational Studies: A Research Companion*. Cheltenham, UK; Northampton, MA: Edward Elgar.

Gittell, J. H., & Douglass, A. (2012). Relational bureaucracy: Structuring reciprocal relationships into roles. *Academy of Management Review*, 37(4), 709–733. doi:10.5465/amr.2010.0438

Hooper, D., Coughlan, J., & Mullen, M. (2008). Structural equation modeling: Guidelines for determining model fit. *The Electronic Journal of Business Research Methods*, 6(1): 53–60.

Hustoft, M., Hetlevik, Ø., Aßmus, J., Størkson, S., Gjesdal, S., & Biringer, E. (2018). Communication and relational ties in inter-professional teams in Norwegian specialized health care: A multicentre study of relational coordination. *International Journal of Integrated Care*, 18(2), 9–9. doi:10.5334/ijic.3432

Nunnally, J. C. (1978). *Psychometric Theory* (2nd ed.). New York: McGraw-Hill.

Pituch, K. A. (2015). *Applied Multivariate Statistics for the Social Sciences*. Oxfordshire, UK: Routledge.

Romanow, D., Rai, A., & Keil, M. (2018). CPOE-enabled coordination: Appropriation for deep structure use and impacts on patient outcomes. *MIS Quarterly*, 42(1), 189–212. doi:10.25300/misq/2018/13275

Schumacker, R. E., & Lomax, R. G. (2016). *A Beginner's Guide to Structural Equation Modeling*. Psychology Press.

Warfield, M. E., & Naim Ali, H. (2020). *Communication and Relationships: How Two Constructs of Relational Coordination Explain the Wellbeing of Family Caregivers in Waiver Program for People with Disability*. Working Paper. Heller School. Brandeis University.

Chapter 7

Visualizing and Analyzing Relational Coordination Data with Matrices and Networks

Because relational coordination is a network measure, matrices and networks can be used to visualize the strength of communication and relationships between roles. Visualizing your relational coordination variables in this way can be highly useful for helping participants to better understand the characteristics of the network in which they are working. These visualizations can also inform the design of interventions, by illustrating which roles are already connected by high levels of relational coordination, and which are not. These visualizations can also be useful for developing testable hypotheses about which management practices are responsible for strengthening or weakening coordination between specific roles, and whether weak coordination between specific roles may be preventing the achievement of desired outcomes. For example, in the study "Is the Doctor In?" the researchers were able to see from the matrix shown in Chapter 5 that patients whose physician was employed as a hospitalist benefited from stronger relational coordination between the physician and nonphysician members of their care team. The researchers were then able to test the hypothesis that the new hospitalist job design was responsible for stronger relational coordination as well as for higher quality and lower cost patient care outcomes. Ultimately, repeating the measurement over multiple time points will reveal the effect of implemented managerial practices and further validate those hypotheses.

The primary goal of this chapter is therefore to help you create useful visualizations of your relational coordination variables. We will then show how network metrics like density and centrality can be applied to your relational coordination data.

Principles of Social Network Analysis

The Oxford Dictionary defines a network as "an interconnected system of groups or people." By this definition, every system can be considered a network given that every human, and even every object, is connected by some means to others. Network analysis—sometimes called graph analysis—has been known and used across different disciplines such as anthropology, sociology, mathematics, communications, physics and computer science. Its modern beginning started in 1930 when Moreno drew a graph of a social network to study interpersonal relations and founded the science of social network visualization also known as sociometry (De Nooy, Mrvar, & Batagelj, 2018). The concept of social networks itself stretches back centuries, with the example of descendant lists mentioned in the Bible and old cultural scripts as a way to distinguish attributes and link them to individual families (Freeman, 2004).

Traditional social science has tended to focus on studying individual behavior and linking it to individual characteristics, neglecting to recognize the impact on individual behavior of dynamic interactions with others (Freeman, 2004). Analyzing systems of relationships has therefore provided social science with fresh perspectives.

All networks are analyzed based on two components—actors and the links that connect them. Different disciplines identify actors in a network or graph analysis using different nomenclatures—for example, nodes, vertices, points or atoms—while the connections are called lines, bridges, links, or ties. The connections can be bidirectional where both actors are connected and contribute equally to the relationship. The line between them is then called an "edge." And when the relation is unilateral, the directed line is called an "arc." Lastly, if a line tracks a node back to itself, then it will be called a "loop." Networks with nodes only connected through one line, undirected or directed, are called "simple networks"; but when a node has multiple lines to the same node, the network is identified as a "multiplex network." Because relational coordination data involve multiple actors with layered relationships, they are multiplex networks. The term *multiplex* comes primarily from telecommunication and computer networks where multiple signals are combined into one signal over a shared medium, for example, as different phone calls are carried using the same wire. Similarly, multiplex in the context of social networks means having multifaceted relationships between two people, also known as having multiple layers of the same relationship (Rousseau, 2012).

In practical terms, multiplex network representations of relational coordination can be mapped using either the overall RC Index or any of the seven dimensions. You can create a network map specifically focused on mutual respect among roles in a workplace, for example, or focused specifically on timely communication. This level of specificity is particularly useful when diagnosing a situation, because it allows you to drill down into areas of opportunity for improvement and facilitate more nuanced conversations among participants. We will return to this topic in Chapter 10 when we explore how to leverage relational coordination to create positive change.

To analyze a social network, we need to identify the nodes of the network. Nodes can be anything—people, communities, cities, countries, even objects as equipment, resources, and information. The second components of a network are the lines that connect the nodes. Lines in social network analysis are dyadic, which means a characteristic that is shared by the two connected nodes (McCulloh, 2013). Some examples of dyadic relations are as follows:

–   Kinship relationships [mother, son, wife...]
–   Other role-based relationships [boss, teacher, neighbor...]
–   Affiliations [same club, same university...]
–   Affective relationships [likes, respects, hates...]
–   Cognitive relationships [knows of, views as....]
–   Actions [talks, has lunch with, attacks...]
–   Other interactions [trades, retweets...]
–   Flows [N cars crossing a road...]
–   Distance [miles traveled...]
–   Co-occurrence [same hair color, religion...]

How do these principles of social networks apply to relational coordination? Relational coordination data are a specific type of social network data that describe the coordination of interdependent tasks. The *nodes in a relational coordination network* therefore represent roles that carry out interdependent tasks, for example, organizations that are working together to repair the national transportation infrastructure or respond to a pandemic or similar crisis. The nodes of a relational coordination network might also represent a set of professionals who are working with the same population of students or patients, or family members who are working together to run a household or plan a trip, or professionals and family members who are working together to care for a family member in need. Whether the nodes are organizations or professional roles, the *lines in a relational coordination network* represent dyadic relations that span across several categories found in social network analysis. These lines represent:

–   Role-based relationships (e.g. doctor/nurse; student/teacher; parent/child; marketing/finance; etc.), and
–   Affective relationships (e.g. mutual respect; shared goals), and
–   Cognitive relationships (e.g. shared knowledge), and
–   Actions (e.g. timely communication, problem-solving communication) consistent with the dimensions of relational coordination.

Matrix Diagrams

We often visualize network data initially as a matrix diagram. Similarly, your relational coordination data can be used to build a matrix diagram to visualize patterns of relational coordination between the roles in the work process you have measured, prior to developing a network map. A matrix such as the

Exhibit 7.1 Symmetric Matrix of Relational Coordination Ties

		Relational Coordination Reported *with* These Roles				
		Physicians	Nurses	Physical Therapists	Case Managers	Social Workers
Relational Coordination Reported *by* These Roles	Physicians	**3.82**	3.94	4.03	3.75	3.70
	Nurses	3.81	**4.48**	4.27	4.03	3.92
	Physical Therapists	3.85	4.25	**4.71**	4.06	3.94
	Case Managers	3.83	4.36	4.43	**4.45**	4.37
	Social Workers	3.93	4.01	4.03	4.17	**4.36**
	All	3.85	4.21	4.29	4.09	4.06

one shown here in Exhibit 7.1 underlies any network map, with the numbers on the diagonal representing the strength of within-role ties, and the numbers on the off-diagonals representing the strength of between-role ties.

Exhibit 7.1 is an example of a matrix diagram that was created for the nine-hospital study of surgical care. This matrix diagram shows patterns of relational coordination among physicians, nurses, therapists, case managers, and social workers, as reported by the respondents in the left-hand column. Within-role ties are highlighted in bold. Because all roles in the work process were surveyed, it is a symmetric matrix, meaning that the same roles are represented along the left-hand column and along the top row. The data collected therefore enable us to observe the strength of ties *between* each of the roles in the work process, and also to observe the strength of ties *within* each of the roles in the work process. We can assess where ties are weakest, and where they are strongest. For example, we can see that within-role ties reported by any given role tend to be stronger than the between-role ties reported by that role (and indeed t-tests showed that these differences are statistically significant). We can also see in this case that the weakest ties reported by any role, except physicians, are their ties with physicians (again, t-tests can be conducted to determine whether these differences are statistically significant).

When you are not able to survey all roles in your work process, your matrix will be *asymmetric*, meaning that only a subset of the roles shown in the top row will also be found in the left-hand column. Exhibit 7.2 shows a matrix diagram from a study of medical care, showing the strength of relational coordination with physicians, residents, nurses, therapists, and case managers, as reported by the roles in the left-hand column. Physicians and residents were determined to be central to the work process but were not

Exhibit 7.2 Asymmetric Matrix of Relational Coordination Ties

		Relational Coordination Reported *with* These Roles				
		Physicians	Residents	Nurses	Therapists	Case Managers
Relational Coordination Reported *by* These Roles	**Nurses**	3.77	3.93	**4.35**	3.86	4.05
	Therapists	2.36	2.46	3.97	**4.28**	3.74
	Case Managers	3.65	3.25	4.23	3.17	**4.52**
	All	3.26	3.21	4.18	3.77	4.10

surveyed in this case; therefore they are represented along the top row but not along the left-hand column. As shown in Exhibit 7.2, the data in an asymmetric matrix enable us to observe the strength of ties *between* each of the surveyed roles, the strength of ties *within* each of the surveyed roles, and the strength of ties *with the unsurveyed roles from the perspective of the surveyed roles.*

To summarize, a matrix diagram—whether symmetric or asymmetric—can be built using the relational coordination data collected for any work process.

Blockmodeling Using Matrix Diagrams

Using a matrix diagram, blockmodeling is a technique to analyze networks and to highlight variations in the strength of the ties within that network. Blockmodeling provides an initial perspective into the patterns that exist between roles in a network and helps us to identify potentially *cohesive* groups or subsets of the network that have relatively stronger ties compared to others. These subsets of the network that are identified as *cohesive* are those that exhibit more frequent, positive, and direct ties with each other (Barends & Rousseau, 2018). Exhibit 7.3 shows a relational coordination matrix representing formal and informal healthcare providers who work with patients at three different stages of care—hospital, rehabilitation center, and home—in the joint replacement surgery process. This example is found in the study "Modularity and the Coordination of Complex Work" (Hagigi, 2008), and is also summarized in *High-Performance Healthcare* (Gittell, 2009).

In this matrix, as in other relational coordination matrices, each cell represents the strength of relational coordination from the perspective of the role listed on the left about the role listed at the top. The strength of ties is indicated by a number ranging from 1 to 5 in each cell. Strong ties in this particular matrix are designated as those that are equal to or greater than 3.0, indicated in bold and with shading. Note that this matrix is asymmetric, similar to the matrix shown in Exhibit 7.2. When a subset of roles

Exhibit 7.3 Blockmodeling Using a Relational Coordination Matrix for Postsurgical Care

Relational Coordination Reported by These Roles	Relational Coordination Reported with These Roles											
	Family Member	Hospital Case Manager	Rehab Case Manager	Hospital Physical Therapist	Rehab Physical Therapist	Home Physical Therapist	Rehab Nurse	Home Care Nurse	Surgeon	Rehab Physician	Primary Care Physician	Managed Care Case Manager
Family Member	---	1.8	2.1	2.4	2.8	3.6	3.0	3.3	3.3	2.1	1.9	1.2
Hospital Case Manager	3.6	1.3	2.6	4.3	2.3	2.2	2.2	2.5	3.5	1.1	2.5	3.9
Rehab Case Manager	3.3	2.2	4.5	1.9	4.4	1.9	4.3	2.2	2.1	3.6	1.8	2.7
Hospital Physical Therapist	1.9	3.8	1.1	4.1	1.4	1.3	1.2	1.1	3.4	1.1	1.1	1.2
Rehab Physical Therapist	3.0	1.7	4.2	2.1	4.6	1.8	4.2	1.5	2.3	3.8	1.4	1.5
Home Physical Therapist	3.3	1.8	1.5	1.9	1.9	4.3	1.6	3.8	3.5	1.6	2.0	2.1
Home Care Nurse	3.4	1.5	1.2	1.3	1.3	4.0	1.2	4.5	2.7	1.2	2.1	1.5
Primary Care Physician	1.9	1.5	1.8	1.3	1.7	1.4	1.7	1.5	2.2	1.4	1.2	1.3

surveyed about their coordination with a larger set of roles, the resulting matrix is asymmetric meaning that some ties are reported from the perspective of one role only.

This matrix in Exhibit 7.3 seems a bit random. However, reorganizing the matrix around the stage of care represented by each of the roles can help convey more useful information about the relational coordination network. Exhibit 7.4 shows this matrix reorganized around the three stages of care––hospital, rehabilitation centers, and home. The researchers placed the roles that worked with patients at all three stages of care at the bottom of the matrix as a separate category of roles that could potentially play the role of system integrators following the logic of a design structure matrix (DSM) used by Steve Eppinger and colleagues to analyze modular systems (Eppinger & Browning, 2012).

Reorganizing the matrix in this way enabled the researchers to visualize the relatively tight clusters of relational coordination within each stage of care, and the relatively weak relational coordination between stages of care. We can see that nearly all coordination within each stage of care met the threshold for being a strong tie, while almost no coordination between the three stages of care met this threshold. The one exception of a strong tie between the stages of care was the tie between hospital-based orthopedic surgeons and physical therapists working with patients postdischarge in their homes.

Now let's turn our attention to the roles that spanned across all three stages of care. We can now ask, which of these roles were functioning as system integrators, in the sense of having strong ties with at least one role within each of the three stages of care? The primary care providers had no strong ties with any of the three stages of care, suggesting they were not playing a system integrator role. Interestingly, the health system represented in this matrix was engaged in an intervention to give the primary care providers a system integrator role. Clearly that intervention was not yet working. The managed case managers had one strong tie—with the hospital case manager. The researchers suggested that the managed care case manager, representing the payor, was particularly interested in moving patients as quickly as feasible out of hospital care, given its high cost. Only the family members of the patients had strong ties with each of the three stages of care. This finding suggests that for better or worse, family members were in fact, and perhaps by default, playing the role of system integrators in this system of care. Only family members in this system had developed central roles and as a result they appeared to act as "brokers" across the three relatively cohesive stage-based care teams that for the most part did not coordinate with each other.

The researchers concluded based on qualitative data they gathered that this pattern was not what was intended by health system leaders. They also concluded that this pattern of coordination was not likely to be equitable given the differential ability of family members to serve as system

Exhibit 7.4 Example of Blockmodeling with the Matrix Reorganized by Stage of Care

| | | | Relational Coordination Reported with These Roles | | | | | | | | | | |
| | | Hospital Stage of Care | | | Rehabilitation Stage of Care | | | | Home Stage of Care | | Across Stages of Care | | |
Relational Coordination Reported by These Roles		Surgeon	Hospital Case Manager	Hospital Physical Therapist	Rehab Physician	Rehab Nurse	Rehab Case Manager	Rehab Physical Therapist	Home Care Nurse	Home Physical Therapist	Primary Care Physician	Family Member	Managed Care Case Manager
Hospital Stage of Care	Hospital Case Manager	3.5	1.3	4.3	1.1	2.2	2.6	2.3	2.5	2.2	2.5	3.6	3.9
	Hospital Physical Therapist	3.4	3.8	4.1	1.1	1.2	1.1	1.4	1.1	1.3	1.1	1.9	1.2
Rehab Stage of Care	Rehab Case Manager	2.1	2.2	1.9	3.6	4.3	4.5	4.4	2.2	1.9	1.8	3.3	2.7
	Rehab Physical Therapist	2.3	1.7	2.1	3.8	4.2	4.2	4.6	1.5	1.8	1.4	3.0	1.5
Home Stage of Care	Home Care Nurse	2.7	1.5	1.3	1.2	1.2	1.2	1.3	4.5	4.0	2.1	3.4	1.5
	Home Physical Therapist	3.5	1.8	1.9	1.6	1.6	1.5	1.9	3.8	4.3	2.0	3.3	2.1
Across Stages of Care	Primary Care Physician	2.2	1.5	1.3	1.4	1.7	1.8	1.7	1.5	1.4	1.2	1.9	1.3
	Family Member	3.3	1.8	2.4	2.1	3.0	2.1	2.8	3.3	3.6	1.9	---	1.2

Exhibit 7.5　Relational Coordination Matrix for Demonstrating Network Manipulation

Department	Relational Coordination Reported by These Roles	Relational Coordination Reported with These Roles								
		Cardiac Physician	Cardiac Nurse	Cardiac Adm.	Surgical Physician	Surgical Nurse	Surgical Adm.	ER Physician	ER Nurse	ER Adm.
Cardiology	Cardiac P.	3.6	4.2	3.3	3.1	3.6	2.1	3.5	3.2	2.8
	Cardiac N.	4.5	4.7	4.1	3.9	4.2	3.9	3.7	3.8	3.6
	Cardiac Adm.	2.9	3.6	3.9	1.9	2.9	3.4	2.1	3	3.1
	Total RC		3.9			3.2			3.2	
Surgery	Surgical P.	4.1	3.9	3.4	4.2	4.4	3.2	3.9	3.7	2.5
	Surgical N.	4.2	4.7	4	4.7	4.8	4.5	4	4.2	3.8
	Surgical Adm.	2.1	3.4	3.4	3.2	4.3	4.5	1.8	1.9	2.9
	Total RC		3.7			4.2			3.2	
Emergency	ER P.	3.9	3.4	3	4.3	4.2	3.5	4.8	4.9	4.2
	ER N.	4.2	4.5	3.8	4.3	4.5	4	4.9	5.0	4.4
	ER Adm.	2	2.4	3	1.4	1.6	2	3.5	4	4.2
	Total RC		3.4			3.3			4.4	

Within Roles		Between Roles	
Weak	< 4.1	Weak	< 3.5
Moderate	4.1–4.6	Moderate	3.5–4.0
Strong	> 4.6	Strong	> 4.0

Norms updated based on terciles of RC data collected 2012-2015 integrators for surgical care, based on their educational, financial resources and time resources, and even their personal social networks. While some families have personal networks that provide easy access to advice from nurses and doctors, for example, others do not.

Network Visualization Analysis

Social network analysis is based on visual analysis of the network, followed by computation of network metrics. The first step to analyze a network is through visualization, in order to assess the structure, shape, and spacing of the network. Digital network drawing and analysis have helped to detect patterns, calculate probability and predict connections. Multiple programs can be used to draw and analyze social networks. The most-used programs include Kumu sumApp, Gephi, Cytoscape, UCInet, NodeXl, Netminer, Pajek, and Social Network Visualizer. Relational Coordination Survey vendors also provide several visualization options for your relational coordination data.

Our eyes are trained to detect patterns and identify parallels. Seeing the network as a whole conveys information that is as important as breaking it down quantitatively and counting the frequency and direction of ties connecting the nodes. Digital graphing of social networks enables many graphical variations to display social networks and enhance visualization as an analytical technique (Borgatti, Everett, & Johnson, 2013).

Manipulation

Social networks—especially multiplex networks—can be viewed in different ways through manipulation. One approach is to select certain clusters or key parts from large networks to boost visualization. These selected clusters form a "partition." Dividing a network into partitions facilitates their description and comparison, allowing us to deduce more information to analyze their importance. This is called a *local view*—the view of a subnetwork extracted from a larger network, displaying only the nodes and lines incident with it. Another analysis tool available through network manipulation is reduction, which means dropping the complex aspect of network loops and multiple lines to visualize the network in its simplest format. This is called a *global view*—a zoom out view that displays connections between subnetworks instead of nodes. Thirdly, digital building of networks has created the option to easily change the focus of how we split and compare parts of networks. Mutually exclusive partitions can be turned into smaller subsets called subnetworks. This is sometimes called a *contextual view*—a detailed view of one partition/subnetwork with all the nodes and lines involved in it, while the rest of the network is reduced and connected to the chosen subnetwork through aggregated ties. Finally, to analyze the power of certain players, an ego network can be constructed. An *ego network* is where one node is extracted out of the network and its ties with other nodes are analyzed, often to visualize and assess high influence actors. In the case of relational coordination networks, an ego network is sometimes shared with each role to enable participants to focus on how well they are meeting the coordination needs of all other roles in their network, and vice versa.

In sum, network manipulation can enhance visual comparison by changing the focus on specific partitions and subnetworks, thus creating multiple views of the same network. The following RC matrix shows the relational coordination ties between different roles in a tertiary hospital, subgrouped by their specialty department. Note that P. signifies physician, while N. signifies nurse, and Adm. signifies administrator.

Based on normalized RC survey data collected between 2012 and 2015, RC scores are categorized to indicate the strength of the ties using distinct colors. Scoring differs if the ties are between roles or within roles, because within role ties tend to be stronger than between role ties. **Between role** RC scores that are below 3.5 indicate weak ties; between 3.5 and 4 indicate moderate ties; and above 4 indicate strong ties. Cutoffs for within role RC scores are set at a higher level. **Within role** RC scores that are below 4.1 indicate weak ties; between 4.1 and 4.6 indicate moderate ties; and above 4.6 indicate strong ties. In both cases, orange or red is typically used to indicate weak ties, blue to indicate moderate ties, and green to indicate strong ties.

The four views shown in Exhibit 7.6 are extracted from this matrix diagram. In all four views, each of the roles is represented as a circle connected to other roles through colored lines. The circles are also colored to indicate the strength of RC ties within the same role.

Alternative Views of the Same Relational Coordination Network

The first, Exhibit 7.6.1, is a *global view* of the whole network of three roles (physicians, nurses, administrators) from three different departments (its matrix is shown in Exhibit 7.5). The *global view* allows the viewer to initially identify key roles, those with higher number or stronger ties compared to others, especially if those ties are between departments. When the research question involves exploration of RC between departments, it is more sensible to start with this global view to see, for example, which role is acting as a boundary spanner or liaison between departments. In this example, nurses, regardless of their department, are reporting stronger ties with roles in other departments than are physicians or administrators.

Exhibit 7.6.2.1 show three views, each of which is a *local view* of ties between roles in the same department. Local views help you to conduct a focused analysis by dividing the global network into smaller partitions using a common attribute filter. In this example, the attribute is the department. The local views identify weak ties between administrators and physicians, especially in the cardiology and surgical departments.

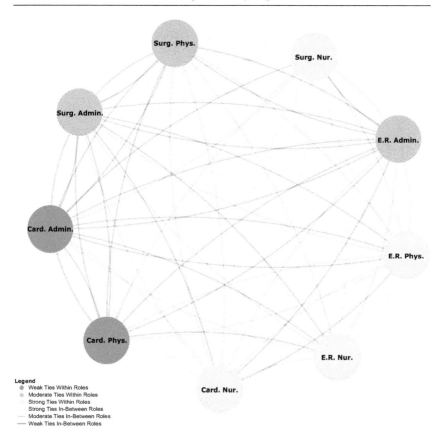

Legend
- Weak Ties Within Roles
- Moderate Ties Within Roles
- Strong Ties Within Roles
- Strong Ties In-Between Roles
- Moderate Ties In-Between Roles
- Weak Ties In-Between Roles

Exhibit 7.6.1 Global View for the Whole Network

On the other hand, a *contextual view* as shown in Exhibit 7.6.3 seeks to provide information relevant to a specific question, where some roles or ties are omitted as they are irrelevant to the question. In our example, the contextual view mainly focuses on interactions between roles on the frontline of care who are working with patients.

Practically speaking, different views can help the viewer to spot patterns and identify findings that motivate further analysis. For example, a local view can quickly pinpoint the presence of weaker ties among a specific set of roles while a global view gives a comprehensive picture of the overall interactions between roles in your network.

The *ego* view is beneficial for focusing on the ties of one key role at a time, either to compare them to other key roles at the same point in time, to compare them to themselves over time if multiple assessments are conducted at different intervals, or simply to enable that role to better understand and improve its ties with other roles in its network. The same network

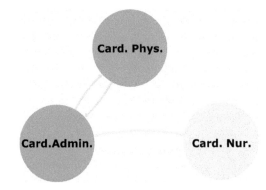

Exhibit 7.6.2.1 Local View for the Cardiology Department

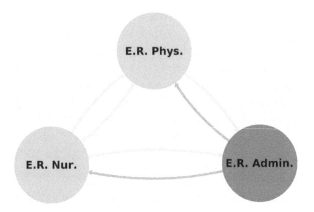

Exhibit 7.6.2.2 Local View for the Emergency Department

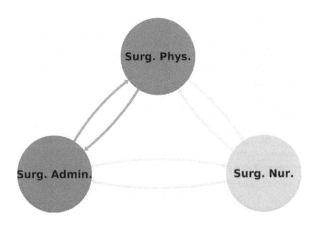

Exhibit 7.6.2.3 Local View for the Surgical Department

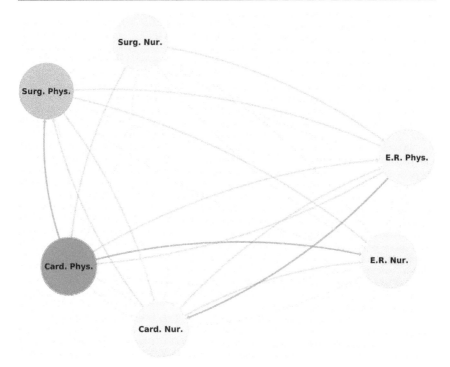

Exhibit 7.6.3 Contextual View for Ties Between Roles on the Frontline Working with Patients

can be decomposed into many ego networks, one for each role, to facilitate separate conversations before bringing all roles together. Exhibit 7.6.4 shows an ego view of Team 2 in a network that is composed of ten teams. We can see both the number and strength of ties reported by Team 2 with the other teams in the network, and vice versa. Note that the color coding for this network is slightly different with yellow instead of blue used to signify moderate strength. Furthermore, because Team 2 did not report any relations with Team 1 or Team 7, there are no lines connecting them. Most importantly, in this graph the ties are split-colored to distinguish the strength of ties as reported in each direction, rather than averaging together the reports provided by the two roles. This split-colored bidirectional approach is an important innovation to build upon going forward, because it allows roles to quickly identify whether their experiences with other roles are reciprocated, or not.

Layout

In addition to the manipulation options described above, choosing which layout to use is also critical for visualization analysis. Network layout is the position of the nodes in the graph. Layout can be in a *random* form. In a

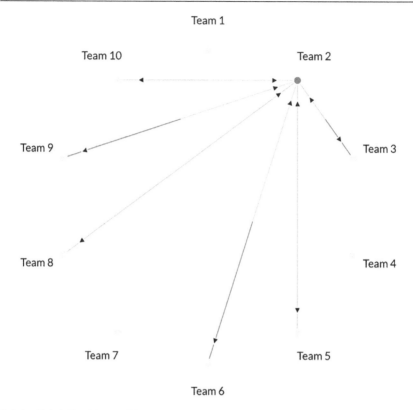

Exhibit 7.6.4 Ego View of Bidirectional Ties with Team 2

random layout, no significant worth is assigned to the spacing between the nodes. Teams are positioned to maximize aesthetic visualization of the network without specific positioning of the teams. Nonrandom layouts are established through positioning network nodes based on specific attributes. *Multidimensional scaling* means positioning nodes in a form that highlights their level of proximity. Nodes' proximities may denote actual physical proximity, for example, the distance between the two cities, between service branches in a company or between continents in a trade network; or it may denote figurative proximity in the sense of strong ties between the nodes. *Hierarchical clustering* is another tool used to shape the layout of social network data, based on contextual manipulation of the nodes and ties to underscore different levels of relations or importance.

Layout Options for Relational Coordination Data

Exhibit 7.7.1 shows an example of random layout option visualizing the relational coordination data between 10 teams (see example of Exhibit 7.6.4), where the teams organized in a circular layout as it provides a better

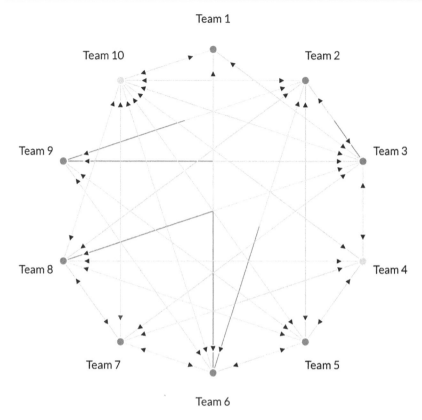

Exhibit 7.7.1 Random Layout

aesthetic and clearer global view output. The *multidimensional scaling* option in Exhibit 7.7.2 shows the ego view of emergency department nurses and their RC ties with the other 8 roles in the network introduced above. The nodes signifying roles from the emergency department (sharing same department) are the closest followed by nodes that denote surgical and cardiac nurses (sharing same work type). In this example, emergency department nurses appear to have strong ties with other roles in their own department. But it also appears that cross-department interaction between roles with a similar professional identify is easier than between roles with different professional identities.

Finally, the *hierarchical clustering* layout option omits and reshapes the nodes and the ties in the network to draw attention to differences using hierarchy as a defining attribute. In social network analysis, hierarchical clustering represents re-ordered layout, where, for example, central players (units) in the work processes are placed in the middle while players in peripheral or outer circumference of the network indicate those who are less involved or active. The Relational Coordination Survey has the analytic

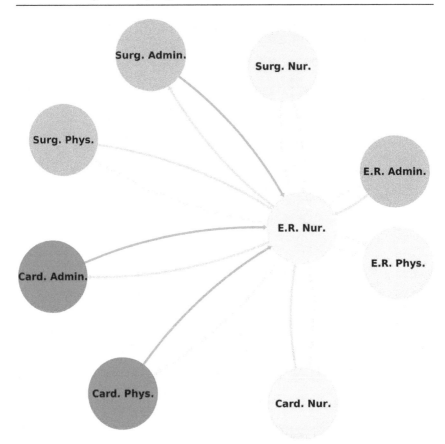

Exhibit 7.7.2 Multidimensional Scaling of an Ego View of Ties between Emergency Nurses and Other Roles

potential to diagnose relations between roles, sites, and organizations through aggregating the scores to describe ties between units at each of these levels. In Exhibit 7.7.3, we can see that roles within departments have mostly moderate to strong ties with each other. When we scale upward to an aggregate view of RC ties between departments, almost all ties are concerningly weak. Hence, the hierarchical clustering layout led the observer to identify a critical flaw in inter-departmental relational coordination.

Other Attributes—Color, Shape and Size

Beyond manipulation and network layout, other attributes of networks can be illustrated by changing the color, shape, and size of the nodes or the lines connecting the nodes. In some instances, we could use a similar shape for all roles while changing the diameter of the shape to imply additional importance or leadership roles.

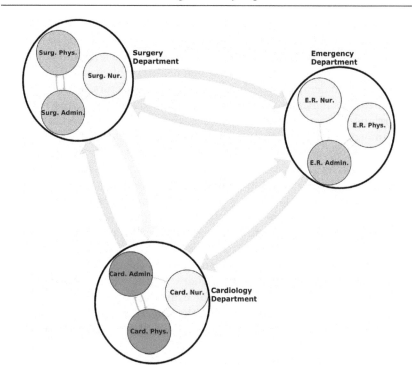

Exhibit 7.7.3 Hierarchical clustering view, where the network visualization shows ties between roles within the departments as well as total RC ties in between departments

Network Metrics—Density, Centrality, Betweenness, Cohesion and Ranking

In addition to visualization, a network can also be described through different metrics that reflect various parameters of the network's nodes and links.

Density

The first metric is *density* which is a measure of cohesion among all actors in a network. Density is defined as the number of ties in the network expressed as a proportion of maximum possible number of ties. The maximum possible number of ties and network density can be calculated through the following equations:

$$\text{Maximium lines} = n \times \frac{(n-1)}{2}$$

$$\text{Density} = \frac{\text{N. of all network lines}}{\text{Maximium lines}}$$

where n = number of nodes in the network

In traditional social network analysis, density of the network indicates cohesion among all actors in the network as measured by *whether or not they are connected*. Thus a network that possesses the maximum number of lines, or in analytical terms is of maximum density, is often called a complete network. When density is low, meaning many of the actors are currently not connected, this indicates that the network has a greater capacity to grow.

In relational coordination analysis, density of the network indicates cohesion among all actors in the network as measured by *the strength of their communicating and relating*. When computing density for relational coordination, tie strength is measured as a continuous variable rather than a yes/no variable. As we learned in Chapter 6, tie strength is computed as the Relational Coordination Index, which ranges from 1 (very weak) to 5 (very strong), using survey responses from the Relational Coordination Survey. Density of a relational coordination network is conceptualized as the average strength of ties across the network, which can be assessed relative to its maximum possible rating of 5. In other words, the density of a relational coordination network equals the RC Index for the whole network divided by the maximum strength of 5. So for example, if the RC Index in your organization at Time 1 is equal to 4.2, the density or strength of your network relative to its maximum strength is 84%. When RC network density is low, meaning that the roles in the network have weak ties on average, this indicates a greater opportunity for improvement.

Centrality and Betweenness

Centrality is a second metric for social network analysis, used to describe the structural importance of the node or in other words, the importance of the node to the network. A node's importance can be due to its connectedness to other nodes in the network, or due to its position, or due to how it establishes a flow across the network—or all of the above! Centrality suggests power—it signifies the ability of the actor represented by the node to influence others in the network. For example, formal and informal leaders often have high levels of centrality. Interacting with these central players can provide an opportunity to carry out interventions to strengthen one's own network. Computing the centrality of each node in a network allows you to divide nodes into three categories, to further predict their role in the network: *peripheral* (with below average centrality), *central connector* (with above average centrality), and *brokers* (with above average betweenness). Betweenness is a type of centrality describing the extent to which a node connects otherwise unconnected networks, as is the case with node X in Exhibit 7.8, who serves as a broker.

To summarize, *density* is a group measure that reports the strength of the whole relational coordination network. *Centrality*, including *betweenness*, is an individual measure that assesses the position of individual roles in relation to others in the network.

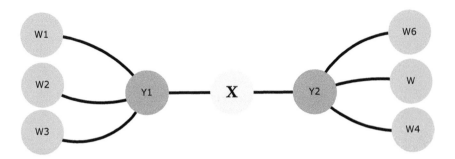

Exhibit 7.8 X as a Broker Due to Above Average Betweenness

Cohesion

In addition to density and centrality, network metrics test two main patterns: cohesion and ranking. *Cohesion* is a pattern of tightness exhibited by certain nodes that present themselves as dense pockets within the network. The theory of cohesive groups asserts that highly interactive groups share more underlying likeness beyond expected network interactions. Usually, if cohesive groups are detected in a network, they will have a sense of solidarity, shared norms, identity, and collective behaviors. As we saw above through blockmodeling of relational coordination data across the postsurgical care continuum in Exhibit 7.4, there were relatively cohesive groups or clusters within acute care, rehabilitation care, and home care, but little cohesion between those groups.

Ranking

Another pattern investigated by social network analysis is *ranking*. Exploring unequal roles and disproportionate interactions of members in any social group through social network analysis, we will be able to distinguish variations in the role and importance of nodes, and subsequently assign more rank and prestige to some actors in the network over the others, for example, based on their centrality (Brass & Borgatti, 2020).

Note that all of these measures are based on mapping ties based on a binary system, where the actors are either connected or not ("yes/no"), while relational coordination ties are measured using the RC Index, which provides continuous variables on a scale of 1 to 5. Researchers who have attempted to explain the variations in interactions between roles based on both social network analysis and relational coordination analysis have sometimes used a three-level Relational Coordination Index (e.g. weak <

Case Study 7.1:   Analyzing Collaboration Among HIV Agencies Through Combining Network Theory and Relational Coordination

(Khosla, Marsteller, Hsu & Elliott, 2016)

Background. People living with HIV need a wide array of services, both medically and socially. Patients with this vicious chronic disease require care from multiple medical specialties, psychological counseling, legal help, and so on. Often, HIV services in the US are delivered through a variety of independent agencies across multiple sectors. One patient with HIV can be receiving his or her services at one point in time from public, private, and nonprofit agencies. When service delivery is so highly distributed, coordination becomes a major challenge with grave consequences for service delivery. Khosla and colleagues thus studied interagency collaboration among agencies that provided or facilitated services for HIV prevention, care and treatment in the city of Baltimore.

Study aim/objectives. Researchers aimed first to map the presence of interactions between these agencies using social network analysis metrics such as centrality, closeness, and betweenness. Secondly, they aimed to investigate the quality of these interactions by measuring the strength of those ties using the Relational Coordination Survey.

Methods. After identifying 62 agencies that fit the pre-set inclusion criteria, researchers collected data about the frequency of interaction between agencies, and about relational coordination between agencies, in two consecutive phases. In phase one, researchers contacted each of the 62 agencies and asked for a representative, often the leading case manager, to report the top 6 agencies with whom they interact, using the 62 preidentified agencies and on the frequency of their interaction with those 6 agencies over the past 12 months. Researchers received 51 responses from the 62 contacted agencies. The data were then used to map an initial social network that included 62 actors / agencies. In phase two, agencies who interacted with at least one-third of the sample were labeled as most active, and asked their employees to complete a survey about their relational coordination with the other 10 agencies. This second survey helped to provide insights on the strength of overall relational coordination ties, and on the strength of each of the underlying seven dimensions.

Results. The social network analysis for the selected 11 agencies revealed a well-connected network, suggesting the potential for a flow of information and service referrals. Moreover, the network had only 20 percent density when ties were measured as monthly or greater contact. If monthly or higher ties represent consequential inter-agencies interactions, then by default, social network analysis showed that most of the

(*Continued*)

Case Study 7.1 (Continued)

contacts were superficial or irrelevant to the agencies' work process. To better understand the variations among agencies, relational coordination data provided an additional explanatory lens, by comparing agencies' relational coordination. Researchers compared network descriptive statistics across the seven dimensions and the Relational Coordination Index to identify the actors who were most successful in collaborating with other agencies. The agency that had the highest problem-solving communication score showed an overwhelming density of 0.98, a nearly complete network.

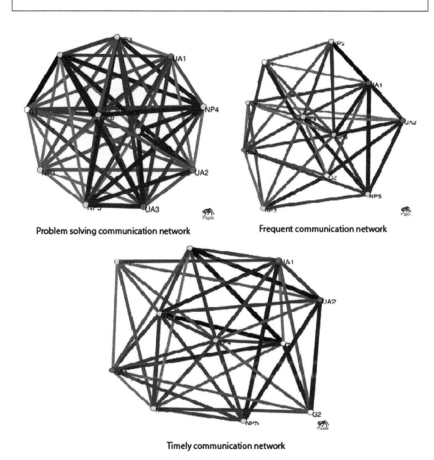

Problem solving communication network

Frequent communication network

Timely communication network

Legend
G1-G3: government-affiliated agencies
NP1-NP5: not-for-profit agencies
UA1-UA3: university-affiliated agencies

Exhibit 7.9 Relational Coordination Networks for Problem-Solving Communication, Frequent Communication, and Timely Communication (Khosla et al., 2016).

2.5, moderate >2.5 and < 3.5, strong > 3.5) to transform continuous RC variables into categorical RC variables.

The following study is to our knowledge the first published attempt to combine social network and relational coordination analysis. Let's take a look, considering how we might deepen the integration of these methods based on what we've learned in this chapter.

Summing Up

In this chapter, we have shared some of the latest additions to relational analytics. We have shown how to integrate the visualization tools and metrics of social network analysis with the visualization tools and metrics of relational coordination to explore patterns in the quality of communicating and relating between roles. The relational coordination network study of community agencies by Khosla and her co-authors is a wonderful starting point, and it is clear that much more is possible. We welcome researchers and practitioners to continue integrating these tools to assess existing patterns of coordination and to gain insight into both strengths and opportunities for improvement.

At the same time, relational coordination is also a theory and research program that explains how these networks drive a broad range of performance outcomes that organizations need for their sustainable success. Relational coordination theory and research also explain how organizations can strengthen or weaken these networks. Join us in the following chapter as we learn how to measure the organizational structures that shape networks of relational coordination for better or worse!

References

Barends, E., & Rousseau, D. M. (2018). *Evidence-based Management: How to Use Evidence to make Better Organizational Decisions*. London, UK: Kogan Page Publishers.

Borgatti, S., Everett, M., & Johnson, J. (2013). *Analyzing Social Networks*. Thousand Oaks, CA: Sage.

Brass, D. J., & Borgatti, S. P. (2020). *Social Networks at Work*. Routledge.

De Nooy, W., Mrvar, A., & Batagelj, V. (2018). *Exploratory Social Network Analysis with Pajek: Revised and Expanded Edition for Updated Software*. Cambridge: Cambridge University Press.

Eppinger, S. D. & Browning, T. R. (2012). *Design Structure Matrix Methods and Applications*. Cambridge, MA: MIT Press.

Freeman, L. C. (2004). *The Development of Social Network Analysis: A Study in The Sociology of Science*. North Charleston: Booksurge, LLC.

Gittell, J. (2009). *High Performance Healthcare: Using the Power of Relationships to Achieve Quality, Efficiency and Resilience*. New York: McGraw-Hill.

Hagigi, F. N. (2008). *Evaluating Coordination as a Key Driver of Performance in Ambulatory Care Clinics.* Brandeis University, PhD Dissertation. ProQuest Dissertations Publishing.

Khosla, N., Marsteller, J. A., Hsu, Y. J., & Elliott, D. L. (2016). Analysing collaboration among HIV agencies through combining network theory and relational coordination. *Social Science & Medicine,* 150, 85–94. doi:10.1016/j.socscimed.2015.12.006

Kolakowsky-Hayner, S. A., Gourley, E. V., 3rd, Kreutzer, J. S., Marwitz, J. H., Meade, M. A., & Cifu, D. X. (2002). Post-injury substance abuse among persons with brain injury and persons with spinal cord injury. *Brain Injury,* 16(7), 583–592. Retrieved from http://resources.library.brandeis.edu/login?url=http://search.ebscohost.com/login.aspx?direct=true&db=mnh&AN=12119077&site=ehost-live&scope=site

McCulloh, I., Armstrong, H. & Johnson, A. (2013). *Social Network Analysis with Applications.* Hoboken, NJ: Wiley.

Rousseau, D. M. (2012). *The Oxford Handbook of Evidence-based Management.* Oxford, UK: Oxford University Press.

Chapter 8

Measuring the Organizational Structures That Shape Relational Coordination

Now that we have measured relational coordination, constructed variables, visualized, and analyzed our data for the groups, organizations, or communities we are working with, many people are likely to be curious about why these patterns exist. We know that organizational structures play a powerful role in shaping relational coordination, for better or worse, as described in relational coordination theory, as demonstrated in our review of the evidence, and as shown in Exhibit 8.1. These organizational structures include human resource practices and coordination mechanisms. They may or may not be easily changed due to leadership resistance, regulatory restrictions, costliness, or simply the lack of time to invest in the process. But in reality these organizational structures have been created by people and they can be re-created by people. To lay the groundwork for possible changes, how do we assess the current state of these organizational structures to see how well they support relational coordination—or not?

In this chapter, we introduce a tool and describe how to customize it to your context to collect the data you will need, and how to display these data in matrix format for the purpose of visualization. At rcsurveyhelp. info you will find the OSAT interview protocol and the commands to conduct all of the analyses described below. Subsequent chapters will show you how to connect your organizational structure data with your relational coordination and performance outcomes data (Chapter 9), and how to use these data to design interventions and create positive change (Chapter 10).

The Organizational Structures Assessment Tool (OSAT)

The Organizational Structures Assessment Tool (OSAT) is an interview protocol accompanied by a scoring grid to measure twelve organizational structures across two domains; human resource practices and coordinating mechanisms. These two domains and the items in them are summarized described briefly in Exhibit 8.2.

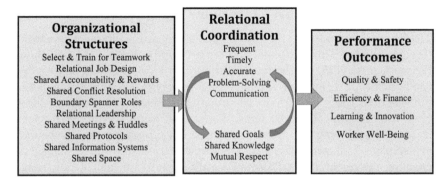

Exhibit 8.1 A High-Performance Work System that Supports Relational Coordination.

Exhibit 8.2 Organizational Structures Assessment Tool (OSAT) Domains and Items

Human Resource Practices

- **Select** staff in each of the relevant roles with attention to their relational competence or teamwork abilities, in addition to their technical competence
- **Train** staff in each of the relevant roles with attention to their relational competence or teamwork abilities, in addition to their technical competence
- Use **relational job design** to create clear expectations regarding the responsibility to coordinate with all relevant roles
- Develop **shared accountability** for outcomes among all relevant roles
- Develop **shared rewards** for outcomes among all relevant roles
- Use **relational leadership** in all supervisory/coaching/mentoring relationships to role model relational coordination with all relevant roles
- Develop **conflict resolution** process for proactively identifying conflicts among all relevant roles and transforming them into growth and learning opportunities

Coordinating Mechanisms

- Create **boundary spanner** roles with sufficient resources and clear responsibilities to facilitate coordination among all relevant roles
- Create **shared meetings** to facilitate coordination among all relevant roles
- Create **shared protocols** to facilitate coordination among all relevant roles
- Create **shared information systems** to facilitate coordination among all relevant roles
- Create **shared space** to facilitate coordination among all relevant roles

Note that a survey based OSAT with the same domains and items is in early stages of testing and development. The survey-based OSAT will be shared at rcsurveyhelp.info when it becomes available.

Customizing the OSAT Interview Questions

The first stage when using the OSAT is to customize the interview questions to your context. This customization requires up-to-date knowledge about the work process that is the focus of the study. This up-to-date knowledge can be achieved through preliminary interviews with key informants. In the nine-hospital study of orthopedic surgery, "A Relational Model of How High-Performance Work Systems Work," for example, the researchers learned through preliminary interviews with key informants that the *boundary spanner role* was played in the surgical context by case managers, enabling the researchers to ask specifically about case managers in stage two of their interviews when asking about the boundary spanner role. The researchers also learned that *shared rewards* could take the form of surplus sharing or risk sharing between independently employed physicians and the hospitals that contracted with them, enabling the researchers to use this language in stage two of their interviews when asking about shared rewards.

As illustrated in this example, the OSAT is always customized to the particular work process in need of coordination. Boundary spanner roles and shared rewards are always relevant to ask about, for example, but the forms those take will vary. Reading Chapters 2 and 3 will help you to understand these organizational structures sufficiently that you can use preliminary interviews with key informants to customize your OSAT interview questions to the context.

Conducting Systematic Interviews

Once you have customized the OSAT interview questions, you will use these questions to conduct systematic interviews with front-line leaders in each of the roles involved in the work process of interest, ideally the same roles that were included in your Relational Coordination Survey. If the roles in your RC Survey included surgeons, nurses, physical therapists, social workers, and case managers, for example, you will want to interview a front-line leader in each of those roles to assess how organizational structures are currently being utilized by workers in that role. For data accuracy, you want leaders who are close enough to the work to know which structures are actually available to workers in each role, and how these structures are being utilized.

These interviews can be conducted either in person, via telephone, or via video chat. Ideally, the interviews will be carried out in a conversational mode to put the interviewee at ease. The interview questions are designed to be specific, yet open-ended, in order to evoke a clear and detailed picture of the organizational structures that are actually available to workers in each role, and how they are actually used. If there is a gap between what the organizational structures are intended to be, and what they actually are in practice, it is useful to capture both to achieve a deeper understanding of the organization and ultimately to assist participants in creating positive organizational change.

While the *intended use* of the organizational structures is of interest for understanding the context and opportunities for change, however, the organizational structures you need to measure to predict existing patterns of relational coordination are the structures as they are *actually used*. If interviewees feel they cannot share this information with you, your data will be subject to social desirability bias and your findings will therefore be less accurate. Below you will see that the question about shared meetings will be coded to indicate which roles attend "never," "sometimes," or "almost always/always." If your interviewee exaggerates and says workers in his or her role "almost always" attend the meetings when the reality is different, your descriptive date will be inaccurate, and your *shared meetings* variable will be less able to predict existing patterns of relational coordination.

The following paragraph summarizes this two-stage process using the example of the surgical study published in "A Relational Model of How High-Performance Work Systems Work" (Gittell, Seidner & Wimbush):

> To measure [organizational structures], front-line administrators were interviewed in each orthopedics unit, including at least one physician, nurse, physical therapist, social worker, and case manager. For each unit, unstructured interviews and observations were conducted in person at the time of the initial site visits, followed up by more systematic structured telephone interviews after the site visits. The interview protocol that we [customized] based on our first stage of interviews and observations was used as a guide for our second stage of interviews.

Coding Your OSAT Interview Data

Whether your interviews were recorded with written notes then typed up afterwards, or recorded with audiotapes then transcribed afterwards, you will use the written output from your interviews to code your data using the scoring grid included in the OSAT interview protocol. Using the example of the surgical study published in "A Relational Model of How High-Performance Work Systems Work," this coding process is illustrated below for six of the organizational structures in the OSAT (Gittell, Seidner & Wimbush, 2010):

> *Selection* was measured by asking administrators in each orthopedics unit about selection criteria for physicians, nurses, and physical therapists, probing as to whether cross-functional teamwork ability was considered an important selection criterion. This variable was coded from 0 to 2 for each of these three roles, 0 indicating that cross-functional

teamwork ability was not considered, 1 indicating that it was considered to some extent, and 2 indicating that it was a consistent criterion for selection.

Conflict resolution was measured by asking about conflict-resolution processes. Questions probed as to whether any formal cross-functional conflict resolution process was in place for physicians, nurses, or physical therapists. This variable was coded 0 or 1 for physicians, nurses, and physical therapists; 0 indicated that the role had no access to a formal cross-functional conflict resolution process and 1 indicated that the role did have access.

Performance measurement [**shared accountability**] was measured by asking about the quality-assurance process and the utilization review process in each hospital, probing as to whether each of these processes were largely focused on identifying the single function that was responsible for a quality or utilization problem or whether the approach was more cross-functional. Responses were coded on a 5-point scale, where 1 = highly functional, 2 = fairly functional, 3 = equally functional/cross-functional, 4 = fairly cross-functional, and 5 = highly cross-functional. Questions also probed interviewees as to whether these two performance-measurement processes were reactive (focused on affixing blame) or proactive (focused on problem solving). Responses were coded on a 5-point scale: 1 = highly reactive, 2 = fairly reactive, 3 = equally reactive/proactive, 4 = fairly proactive, and 5 = highly proactive.

Shared rewards were measured by asking about the criteria for rewards for physicians, nurses, and physical therapists, probing as to whether rewards were based purely on individual performance or whether they were based on some cross-functional performance criteria as well. This variable was coded from 0 to 2. For nurses and physical therapists, 0 indicated no performance-based rewards, 1 indicated individual rewards only, and 2 indicated some cross-functional team rewards. For physicians, 0 indicated individual rewards only, 1 indicated surplus sharing with the hospital (potential for sharing positive financial outcomes), and 2 indicated risk sharing with the hospital (potential for sharing both positive and negative financial outcomes).

Meetings were measured by asking key informants about participation in physician rounds and nursing rounds, probing to find out which functional groups participated in those rounds and the consistency of their participation. Rounds are the primary form of meeting used for coordinating patient care. These variables were coded on a 0–2 scale, with 0 indicating that the functional group did not participate in the rounds, 1 indicating that they participated sometimes, and 2 indicating that they participated usually or always.

Boundary spanner was measured by asking about the caseload and roles of the case managers who worked with joint replacement patients and whether the primary nursing model was in place on that unit (i.e., the practice of assigning one nurse to assume primary responsibility for a patient throughout his or her stay and to serve as a point person for coordinating that patient's care). Caseload, the number of patients for whom case managers were typically responsible at a time, was measured as a continuous variable, ranging across hospitals from 6.7 to 40. Each of the case manager roles—leadership of rounds and planning for patient discharge—was coded as 0 or 1, with 0 indicating that the role was not expected and 1 indicating that it was expected of case managers. Primary nursing [another boundary spanner role in this context] was coded as 1 if the model was in place and 0 if not.

This excerpt provides an example of how the OSAT interviewing and data coding processes worked in one of the earliest studies. But we recommend that you use the OSAT interview protocol and coding scheme at rcsurvey-help.info for the most complete and up to date guidance.

Creating Variables for Each Organizational Structure and an Index for All Structures

The next stage of the process is to use the coded data from the previous stage to create a variable for each organizational structure. That variable describes the inclusiveness or extent of that organizational structure as it is actually used in a particular site you are studying. For example, you will combine coded data for shared meetings, as gathered from each role, to create a variable that indicates the inclusiveness of shared meetings in a particular site.

Depending on your needs, you may or may not want to also create an index for the overall system of organizational structures. If you do create an index measuring the overall bundle or system of organizational structures, you must first test whether your variables are correlated with each other, which is only possible if you are carrying out a multisite study, or a perhaps a single-site study with multiple waves or measurement. If they are correlated, you can proceed to test the construct validity of an Organizational Structures Index, using methods similar to those you used for creating the Relational Coordination Index. In "A Relational Model of How High-Performance Work Systems Work," the focus was on six of the organizational structures identified in relational coordination theory—selection for teamwork, shared conflict resolution, performance measurement/shared accountability, shared rewards, shared meetings, and boundary spanners, and the Organizational Structures Index was called a High-Performance Work Practices Index in keeping with the human resource management literature. The process of creating that index was described as follows (Gittell, Seidner & Wimbush, 2010):

> Because these six work practices were correlated with one another, forming a 'bundle' of work practices, we combined the above measures into an index of high-performance work practices. Exploratory factor

analysis suggested that these high-performance work practices can be characterized fairly well as a single factor. Nineteen of the original 23 items had factor 1 loadings greater than 0.40 and were retained; see Table 1 for factor loadings. Four items with loadings less than 0.40 were dropped, including cross-functional approach to utilization review (1 item), participation in nursing rounds (2 items), and coordination role for case managers in nursing rounds (1 item). The eigenvalue for Factor 1 was 8.53, and the eigenvalue for Factor 2 was 3.08. Checking for cross-loadings, we found that 6 of the 19 variables in the high-performance work practices index also loaded onto Factor 2 with loadings of 0.40 or higher. If we drop these six items from our high-performance work practices, our regression results remain virtually the same, with no changes in the significance level of our key independent variables and no change in the significance of mediation as measured by the Sobel test. We therefore elected to retain all 19 items.

All items in the high-performance work practices index had item-to-total correlation scores of 0.40 or greater, suggesting that our index meets standards for convergent validity. An additive scaling method was used in which each item that loaded onto factor 1 with loading of 0.40 or more was standardized with a mean of 0 and a standard deviation of 1 so that each item in the high-performance work practices index was equally weighted. A joint test for skewness and kurtosis indicated that normal distribution of the high-performance work practices index could not be rejected (chi square 2.01, prob (chi square) = 0.3654). Cronbach's alpha for the high-performance work practices index was 0.93, suggesting that this construct has a high level of reliability.

We selected an additive rather than a multiplicative approach for aggregating high-performance work practices into an index because the additive approach is more comprehensive, withstands missing human resource practices, and reflects the entire gestalt (Becker & Gerhart, 1996; Delery, 1998; Youndt, Snell, Dean, & Lepak, 1996). Moreover, additive models assume each practice is equally important within the index, an appropriate assumption for our study given that we have offered no hypotheses that indicate otherwise. A multiplicative approach is more appropriate when the practices together are expected to add up to more than the sum of the individual practices because of their fit with each other. Although this may be the case with the high-performance work practices presented here, the theoretical construct as developed thus far does not include explicit arguments regarding fit. As with other types of high-performance work practices, organizations can improve performance either by increasing the number of work practices they employ within the system or by using the practices within the system in a more comprehensive and widespread manner, for example, by extending their reach to cover a wider array of employee roles.

Exhibit 8.3 Organizational Structures Assessment Tool (OSAT) Sample Report Summarizing Data Across Nine Sites

	Factor loading	Range	Mean	SD	No. of observations
Cross-functional selection					
Physicians selected for cross functional teamwork	0.701	0–2	0.44	0.88	9
Nurses selected for cross functional teamwork	0.760	0–2	1.44	0.73	9
Physical therapists selected for cross functional teamwork	0.570	0–2	1.67	0.88	9
Cross-functional conflict resolution					
Physician access to cross-functional process	0.916	0–1	0.44	0.53	9
Nurse access to cross-functional process	0.700	0–1	0.22	0.44	9
Physical therapist access to cross-functional process	0.438	0–1	0.33	0.50	9
Cross-functional performance measurement					
Cross-functional approach to quality measurement	0.544	1–5	3.33	1.41	9
Problem-solving approach to quality measurement	0.729	1–5	2.78	1.39	9
Cross-functional approach to efficiency measurement		1–5	2.56	1.88	9
Problem-solving approach to efficiency measurement	0.834	1–5	3.00	1.58	9
Cross-functional rewards					
Physicians rewarded for cross-functional teamwork	0.438	0–3	0.22	0.67	9
Nurses rewarded for cross-functional teamwork	0.560	0–2	0.56	0.88	9
Physical therapists rewarded for cross-functional teamwork	0.803	0–2	1.11	1.05	9
Cross-functional meetings					
Nurses included in physician rounds	0.548	0–2	1.33	0.87	9
Physical therapists included in physician rounds	0.691	0–2	0.56	0.88	9
Case managers included in physician rounds	0.677	0–2	0.67	0.87	9
Physicians included in nursing rounds	−0.210	0–2	0.78	0.44	9
Physical therapists included in nursing rounds	−0.112	0–2	1.44	0.73	9
Case managers included in nursing rounds	0.642	0–2	1.33	1	9

(*Continued*)

Exhibit 8.3 (Continued)

	Factor loading	Range	Mean	SD	No. of observations
Cross-functional boundary spanners					
Case manager caseload	−0.740	6.7–40	26.30	10.80	9
Case manager discharge planning role	0.515	0–1	0.89	0.33	9
Case manager coordination role [a]	0.368	0–1	0.44	0.53	9
Primary nursing model	0.746	0–1	0.56	0.53	9
High-performance work practices index ($\alpha = 0.93$)					

Analyzing and Reporting Results from the OSAT for Practitioners

Alternatively, the data from your Organizational Structures Assessment Tool can be displayed visually in a matrix format, by ranking each organizational structure as weak, moderate, or strong in its support of each role. See Exhibit 8.4. This data visualization is helpful for enabling participants

Exhibit 8.4 Visualization of OSAT Data Using a Matrix Format

Organizational Structures	Roles					
	Nurses	Therapists	Residents	Physicians	Case Managers	Social Workers
Selected for Teamwork						
Trained for Teamwork						
Relational Job Design						
Shared Accountability for Outcomes						
Shared Rewards for Outcomes						
Shared Conflict Resolution Process						
Shared Boundary Spanner						
Shared Meetings & Huddles						
Shared Protocols						
Shared Information Systems						

to identify opportunities to strengthen relational coordination and drive positive organizational change.

Alternatively, this matrix can be created by multi-stakeholder teams through a facilitated conversation, to visualize the organizational structures that are shaping the relational patterns they are experiencing. Whether you use a formal interview process or a facilitated group conversation, this is a useful activity to offer after you have shared Relational Coordination Survey data with participants when they will likely be very curious about what is causing these relational patterns and how current organizational structures may be playing a role.

Summing Up

In this chapter, you have learned how to use the OSAT to assess the current state of organizational structures in a group, organization, or community to see how well they are currently designed to support relational coordination. You may want to share the resulting data with the participants themselves in order to engage them in redesigning these structures to better support relational coordination. In Chapter 10, we will describe the use of OSAT data to carry out structural interventions as a key element of creating—and sustaining—positive change.

But first, you may want to use your OSAT data and Relational Coordination Survey data to explore which of these organizational structures are shaping relational coordination in your context, and whether relational coordination is driving the outcomes of interest to your key stakeholders. If so, please read Chapter 9!

References

Becker, B., & Gerhart, B. (1996). The impact of human resource management on organizational performance: Progress and prospects. *Academy of Management Journal*, 39(4), 779–801. doi:10.2307/256712

Delery, J. E. (1998). Issues of fit in strategic human resource management: Implications for research. *Human Resource Management Review*, 8(3), 289–309. doi:10.1016/s1053-4822(98)90006-7

Gittell, J. H., Seidner, R., & Wimbush, J. (2010). A relational model of how high-performance work systems work. *Organization Science*, 21(2), 490–506.

Youndt, M. A., Snell, S. A., Dean, J. J. W., & Lepak, D. P. (1996). Human resource management, manufacturing strategy, and firm performance. *Academy of Management Journal*, 39(4), 836–866. doi:10.2307/256714

Chapter 9

Analyzing the Outcomes and Predictors of Relational Coordination

You have learned how to measure relational coordination, and the organizational structures that tend to shape relational coordination for better or worse. You are now ready to analyze the outcomes of relational coordination that matter to your key stakeholders, and the organizational structures that predict relational coordination in your context. In this chapter, we introduce various ways to analyze your relational coordination data. Specifically, we walk you through the process of testing for differences across sites and over time, analyzing both the outcomes and predictors of relational coordination, and analyzing the mediators and moderators of relational coordination. At rcsurveyhelp.info you will find the commands to conduct each of these analyses, along with sample data sets to practice carrying out these analyses.

Testing for Differences between Sites, Groups, Organizations, and More

To start, we are often very interested in assessing differences in the strength of relational coordination ties between different sites, or between relational coordination in intervention and nonintervention groups within the same site. To assess these differences, you first conduct analyses of variance to find whether you have significant differences in relational coordination between your units of analysis (e.g., between sites, or between intervention and nonintervention groups). In the original flight departure study, significant cross-site differences ($p < 0.0001$), as well as significant cross-role differences ($p < 0.0001$), were found in relational coordination. When site-level and role-level differences were considered jointly, site-level differences remained significant with an F-statistic of 0.0003. The intra-site correlation for relational coordination was significantly greater than zero ($p < 0.001$). Taken together, these results were consistent with treating relational coordination as a site-level construct.

For the original patient care study, similar descriptive analyses were conducted with some additional details. Using one-way analysis of variance, significant cross-site differences in relational coordination were found, $F(8,327) = 5.32$, $p < 0.001$, as well as significant cross-role differences in relational coordination, $F(5,330) = 2.89$, $p < 0.05$. When site-level and role-level differences were considered jointly, site-level differences remained significant, $F(8,322) = 4.51$, $p < 0.001$, while role-level differences became insignificant, $F(5,322) = 1.75$, $p = 0.12$. To further assess treating relational coordination as a site-level construct, we computed intra-class correlations ICC(1) and ICC(2). ICC(1) is the proportion of total variance that is explained by site membership with values ranging from −1 to +1 and values between 0.05 and 0.30 being most typical. This number provides an estimate of the reliability of a single respondent's assessment of the site mean. ICC(2) provides an overall estimate of the reliability of site means, with values equal to or above 0.70 being acceptable. For relational coordination, ICC(1) = 0.25 and ICC(2) = 0.81. We concluded that relational coordination performed well on both forms of intra-class correlation. Taken together, these results were consistent with treating relational coordination as a site-level construct.

Analyzing Predictors of Relational Coordination

The organizational structures that are predicted to support relational coordination (perhaps measured using the Organizational Structures Assessment Tool introduced in Chapter 8) are typically measured at the site-level of analysis. To assess their impact on relational coordination, you can use a model in which the unit of analysis is the individual respondent to the Relational Coordination Survey. In this multilevel model, the organizational structure or set of structures serves as the independent variable, the control variables or covariates are the role identity of the individual respondents (and any other individual-level predictors you want to include), and the dependent variables are the individual-level measure of relational coordination. This model allows the effects of organizational structures on relational coordination to be tested at the level of the individual participant, controlling for his or her role identity.

Multilevel regression analysis can again be used to adjust coefficients and standard errors for the multilevel nature of the data (individual observations within multiple sites). The unit of analysis when predicting relational coordination is the individual participant within the site. The random effect is the site. As before, the analysis will produce both a within-site R square, and a between-site R square. Within-site R square indicates the percent of within-site variation that is explained by the variables in the models. Between-site R square indicates the percent of between-site variation that is explained by the variables in the model. Either or both R squares can be reported, so long as they are labeled clearly and explained to readers.

To learn more about random effects regression modeling, see Hausman (1978) and (Bryk & Raudenbush, 1992; Hausman, 1978). Random effects models are increasingly common, and a sentence such as the following can be used to explain their use: "For the above analyses, random effects modeling was used to adjust standard errors for the multi-level nature of the data, accounting for non-independence of the error terms" (Bryk & Raudenbush, 1992).

Analyzing Outcomes of Relational Coordination

According to relational coordination theory (see Chapter 2) and consistent with much of the evidence thus far (see Chapter 3), relational coordination improves performance outcomes for multiple stakeholders—quality, efficiency, worker well-being, learning, and innovation—particularly in contexts that are characterized by high levels of task interdependence, uncertainty, and time constraints. You should choose performance measures that are clearly related to the focal work process of interest and that reflect desired outcomes for key stakeholders. In the flight departure study, the impact of relational coordination was evaluated for efficiency (gate time per departure; employees per passenger) as well as quality (on-time performance; baggage handling performance; customer satisfaction) (Gittell, 2001). In the patient care study, the impact of relational coordination was evaluated for efficiency (length of stay), as well as quality (postoperative pain; postoperative functioning; patient satisfaction) (Gittell et al., 2000). It is a good idea to choose these performance measures based on a consensus among practitioners regarding the performance outcomes that are vital for sustainable success in their industry.

In order to assess the impact of relational coordination on performance, one must also understand and measure the other factors that affect those performance outcomes. For the flight departure study, these covariates included scale of operations (flights/month); size of flight (passengers/departure); length of flight (miles/departure); percent connections (passengers connecting/total passengers); and freight loading requirements (tons of freight/departure). For the patient care study, these covariates included site-level volume (surgeries/month); as well as patient age; comorbid conditions; type of surgery; preoperative pain and functioning; overall health; psychological well-being; marital status; race; and gender. If you do not "risk adjust" your models by including the appropriate covariates, you are likely to find that the performance effects of your variable of interest – relational coordination – are insignificant. Again, industry practitioners can be a vital source of information.

In models that predict performance, the independent variable of interest is relational coordination, measured at the site-level unless you decided to collect a separate measure of relational coordination for each client. The covariates are also included as independent variables in the model. The dependent variables are the performance measures themselves. A separate regression model should be run to predict each measure of performance, unless you decide to create an index of performance outcomes using a construct validation process as described in Chapter 5. Multilevel regression analysis should be used to adjust coefficients and standard errors for the multilevel nature of the data. Previous analyses of the performance effects of relational coordination have nearly always used random-effects models, a form of multilevel analysis. The unit of analysis is the individual client or monthly observation within the site. The random effect is the site. Random effects regressions will produce both a within-site R square, and a between-site R square. Within-site R square indicates the percent of within-site variation that is explained by the variables in the models. Between-site R square indicates the percent of between-site variation that is explained by the variables in the model. Either or both can be reported, but should be labeled and explained to readers. To learn more about random effects regression modeling, see Hausman (1978) and Bryk and Raudenbush (1992).

Random effects models are increasingly common, and a sentence such as the following can be used to explain their use: "For the above analyses, random effects modeling was used to adjust standard errors for the multi-level nature of the data, accounting for non-independence of the error terms" (Bryk & Raudenbush, 1992).

Analyzing Mediation

If you have been able to measure relational coordination, performance outcomes, and some of the organizational structures you expect to influence relational coordination in your context of interest, you may be interested in testing a mediation hypothesis. This hypothesis will take the form: "Organizational structure X is expected to affect performance outcome Y *through its effect* on relational coordination." In other words, relational coordination is expected to mediate (either wholly or partially) the effect of certain organizational structures on performance. Relational coordination is a multilevel theory that operates across multiple levels of analysis, and mediation can be tested across these multiple levels of analysis, consistent with previous studies of relational coordination (Gittell, 2001, 2002).

Following the method developed by Baron and Kenny (1986), evaluating the mediation hypothesis requires three equations and a test of the path's overall significance (Baron & Kenny, 1986). First, the organizational structure must have a significant effect on relational coordination. Second, the organizational structure must have a significant effect on the performance outcomes of interest. Third, if the coefficient on the organizational structure becomes insignificant when relational coordination is added to the outcomes equation, this result suggests that relational coordination mediates the impact of the organizational structure on the outcome, or in other words the organizational structure influences the outcome *through its effect* on relational coordination. Finally, the overall path must be significant.

The Sobel test can be used to determine whether the association between organizational structures and performance is reduced significantly when controlling for the mediator of relational coordination, drawing upon the critical values identified by MacKinnon et al. (2002) to determine whether the results are supportive of mediation (MacKinnon, Lockwood, Hoffman, West, & Sheets, 2002).

An example from "A Relational Model of How High-Performance Work Systems Work" (Gittell, Seidner, & Wimbush, 2010) can be used to illustrate the use of this method for testing the theory of relational coordination. Results of the Sobel test were reported as follows:

> Results of the Sobel test suggest that the association between high performance work practices and quality of care is significantly mediated by relational coordination ($z' = 1.87$, $p < 0.01$). Together, these results suggest that high performance work practices predict quality outcomes, and that they do so by strengthening relational coordination among employees in different roles (*Hypothesis 2*)." And later: "Results of the Sobel test suggest that the association between high performance work practices and length of stay is significantly mediated by relational coordination ($z' = 2.40$, $p < 0.01$). Together, these results suggest that high performance work practices predict efficiency outcomes, and that they do so by strengthening relational coordination among employees in different roles (*Hypothesis 3*).

To learn more about the Sobel test and interpreting its results, please see MacKinnon, et al. (2002). Exhibit 9.1 shows a visual example of the mediation model that was tested above.

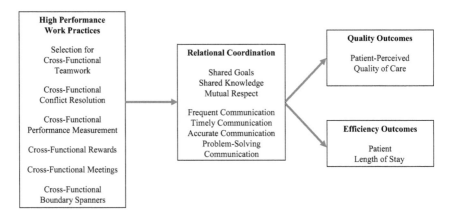

Exhibit 9.1 Example of a Mediation Model

Analyzing Moderation

If you have been able to measure relational coordination, performance outcomes, and some of the factors that are expected to increase the impact of relational coordination on performance, you may be interested in articulating and testing a moderation hypothesis. This hypothesis will take the form: "Contingency factor X (task interdependence, uncertainty or time constraints) is expected to increase (or decrease) the impact of relational coordination on performance outcome Y." In other words, contingency factor X is expected to moderate the effect of relational coordination on performance.

Following the method developed by Baron and Kenny (1986), evaluating the moderation hypothesis requires testing two equations (Baron & Kenny, 1986). First, relational coordination must have a significant effect on performance outcome Y, controlling for contingency factor X. In a second equation, the product of relational coordination and contingency factor X (RC*X) must have a significant effect on performance, controlling for both relational coordination and contingency factor X. This approach is consistent with the recommendation of organizational theorist Schoonhoven (1981) for operationalizing contingency hypotheses (Schoonhoven, 1981).

An example from "Coordinating Mechanisms in Care Provider Groups" (Gittell, 2002) can be used to illustrate the use of this method for testing the theory of relational coordination. First, a random-effects regression equation showed that relational coordination was associated with increased quality of care ($r = 0.23, p < 0.01$), and with reduced hospital lengths of stay ($r = -0.31, p < 0.01$). In addition, the product of relational coordination and input uncertainty was associated with increased quality of care ($r = 0.14, p < 0.05$) and reduced hospital lengths of stay ($r = -0.20, p < 0.01$), suggesting that input uncertainty increased the impact of relational coordination on performance outcomes of interest. Exhibit 9.2 illustrates this moderation model.

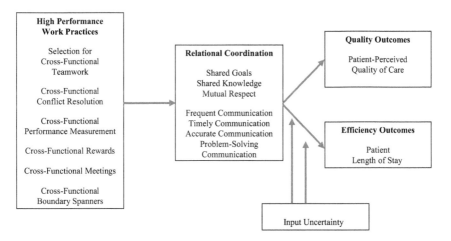

Exhibit 9.2 Example of a Moderation Model That Also Includes Mediation

Analyzing the Dynamic Relational Model of Organizational Change

As people have learned about the performance effects of relational coordination, they have become interested in finding ways to strengthen relational coordination in the organizations they work with. Their work led to the creation a community of researchers and practitioners called the Relational Coordination Collaborative working together to "transform relationships for high performance," and inspired the Relational Model of Organizational Change (Gittell, 2016). As a result, the Relational Coordination Survey is now used to measure changes over time in how people work together, requiring methodologies to analyze the statistical significance of changes in the RC Index and the seven dimensions of RC over time, in response to interventions.

Research on relational coordination is therefore evolving from these relatively static, linear models that use comparative methods to assess the impact of structures on outcomes through their impact on relational coordination. Rather than structures supporting relational coordination in a linear way as originally theorized, the newer more dynamic model shown in Exhibit 9.3 suggests that cross-cutting organizational structures such as relational job design, shared information systems, and boundary spanner roles require a strong relational context for their effective implementation, and only then can they help to strengthen and sustain relational coordination (Claggett & Karahanna, 2018; Gittell, 2016; Gittell, Godfrey, & Thistlethwaite, 2012; Thomas, Sugiyama, Rochford, Stephens, & Kanov, 2018). While this logic seems circular at first glance, we see it instead as process of structuration, or bootstrapping. The idea that effective adoption of relational organizational

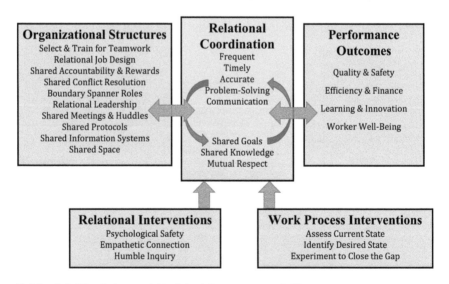

Exhibit 9.3 The Relational Model of Organizational Change

structures may require some baseline level of relational coordination to enable participants to embrace and effectively use them is consistent not only with our Relational Model of Organizational Change (Gittell, 2016; Thomas, et al., 2018) but also with other relational theories of organizational change (Feldman & Rafaeli, 2002; Fletcher, Bailyn, & Beard, 2009). This is why the arrow between structures and relational coordination is bidirectional in the Relational Model of Organizational Change, while it was unidirectional in the linear model of change.

This bidirectional arrow suggests more choices regarding where to intervene, but it also suggests the potential for a mutually reinforcing causal loop that might be difficult to interrupt. How can change agents intervene effectively? Researchers have shown that change agents can engage in *relational interventions* such as humble inquiry and empathetic connection to establish a safe space to reflect on and transform existing patterns and power dynamics, consistent with the studies we reviewed above (Abu-Rish Blakeney et al., 2019; Perloff et al., 2017; Torring, et al., 2019; Purdy et al., 2020). As relational coordination begins to gain strength, participants are able to more effectively implement *structural interventions* that reinforce relational coordination—and the outcomes associated with it.

To more deeply understand the dynamic path of these iterative change processes, we will need longitudinal research designs that pay close attention to the interaction between structures and relationships as the process unfolds, as well as quasi-experimental designs that include relational interventions in some sites, and purely structural interventions in other sites. The study that has come closest to doing this was reported in Gebo and Bond (2020)(Gebo & Bond, 2020), who found that relational and work process interventions increased relational coordination over time in two sites but that the increases were only sustained in the site that also carried out structural interventions.

Analyzing Changes in Relational Coordination Over Time, Pre- and Postintervention

There are some standard methodologies for statistically assessing changes in measures over time, and these can be applied to the analysis of changes in relational coordination over time, pre- and postintervention. We will discuss two of these statistical tests here—*t*-tests, and difference in difference modeling. For *t*-tests, a two-sample *t*-test (also called independent *t*-test) or a paired *t*-test can be used depending on independence across observations. In other words, a two-sample *t*-test is used when you intend to compare means of RC between two different groups while a paired *t*-test is used when you follow the same cohort over time and intend to make comparisons of RC between the same cohort. Both *t*-tests are often used (or can be used) to assess the statistical significance of change between two time periods when there is no comparison group who is surveyed over time.

Difference in difference modeling is appropriate for assessing the statistical significance of change in RC between two time periods when you have both a treatment group and a comparison group that are surveyed before and after the RC intervention. To run a difference in difference model, you need a treatment dummy variable (treatment group=1, comparison group=0) and a time dummy variable (preintervention=0, postintervention=1). These two dummy variables are then entered into a regression model that includes RC scores as an outcome measure. You regress RC scores from the treatment and comparison groups between preintervention and postintervention periods on a treatment dummy variable, a time dummy variable, and an interaction term between the treatment and time dummy variables, and other control variables, if any. The simple difference-in-difference regression model can be presented as $Y = \beta_0 + \beta_1*[\text{Time}] + \beta_2*[\text{Intervention}] + \beta_3*[\text{Time}*\text{Intervention}] + \beta_4*[\text{Covariates}]+\varepsilon$. The coefficient for the interaction term, β_3, is the estimate of the treatment effect, indicating difference in changes over time between the treatment and the comparison group. If β_3 is significant, this supports the hypothesis that the intervention had an effect on relational coordination.

Summing Up

In this chapter, you have learned how to analyze your relational coordination, organizational structures, and performance outcome data to understand how relational coordination works in a particular context, and to identify the potential levers for change. While the change process can be informed by data, data is not sufficient for creating change. To create positive change in a context where work is interdependent, uncertain and time constrained, you are likely to need methods that bring multiple stakeholders together to make sense of the current state, informed by data that connects with their own lived experiences. The following chapter describes this process, while acknowledging there is still a great deal to learn about how it works.

References

Abu-Rish Blakeney, E., Lavallee, D. C., Baik, D., Pambianco, S., O'Brien, K. D., & Zierler, B. K. (2019). Purposeful interprofessional team intervention improves relational coordination among advanced heart failure care teams. *Journal of Interprofessional Care*, 33(5), 481–489. doi:10.1080/13561820.2018.1560248

Baron, R. M., & Kenny, D. A. (1986). The moderator–mediator variable distinction in social psychological research: Conceptual, strategic, and statistical considerations. *Journal of Personality and Social Psychology*, 51(6), 1173–1182. doi:10.1037/0022-3514.51.6.1173

Bryk, A. S., & Raudenbush, S. W. (1992). *Hierarchical Linear Models: Applications and Data Analysis Methods*. Newbury Park: Sage Publ.

Claggett, J. L., & Karahanna, E. (2018). Unpacking the structure of coordination mechanisms and the role of relational coordination in an era of digitally mediated work processes. *Academy of Management Review*, 43(4), 704–722. doi:10.5465/amr.2016.0325

Feldman, M. S., & Rafaeli, A. (2002). Organizational routines as sources of connections and understandings. *Journal of Management Studies*, 39(3), 309–331. doi:10.1111/1467-6486.00294

Fletcher, J. K., Bailyn, L., & Beard, S. B. (2009). Practical pushing: Creating discursive space in organizational narratives. In *Critical Management Studies at Work*. Edward Elgar Publishing.

Gebo, E., & Bond, B. J. (2020). Improving interorganizational collaborations: An application in a violence reduction context. *The Social Science Journal*, 1–12. doi:10.1016/j.soscij.2019.09.008

Gittell, J. H. (2001). Supervisory span, relational coordination and flight departure performance: A reassessment of postbureaucracy theory. *Organization Science*, 12(4), 468–483. doi:10.1287/orsc.12.4.468.10636

Gittell, J. H. (2002). Coordinating mechanisms in care provider groups: Relational coordination as a mediator and input uncertainty as a moderator of performance effects. *Management Science*, 48(11), 1408–1426. doi:10.1287/mnsc.48.11.1408.268

Gittell, J. H. (2016). *Transforming Relationships for High Performance: The Power of Relational Coordination*. Palo Alto, CA: Stanford University Press.

Gittell, J. H., Fairfield, K. M., Bierbaum, B., Head, W., Jackson, R., Kelly, M., ... & Zuckerman, J. (2000). Impact of relational coordination on quality of care, postoperative pain and functioning, and length of stay: a nine-hospital study of surgical patients. *Medical Care*, 807–819.

Gittell, J. H., Godfrey, M., & Thistlethwaite, J. (2012). Interprofessional collaborative practice and relational coordination: Improving healthcare through relationships. *Journal of Interprofessional Care*, 27(3), 210–213. doi:10.3109/13561820.2012.730564

Gittell, J. H., Seidner, R., & Wimbush, J. (2010). A relational model of how high-performance work systems work. *Organization Science*, 21(2), 490–506. doi:10.1287/orsc.1090.0446

Hausman, J. A. (1978). Specification tests in econometrics. *Econometrica*, 46(6), 1251. doi:10.2307/1913827

MacKinnon, D. P., Lockwood, C. M., Hoffman, J. M., West, S. G., & Sheets, V. (2002). A comparison of methods to test mediation and other intervening variable effects. *Psychological Methods*, 7(1), 83–104. doi:10.1037//1082-989X.7.1.83

Perloff, J., Rushforth, A., Welch, L., Daudelin, D., Suchman, A., Gittell, J., ... Selker, H. (2017). Intervening to enhance collaboration in translational research: A relational coordination approach. *Journal of Clinical and Translational Science*, 1, 1–8. doi:10.1017/cts.2017.10

Purdy, E. I., McLean, D., Alexander, C., Scott, M., Donohue, A., Campbell, D., ... Brazil, V. (2020). Doing our work better, together: A relationship-based approach to defining the quality improvement agenda in trauma care. *BMJ Open Quality*, 9(1), e000749. doi:10.1136/bmjoq-2019-000749

Schoonhoven, C. B. (1981). Problems with contingency theory: Testing assumptions hidden within the language of contingency "Theory". *Administrative Science Quarterly*, 26(3), 349–377. doi:10.2307/2392512

Thomas, N. K., Sugiyama, K., Rochford, K. C., Stephens, J. P., & Kanov, J. (2018). Experiential organizing: Pursuing relational and bureaucratic goals through symbolically and experientially oriented work. *Academy of Management Review*, 43(4), 749–771. doi:10.5465/amr.2016.0348

Tørring, B., Gittell, J. H., Laursen, M., Rasmussen, B. S., & Sørensen, E. E. (2019). Communication and relationship dynamics in surgical teams in the operating room: An ethnographic study. *BMC Health Services Research*, 19(1), 1–16

Chapter 10

Leveraging Relational Analytics to Create Positive Change

In the years since relational coordination was first discovered, the most significant evolution we have seen is the growing interest in using it to create positive change. As people have learned about the beneficial outcomes of relational coordination, including enhanced well-being for co-workers and the clients they serve, they have become more and more interested in finding ways to strengthen it in their own organizations. This interest led to the creation of a community of researchers and practitioners—the Relational Coordination Collaborative—that works together to "transform relationships for high performance." In this chapter, we introduce the Six Stages of Change, inspired by scholar practitioner Tony Suchman, to show how the Relational Model of Organizational Change works in practice. See Exhibit 10.1 for the Six Stages of Change.

Stage 1: Explore the Context and Introduce Relational Coordination

The change process begins when you begin to reflect on the current state, engaging in conversations to explore the situation more broadly and deeply. The initiative may come from top management, from a manager closer to the work, from a frontline worker, or from a funder or accreditation body with a responsibility for oversight asking: What are the major coordination challenges we are facing? Who are the key stakeholders who are involved in solving that challenge, or who should be involved? What are the current outcomes, versus the outcomes that are desired by our stakeholders? If coordination appears to be a significant challenge due to high levels of interdependence, uncertainty or time constraints, consider introducing the principles of relational coordination.

Exhibit 10.1 Six Stages of Change

Stage 1	Explore the context and introduce relational coordination
Stage 2	Create a multi-stakeholder change team with space to disagree respectfully
Stage 3	Assess relational coordination from the perspective of all participants
Stage 4	Reflect on findings and engage in sensemaking
Stage 5	Design and implement interventions
Stage 6	Assess impact and refine interventions as needed

Stage 2: Create a Multi-Stakeholder Change Team

From here, you may choose to create a change team that represents the key stakeholders. The first challenge may be to motivate these stakeholders to contribute their time and effort to a change process. Representatives should be invited who have credibility with the stakeholder group they are asked to speak for. Given the distinct perspectives and unequal power held by these stakeholders, a trusted facilitator should be selected to facilitate sensitive discussions on the change team by creating a safe space for participants to disagree respectfully. The change team can engage in relational mapping to begin to see more clearly the situation that they are part of, and to begin to assess the current state of shared goals, shared knowledge, and mutual respect among the key stakeholders they represent. Relational mapping is a useful visualization tool that is complementary to work process mapping or value stream mapping. See Exhibit 10.2 for illustrations of relational mapping, with guidelines for how to facilitate relational mapping available at rcsurveyhelp.info.

Exhibit 10.2 Relational Mapping With Your Change Team

Stage 3: Measure Relational Coordination, Structures, and Outcomes

To see the situation more inclusively and from more perspectives, participants from each key stakeholder group can be surveyed using the Relational Coordination Survey. These questions reflect the seven dimensions of relational coordination, assessing the strength of shared goals, shared knowledge, mutual respect among each of the stakeholder groups, and the extent to which communication is sufficiently frequent, timely, accurate, and focused on problem-solving rather than blaming. As we have learned in previous chapters, the Relational Coordination Survey is a network survey that aims to capture the intersubjective experience of participants in coordinating their work, and to reflect those experiences back to them in a useful way. At the same time, the Organizational Structures Assessment Tool (OSAT) can be used to assess how supportive—or unsupportive—the current organizational structures are.

This is a good time to ensure you have identified the outcomes you are hoping to change—whether they include a broad range of outcomes such as quality, efficiency, worker well-being, innovation, or a single outcome such as reducing errors, or reducing worker turnover—and ensure that you will be able to measure these outcomes regularly to assess progress. Members of the change team could divide up responsibilities to oversee these three broad areas of measurement—(1) relational coordination, (2) organizational structures, and (3) performance outcomes—and engage with colleagues to contribute to data collection as needed. To measure relational coordination accurately and inclusively, it is particularly important to engage participants from each relevant stakeholder group, drawing upon your findings from the relational mapping process in Stage 2.

Stage 4: Reflect on Findings and Engage in Sensemaking

Once measurement has been completed, the interpretation begins. The change team should first dedicate time to making sense of the data among themselves. Relational coordination data can be analyzed electronically and shared back in a multi-page report to generate dialogue. Survey results provide visual feedback on the strengths and weaknesses of relational coordination, for each of the seven dimensions of relational coordination, as well as network maps that identify weak, moderate, and strong ties. Findings can then be presented to key stakeholders, and used to engage stakeholders in reflective discussion to make sense of the findings by connecting them to examples and stories that reflect their daily experiences. The graphical representation of these findings as shown in Exhibit 10.3 enables participants to see the system, look into the mirror, or put the elephant on table, creating a starting point for new conversations, collective sense-making, reflection, and change. In a sense these graphical representations serve as boundary objects, helping participants to create shared meaning among themselves.

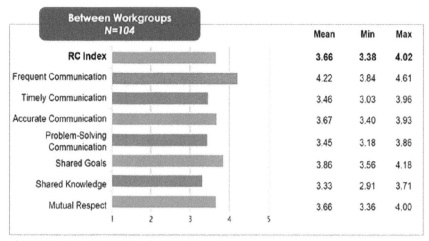

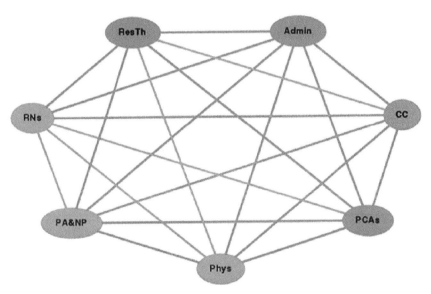

Exhibit 10.3 Sample Relational Coordination Data to Feedback to Participants. (1) Bar graph for the relational coordination scores, colored based on strength of the ties; (2) Network map of the roles in the study and the relational coordination ties between them, colored based on strength of the ties;

(Continued)

			Ratings of					
		Admin	CC	PCAs	Phys	PA&NP	RNs	ResTh
R a t i n g s b y	Administrative Support	1.79	1.79	1.79	1.79	1.79	1.79	1.79
	Care Coordination	4.43	4.86	4.29	4.52	4.71	4.67	3.86
	Personal Care Assistants (PCAs)	2.62	2.40	4.02	2.29	2.29	3.50	2.40
	Physicians	3.58	4.26	3.47	4.25	4.19	3.84	3.50
	Physicians' Assistants and Nurse Practitioners (PAs & NPs)	3.75	4.29	3.39	4.30	4.55	3.96	3.20
	Registered Nurses	3.37	4.08	3.70	3.55	3.98	4.22	3.49
	Respiratory Therapy	2.57	2.57	2.57	3.14	3.14	3.43	4.00

Exhibit 10.3 (Continued)(3) A matrix of the roles and their relational coordination scores, colored based on strength of the ties

Tony Suchman, who pioneered the use of the Relational Coordination Survey for participatory change, reflected after one engagement that: "The survey was the perfect way to help them open up a conversation and to name some elephants to release their hold over the group."

Using a data-driven improvement process, the change team in partnership with the stakeholders they represent can interpret the data in order to decide how to intervene. Ties that have a significant impact on performance, *and* that are particularly weak, whether in an individual team, or for the organization or the industry as a whole, should become a priority for improvement. We sometimes find in surgical care teams that ties between surgeons and anesthesiologists are particularly weak. These ties may require particular targeted interventions (or countermeasures, in the language of lean) that could be similar or different than the interventions targeted at weak ties found between surgeons and scrub techs.

We can also easily imagine how these two different dyads would impact different outcomes. Weak ties between surgeons and anesthesiologists may impact safety outcomes related to the circulatory and respiratory systems, whereas weak ties between surgeons and scrub techs may impact safety outcomes related to infection. One must also be attentive to the power gradients involved when carrying out interventions to address relational coordination. For example, weak ties between surgeons and anesthesiologists can be addressed as a dynamic between two powerful groups, whereas weak ties between surgeons and scrub techs must be addressed as a dynamic between unequally powerful groups, with greater attention to psychological safety.

It is also worth noting that these dyadic interactions, positive or negative, have the potential for spillover effects beyond the immediate dyad that is involved. Tensions between any two roles can disrupt the focus and flow in a shared space such that the group as a whole becomes more prone to errors, delays, and burnout. Those involved on a team with one particularly weak tie may even find their interactions with the next patient are disrupted. We are human after all, and these relational coordination ties are not just technical, they are also emotional.

Sharing Relational Data with Participants

Sharing relational data with participants is a key element of the change process. Like people analytics, relational analytics can be used to control workers and customers in unwelcome ways, by using data about them to direct, evaluate and discipline them. Imagine for example that your organization was impressed by the evidence that relational coordination among workers is a significant driver of quality, safety, efficiency, and financial performance, as well as worker well-being, learning, and innovation. In seeking to strengthen relational coordination, top management might decide to hold every manager accountable FOR achieving high levels of relational coordination within their team, and between their team and other key functions and stakeholders. On the one hand, this could be excellent news—management is taking relational coordination seriously! On the other hand, there is now the potential that relational coordination scores will be used in a way that is punitive rather than developmental, reflective of hierarchical rather than relational leadership.

It was based on this concern that two scholar practitioners—Edgar Schein and Tony Suchman—made a statement regarding the potential misuse of relational coordination data in 2011, the year the Relational Coordination Collaborative (formerly the Relational Coordination Research Collaborative) launched:

> While the RC Survey is well established as an observational research tool, its use as an intervention is still at relatively early stages of development. It would be easy to underestimate the complexity of this work. Overly simplistic interpretations can cause harm. Reviewing RC scores can elicit shame, defensiveness, projection, triangulation, and scapegoating; it can exacerbate conflict and compromise performance. The lower the level of relational coordination (and thus the greater the need for an intervention), the greater the likelihood of a dysfunctional response to the scores.
>
> As elegant and straightforward as the RC Survey is as a measure, it is not a magic bullet for improving team performance or organizational culture. It needs to be used as one part of a broader intervention that

includes longitudinal individual and team coaching, trustworthy processes for relational learning and accountability, and leadership development to assure consistent parallel process across levels of the team or organization. Such work requires the involvement of skilled coaches/consultants with deep experience in group dynamics, systems work, conflict resolution and the teaching of emotional self-management.

For all these reasons, we urge you not to tread lightly or naively into the realm of interventions. Be prepared to invest the necessary time and resources and be sure you have access to the skills and experience that the work requires.

Thanks to this cautionary note and its influence on the Relational Coordination Collaborative, the analytics that are conducted with relational coordination data for interventional purposes are used responsibly in many cases, though certainly not all.

Opacity regarding the logic behind data can also contribute to increasing the power of some over others, a negative aspect of algorithmic control (Kellogg, Valentine, & Christin, 2020). One of the key insights arising from practitioners in the Relational Coordination Collaborative has been to become more transparent rather than less transparent with the data, sharing more of it rather than less of it with more people along with clear insights into where those data come from.

Many practitioners agree that transparency regarding where the data come from, while protecting the confidentiality of respondents, is essential for a positive learning experience and for minimizing unhealthy power dynamics that could get in the way. Tony Suchman often reminds colleagues to share with participants—before sharing their data with them—the exact seven questions that were used to assess relational coordination. As participants look at each dimension—frequent communication, timely communication, accurate communication, problem-solving communication, shared goals, shared knowledge, and mutual respect—they are reminded about how each dimension was explained to respondents as they completed the survey. Perhaps most impactful is telling participants the Relational Coordination Survey data is *their* data, and then acting as though it belongs to them. Suchman will say: "This is not a report card. Think of it as looking in the mirror together. It is a reflection of how you felt about working together at the point in time when you completed this survey—that can change and you can change it together." Practitioners tend to agree wholeheartedly with this advice. Most who are drawn to the practice of relational coordination want to share back data in an empowering process to help participants make change. They want people to understand where the data comes from and to own it. That way, when it's time to make change, participants are better prepared to take the lead.

What practitioners tend to disagree about is *how much* of the data to share and *with whom*. The more cautious school of thought is to share only the seven dimensions aggregated across all roles to show how they are experienced by everybody about everybody. These practitioners believe that sharing data on the quality of communication and the quality of relationships for all roles as a whole is more than enough to stimulate productive conversations. Is our communication, on the whole, sufficiently frequent, timely, accurate, focused on problem-solving? Do we have shared goals, shared knowledge, and mutual respect, on the whole? As coaches or consultants, they appreciate having the matrices and networks to identify where there are weak and strong ties between specific roles, but they tend to feel that data about specific role relationships is riskier to share especially when the level of respect is low and professional facilitation is not available to help conflicted groups talk with each other. While the process for creating the data should be highly transparent, the data themselves should be more opaque due to the high potential for the more explicitly relational data to "...elicit shame, defensiveness, projection, triangulation, and scapegoating; it can exacerbate conflict and compromise performance. The lower the level of relational coordination (and thus the greater the need for an intervention), the greater the likelihood of a dysfunctional response to the scores," as Suchman and Schein cautioned above.

On one hand, this makes sense. As we know, even technical data about errors can be fraught with tension and meaning, because there is insufficient psychological safety, or because the well-being of the organization and its stakeholders is at stake, or both.

Others take another path, sharing more than just the seven dimensions aggregated across all roles, and looking at the network maps and matrices that show how each role is related to each other role. As we saw in Chapter 7, relational coordination measures are based on a 360-degree evaluation of each role. When presented this way, the data could be used to help people to coordinate more effectively with each other, by breaking down the specific metrics for each role. Or one could instead step back and ask: "What kinds of patterns are you seeing here? Anything that reflects your experience? Anything surprising?" This greater transparency carries risks but these may be offset by the benefits. One scholar practitioner in this school of thought, Carsten Hornstrup, explained that he was more concerned about lack of transparency than people's ability to respond productively to the data.

> Maybe I'm not a sensitive guy, but this survey is not asking "do you love me?" —it's just asking: "do people respect each other's contribution to how we do our job?" I mean, it's the voices of people, so I would think not to use the data rather openly would not be sensitive to the people who answered this survey. And of course, I've had separate discussions with those groups that have really low numbers. But they are not surprised. Because they know. The ones who are going to get the lowest score, they know before they get them. That's often why they're a bit defensive.

While he wants people to become comfortable with seeing and making sense of relational data, Hornstrup is quite thoughtful about who should get the data, and in what sequence. Like others, Hornstrup shares data first with those who are most accountable for performance outcomes.

> That's where I'm very careful. Who to share the data with first. Don't go senior. Don't go to the employees. Instead go to the people who are pointed at, who are accountable for results, who have all the pressures—the frontline leaders. We need to talk to them first.

Stage 5: Design and Implement Interventions

Based on what is learned from sharing the data and engaging in dialogue across stakeholders, the change team can then develop a plan of action for improving relational coordination in order to more easily achieve desired outcomes for multiple stakeholders. Which role relationships are most in need of strengthening? Which dimensions would be most impactful to strengthen—mutual respect, or perhaps timely communication? And which types of interventions are needed to strengthen relational coordination in a sustainable way? Systems have relational, work process, and structural elements, so to change working relationships in a sustainable way, all three types of interventions are needed (Gittell, 2016). The Relational Model of Organizational Change in Exhibit 10.4 shows how these three types of interventions interact to support and sustain the development of relational coordination in order to achieve desired outcomes.

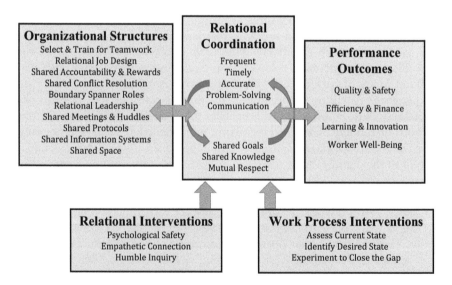

Exhibit 10.4 The Relational Model of Organizational Change

Relational Interventions

Relational interventions can be carried out to jump start a culture of relational coordination by enabling diverse stakeholders to build shared goals, shared knowledge, and mutual respect across their differences. Relational interventions include tools such as humble inquiry (Schein, 2013) to create mutual respect and power-with, conversations of interdependence to create shared knowledge (Suchman & Rawlins, 2020), and safe spaces to create the psychological safety that is needed to address negative emotions that arise from the loss of power-over (Edmondson & Harvey, 2017; Kahn, 1990). By seeing their interdependence, participants can begin to develop shared knowledge of the situation and how each party contributes to it. As a result, they can more readily identify shared goals that they cannot achieve without help from each other. Based on this, mutual respect can begin to develop, setting off a positive self-reinforcing cycle. These relationships of shared goals, shared knowledge, and mutual respect give rise to communication that is frequent, timely, accurate, and based on problem-solving rather than blaming, which further supports the development of shared goals, shared knowledge, and mutual respect. The result is a mutually reinforcing process of communicating and relating for the purpose of task integration. Exhibit 10.5 provides a Relational Intervention Toolbox with examples that may help you to generate ideas. Note that a continuously updated toolbox is available through the Relational Coordination Collaborative.

To achieve high levels of relational coordination, interventions are needed at the emotional level so that the parties can engage the process of identifying the real issues. To begin this process, it is not necessary that people love or even like each other. Rather, what is needed is to identify shared goals, create shared knowledge, and establish mutual respect among key stakeholders. The first step is to ensure there is adequate mutual respect, because when the stakeholders feel disrespected, little progress can occur. In effect, the emotional impact of feeling disrespected is likely to make productive discourse impossible.

Graham Wright offers one such first step. He notes that even in circumstances of extreme polarization, there is an opportunity to move toward integration if both parties are willing to break the conflict into its component parts and *to recognize and discuss* the aspects of their position on which they would prefer to remain silent or on which they have not yet reflected (Wright, 2018). This is an important step because, as he argues, in instances of extreme conflict, each side is generally silent on the aspect of the conflict that is of most interest to the other. Trusting enough to listen to the main concern of the other side—and acknowledge the silence we have likely maintained on our side—is one way of extending an invitation to integration. Extending such an invitation, of course, does not guarantee a reciprocal response.

Exhibit 10.5 Relational Intervention Toolbox from Relationship-Centered
             Health Care

Mutual Respect

- Story telling (e.g. stepping-stone stories)
- Dialog skills (reflective listening, open honest questions, humble inquiry)
- Empathy listening—Scharmer's *Theory U*
- Nonviolent communication
- Multiple perspective tasking skills (cone in the box)
- Emotional intelligence—EQ
- Unconscious bias workshop
- Understand value of each role—what would happen if each role stopped?
- Small group and 1:1 coaching to increase self-awareness

Shared Goals

- Retreat using Appreciative Inquiry dialog around vision, goals differentiation
- World café
- Future search / vision conference
- Open space
- Sticky note mind map
- Fishbowl dialog with multiple stakeholder groups

Shared Knowledge

- Process mapping with sticky notes
- Scope of practice discussions—use of evidence-based tools
- Walk in my shoes.... learning journey
- Speed dating questions
- Conversations of interdependence

But we believe strategies such as this have the potential to create the kind of psychological safety needed to move toward integrative solutions.

Work Process Interventions

Process improvement seeks to improve outcomes through improved coordination of the work and many approaches seek to do so in a participatory fashion. However, process improvement is often carried out in a purely technical way, thus missing the relational dynamics that provide participants with the shared goals and shared knowledge that would help them to succeed. Relational analytics can help participants to visualize the current state of communicating and relating, and to visualize each part of the system in relation to the whole, thus enabling them to engage more easily in systems thinking. They can then use standard process improvement tools like work process mapping in a more relational way to analyze the work, identify and measure the desired state, and improve the work to achieve that desired state. This suggests why relational mapping and work process mapping are such complementary tools.

Structural Interventions

To support and sustain these new patterns of communicating and relating, new organizational structures must be designed. Moreover, the new working relationships themselves can be the source of this new design as participants identify structures that will sustain the new ways of communicating and relating and the ability to achieve desired outcomes. Structural solutions that have emerged in interventions based on this model include selecting and training participants for relational competence, creating shared accountability and rewards among participants, creating shared conflict resolution processes, boundary spanner roles, shared meetings, shared protocols to guide behavior, and shared information systems to keep participants informed in a timely, accurate way. These structures help to reinforce and support new relationships as they emerge (Gittell, 2016).

The process of using the Organizational Structures Assessment Tool (OSAT) to facilitate a design conversation among key stakeholders is explained at rcsurveyhelp.info. Jon Erik Borreson's experience with using the OSAT in this way suggests that leaders can create accountability among their top management team members for transforming these structures to be more supportive of relational coordination. Others have coached mid-level leaders to use a conversational version of the OSAT to create the above matrix, gaining visibility into the strengths of the existing structures and the opportunities for their improvement.

The challenge you may encounter is that when mid-level leaders become aware of instances where these structures are not well-designed to support relational coordination, they may not be in a position to redesign all of them. This is especially true of accountability and reward structures, which often fall short of what is needed to support relational coordination, but these structures are typically established higher in the organizational hierarchy or even outside the organization by boards of trustees, payers, regulators, and/or accrediting bodies. Changing accountability and reward structures may require building a broader change team of stakeholders who are needed to design and approve and implement such structural changes. In some cases, a crisis may be needed in your organization, industry, or sector for these macro institutional changes to occur.

In the meantime, creating local reward structures can be very powerful, especially when leaders role model the behaviors they are rewarding. Consider for example how RC Bingo was used in the Billings Clinic intensive care unit to bring attention to the seven dimensions of relational coordination, and to reward participants for demonstrating these relational behaviors towards their colleagues and their patients. For more about this and other creative interventions, please see *Transforming Relationships for High Performance* (Gittell, 2016) and other resources to be shared by the Relational Coordination Collaborative and highlighted at rcsurveyhelp. info as they become available.

Stage 6: Assess Impact and Refine Interventions As Needed

Lastly, in any significant change process, ongoing assessment is needed by the change team to understand what is working and what is not, and to adjust as needed. These assessments can include the Relational Coordination Survey and the OSAT, as well as the measurement of desired performance outcomes. To the extent that these data were collected earlier in the process, they can be collected again and compared to the earlier data. Chapter 9 showed how to assess changes in relational coordination over time; the same or similar analytic methods can be used to assess changes in organizational structures and desired outcomes over time.

Sustainability is an important aspect of successful change. As we found in the Gebo and Bond study, for example, both intervention sites experienced significant positive changes in relational coordination, but after four time periods of measurement, only one of those sites had sustained the change. It was the site that had adopted a structural intervention—a city-wide boundary spanner role—to ensure stakeholders would continue to meet over time to coordinate their efforts on behalf of troubled youth. In addition to sustaining positive change, there is also the potential that positive change did not occur in a measurable way in the first cycle, and may require adapting efforts to address the challenges that exist. Finally, even once positive change has occurred and has been sustained, you may need to continue the cycle over time as the situation continues to evolve in both expected and unexpected ways; for example, the arrival of new leaders, new performance pressures, or new stakeholders with new needs.

Summing Up

In this chapter, you have learned a bit about using relational analytics to create positive change. Probably the most exciting thing we have seen is how relational analytics bring attention to relationships and how they can transform how people understand themselves and the role they play whether in a simple or complex process. Any use of data is sensitive, however, given the experiences many of us have had with data that have been used as a judgmental report card for ranking purposes. Providing relational data does not solve that challenge by itself. There is still a need to facilitate a relational process of understanding relational data in a way that can foster collective self-control by the group. In this chapter, we have provided some insight into this facilitation challenge, and also into the importance of structural interventions for supporting and sustaining positive change. But there is much more to learn, so we invite you to join the global learning community called the Relational Coordination Collaborative. Lead practitioners and researchers in the RCC are continuously sharing their results in writing, in webinars, and in workshops, so join if you can and share what you are learning as well.

References

Edmondson, A. C., & Harvey, J. F. (2017). *Extreme Teaming: Lessons in Complex, Cross-sector Leadership*. Bingley: Emerald Publishing.

Gittell, J. H. (2016). *Transforming Relationships for High Performance: The Power of Relational Coordination*. Palo Alto, CA: Stanford University Press.

Gittell, J. H., & Fletcher, J. K. (2018). Integrative solutions in a divided world: A relational model of change. In M. Stout (Ed.), *The Future of Progressivism: Applying Follettian Thinking to Contemporary Issues*. Anoka, MN: Process Century Press.

Kahn, W. A. (1990). Psychological conditions of personal engagement and disengagement at work. *Academy of Management Journal*, 33(4), 692–724. doi:10.5465/256287

Kellogg, K. C., Valentine, M. A., & Christin, A. (2020). Algorithms at work: The new contested terrain of control. *Academy of Management Annals*, 14(1), 366–410. doi:10.5465/annals.2018.0174

Schein, E. H. (2013). *Humble Inquiry: The Gentle Art of Asking Instead of Telling*. Oakland: Berrett-Koehler Publishers.

Suchman, A., & Rawlins, D. (2020, July 23) Personal Communication/Interviewer: J. H. Gittell.

Wright, G. (2018). From domination to integration: Dealing with polarized views of race in contemporary American politics. In M. Stout (Ed.), *The Future of Progressivism: Applying Follettian Thinking to Contemporary Issues*. Anoka, MN: Process Century Press.

Chapter 11

Moving Forward with Research and Action

We are grateful that you have joined us on this journey into the expanding world of relational analytics. Relational analytics share in common with people analytics the use of algorithms to understand and shape human behavior. Beyond that, however, relational analytics are quite different given their focus on managing interdependence rather than controlling individual behavior. Analytics are clearly not neutral. They can give power or take power away. They can shape behavior by shaping how we see ourselves in relationship to our work and in relationship to each other.

What We've Tried To Do In This Book

Relational analytics are highly relevant to both researchers and practitioners. Given this, we designed these guidelines for *practitioners* to successfully use relational analytics to drive organizational change and achieve desired performance outcomes for multiple stakeholders, and for *researchers* to replicate, improve and expand upon the research that has been conducted to date, preferably in close partnership with practitioners. We expect that these guidelines will be particularly useful for practitioners and researchers who are working together to develop and test innovative solutions to significant coordination challenges. These coordination challenges may be found in teams, in organizations, and in networks of organizations that are working together to solve complex problems.

To meet their needs, we have introduced relational coordination as a conceptual foundation for doing relational analytics, building upon the strengths of both social networks and social capital. We've shown the considerable body of evidence for the theory to date, and we've mapped out some of the areas that are in need of further exploration. We've walked you through the process of setting up your research or evaluation design, then collecting your data, creating your variables, visualizing your data, and analyzing your data. We've shown how to assess the organizational structures that are known to strengthen or weaken relational coordination depending on their design. Perhaps most importantly for some readers, we have shown how you can leverage the tools of relational analytics to help create positive change.

New Frontiers

Probably the most significant evolution in the theory, measurement, and analysis of relational coordination between 2011 and 2020 was the increased interest in using relational coordination principles and metrics to create change. As people have learned about the performance effects of relational coordination, they have become more and more interested in finding ways to strengthen it. As we showed in Chapter 10, their work has informed the Relational Model of Organizational Change, and has given birth to the creation of a global community of researchers and practitioners working together to "transform relationships for high performance" (visit the Relational Coordination Collaborative; see also (Gittell, 2016; Gittell & Douglass, 2012). As a result, the Relational Coordination Survey is now being used to measure changes over time in how people work together, requiring methodologies to analyze the statistical significance of changes in the Relational Coordination Index and the underlying seven dimensions over time. Some of these statistical methodologies were introduced in Chapter 9. But there is much more learning needed to fully understand how to create—and measure—changes in relational coordination.

Going forward we expect new frontiers will include innovations in the measurement tool itself to provide more of a moving picture rather than a snapshot of coordination patterns at a particular moment in time. In addition, unexpected findings from our review of the literature suggest opportunities to extend research in new directions, including the following.

Variable Effects of Boundary Spanners on Relational Coordination

As we saw in the systematic review in Chapter 3, one inconsistent finding about organizational structures thus far has been regarding the role of boundary spanners in strengthening relational coordination. A more nuanced hypothesis is that boundary spanners such as care coordinators or project managers can facilitate strong relationships in teams that are already striving for relational coordination, but in teams that are siloed, team members tend instead to "farm out" relationship work to the boundary spanner and in so doing may reduce the overall level of relational coordination. So instead of asking whether a boundary spanner role makes a difference for relational coordination, we might ask instead how and under which circumstances do boundary spanners help others to build relational coordination? The conditions might include designing the boundary spanner role appropriately with clear expectations of facilitating coordination among others rather than taking personal responsibility for all coordination. Or it may come down to a recognition that participants in a siloed organization must begin to overcome their silos in order to use the boundary spanner role appropriately—as a support for everyone to coordinate with one another rather than a role that absolves others of their coordination responsibilities. Once the boundary spanner role is clearly defined, other predictors might include selecting people who have the right competencies—perhaps including some content knowledge regarding the work of each role whose work they are seeking to coordinate, and the systems thinking to build relational coordination across these differences.

Conflict Resolution and Shared Spaces Need More Attention

While some aspects of relational coordination have been well-studied, other aspects are in need of greater attention, as we learned in Chapter 3. For example, only a handful of studies have explored the impact of conflict resolution on relational coordination. While nearly all have found the expected positive relationship, we still have more to learn about which forms of conflict resolution are most effective for strengthening relational coordination, in which contexts. For example, the most effective form of conflict resolution may depend on the size of the power differences that exist between the parties who are in conflict, or the geographical proximity and/or familiarity between the parties.

Similarly, only a handful of studies have explored the impact of shared space on relational coordination. All but one study found that shared space is conducive to relational coordination. The other—a study of venture investing—found that spatial proximity was not necessary for relational coordination; the author argued that relational coordination is itself a form of proximity that does not depend on spatial proximity (Kuebart, 2019). This topic deserves greater attention given the increasing trend toward distributed work in digitally mediated work processes (Claggett & Karahanna, 2018), accelerated by the global pandemic of 2020.

From Information Technology to Artificial Intelligence

Findings thus far about the impact of IT on relational coordination have been quite consistent with the theory that when IT spans across role boundaries, it helps to strengthen relational coordination *so long as it is used to complement rather than replace personal communication*, as we learned in Chapter 3. Given recent trends, it will be increasingly important to ask how relational coordination might look in a world with social media and artificial intelligence in the workplace. A study by Aristidou and Barrett explored how social media impacted relationships in community-based care, and found that approaches that work well in the face-to-face environment may not work in the virtual environment (Aristidou & Barrett, 2018). How might the shift toward virtual coordination and/or machine-driven coordination influence the ability to foster relational coordination, or the importance of relational coordination for achieving desired outcomes? Perhaps relational coordination itself serves as a form of proximity, as argued above, but what does that mean? We may also want to know how artificial intelligence can be used to create data that are more transparent and more amenable to collective self-control, thus addressing the concerns of Kate Kellogg and co-authors (2020) (Kellogg, Valentine, & Christin, 2020).

Impact of Diversity on Relational Coordination

Occupational diversity is implicitly at the heart of coordination theory as people struggle to coordinate across different occupational thought worlds (Dougherty, 1992). The impact of demographic diversity and how it can be leveraged to foster relational coordination has been relatively neglected, however. Demographic diversity has emerged as a covariate in some relational coordination research. One study in our review found that female physicians experienced significantly lower levels of relational coordination from colleagues than did male physicians (Manski-Nankervis, Furler, Young, Patterson, & Blackberry, 2015), for example, while another found that relational coordination was significantly stronger in interprofessional teams with a higher percentage of women (Hustoft et al., 2018). In addition, the relational dimensions of relational coordination positively predict identity freedom at work (Singh, Selvarajan, & Chapa, 2019).

Lee and Kim (2019) have explicitly incorporated demographic diversity into relational coordination theory (Lee & Kim, 2019). The authors proposed that demographic diversity is associated with weaker relational coordination, but that these same forms of diversity can promote higher levels of relational coordination and a range of positive performance outcomes in the presence of organizational structures that promote shared accountability for outcomes. Their study of manufacturing firms in South Korea found evidence for this proposition. They concluded that relational coordination is more challenging to achieve in the presence of diversity, but that cross-cutting organizational structures can neutralize these effects and transform diversity into an asset for increasing relational coordination and performance. Given the increasing diversity in organizations, research on structures that positively leverage diversity to strengthen relational coordination and its impact on team and organizational performance outcomes should receive serious attention going forward.

Noncore Roles and Relational Coordination

The impact of "noncore" roles on relational coordination is worthy of greater attention due to the increasing trend to rely on semi-professionals, for example in health, education, and law. Consider recent discussions about the role of "noncore" workers (Bolinger, Klotz, & Leavitt, 2018). Also consider findings from a recent study of Beth Israel Deaconess

Medical Center regarding "noncore" workers whose work is relatively invisible, described in Chapter 5 (Olaleye, 2020). Interestingly, even in the relatively egalitarian context of Denmark, the lowest educated and lowest status workers who spend the most amount of time with clients tend to be removed from the situation when big decisions need to be made, meaning that their knowledge is lost (Hornstrup, 2020). To further understand the value created by "noncore" workers, it may be useful to consider Kate Kellogg's research on medical assistants, and Ruth Blatt's research on contingent workers (Blatt, 2008; Kellogg, 2018).

Distributional Consequences of Relational Coordination

Our concern with the dynamics between core and noncore roles raises the question of who benefits from relational coordination. Even though the theory suggests that relational coordination creates value by helping participants to manage interdependence, thus pushing out the production possibilities frontier and relaxing tradeoffs (Caldwell, Roehrich, & George, 2017; Pagell, Klassen, Johnston, Shevchenko, & Sharma, 2015), there is no theorizing to date on its distributional consequences.

The value that is created through relational coordination may not be equitably shared with the less powerful workers who may be essential to its creation. Data show steadily increasing productivity in the U.S. since the early 1970s with real wages growing far more slowly, suggesting that productivity gains have not been equitably shared. Other countries have done better but the trends are similar. Our systematic review suggests that firms benefit from the increased efficiency, quality, client engagement, learning and innovation that are associated with relational coordination, and that their workers benefit from increased job satisfaction, engagement, and reduced burnout. But we have not explored whether workers share in the financial rewards created by relational coordination, and we suspect that low status, so-called "noncore" workers, do not.

The Relational Model of Organizational Change provides some initial insight into how relational coordination could help to achieve a more equitable distribution of benefits. According to this model, when participants are able to visualize the coordination networks through which value is created, they gain a new perspective on the interdependence through which value is created, and their role in that value creation process (Gittell, 2016). Visualizing work as a horizontal process coordinated through networks offers a sharp contrast to visualizing work as a top-down process with frontline workers in subordinate roles. This visualization is expected to be particularly useful in contexts when status differences make some participants invisible, silencing voices that are essential for progress to occur (Bolinger et al., 2018; Havens, Gittell, & Vasey, 2018). Relational interventions that include high- and low-status workers may increase awareness of interdependence such that lower status workers become aware of their power, and higher status workers become aware of their dependence upon others to achieve desired outcomes. With this increased awareness of interdependence, participants may have a greater sense of jointly owning the results of their labor and be able to negotiate more equitable financial rewards. Shared rewards are expected in turn to strengthen relational coordination and performance outcomes, thus creating a positive feedback loop.

Interventional Uses of Relational Analytics

Much more work is needed to inform the practice of relational coordination. For example, we have much to learn about the impact of sharing relational coordination measures with participants in order to start new conversations among them and to shift how they see themselves in relation to each other. How to do this in a way that is productive rather than counterproductive? How to shift from a report card mentality to a learning mindset?

While the interventional use of relational analytics has much room for innovation and development, it has already been successfully deployed in a wide range of organizational settings. Given new developments by practitioners, relational analytics can now be used to *assess the current state* in your team, your organization, or your ecosystem, *design interventions,* and *measure changes* over time. Consistent with the principles of relational coordination and what we know about organizational learning, we have recommended that relational analytics be used in a way that is nonprescriptive, beginning with the introduction of the relational coordination framework, and creation of a change team, with participants using a range of tools including relational mapping to identify the core set of roles who are required to coordinate their work in order to produce the desired performance outcomes. Subsequent stages involve communication planning and deployment of the Relational Coordination Survey, followed by presentation and sense-making of findings with key stakeholders, inclusive of senior leaders and front-line staff engaged in the work process, in a facilitated context to generate dialogue about the strengths and opportunities that exist within a particular context. With outside facilitation by a consultant or by developing internal consulting capacity, participants then design and implement interventions, assessing their progress with periodic assessments of relational coordination and desired performance outcomes.

In this book, we have offered a model for using relational analytics to help participants to see the pattern of relationships in which they are engaged. This way of seeing can create greater awareness of the situation and can help to provide perspective and a sense of objectivity regarding the pattern of relationships. Creating visibility can be particularly useful when interrelating is fraught with conflict both spoken and unspoken, and when power differentials and the invisibility of some participants have silenced voices that are essential for progress to occur. The awareness of interdependence is increased in this process. As more powerful participants become aware of their dependence on less powerful participants to achieve their desired outcomes, including their mutual well-being, this awareness helps to mitigate the impact of power differentials.

In this context, participants can identify additional stakeholders to involve, then negotiate the implementation of structural interventions to support and sustain these new relational dynamics, thus helping to achieve mutually desired outcomes. Organizational structures such as training, accountability, rewards, conflict resolution, boundary spanner roles, meetings, protocols, and information systems are then designed by a wider group of stakeholders based on principles of relational coordination to further reinforce and sustain relational coordination.

Because the model centers around the development of high-quality relational networks, it can be applied at multiple levels of systems change, including the coordination among diverse stakeholders to achieve broad social change. For example, as we learned in Chapter 4, Erika Gebo and Brenda Bond (Gebo & Bond, 2016, 2020) have been using this model to address youth violence in Massachusetts cities, with baseline data from one city shown in Exhibit 11.1.

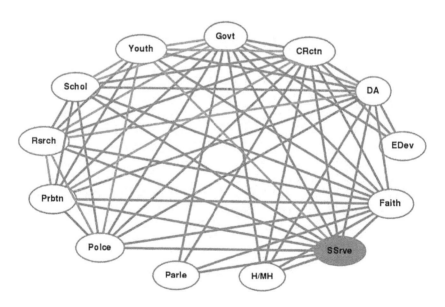

Exhibit 11.1 Relational Coordination Network Map for Youth Violence Initiative

Micro Mechanisms for Developing Relational Coordination

Because the theory has mostly been developed at the meso level of coordination across roles, there has been only preliminary attention to what is happening at the micro level. Psychological safety has been identified as a key element for developing the relationships across roles that enable participants to coordinate their work across the differences in power and status that can be threatening. Based on case studies, Gittell (2016) theorized that this process begins with relational interventions such as creating safe spaces for humble inquiry, led by participants who are willing and able to model the change they wish to see (Schein, 2013).

But in addition to psychological safety, Stephens offers another micro-level mechanism for learning to coordinate (Stephens, 2020). He identifies an aesthetic process through which participants notice fragmentation, which triggers a negative emotional response, which motivates efforts to repair the fragmentation by attending to the actions of others and coordinating more closely with them until coherence or wholeness is restored. This process requires a shared aesthetic sense of the whole and it is not yet clear whether that sense of the whole is negotiated among participants from their distinct perspectives or provided by a single authoritative source. Still the insight is useful for understanding how we learn to coordinate.

A third micro mechanism for learning to coordinate is empathy. Humans have evolved as an empathetic species and this empathy has arguably been central to our evolutionary success (Wilson, 2019). Yet as interdependence has expanded across networks of strangers, our ability to build empathetic connections with diverse others has not caught up (Gutsell & Inzlicht, 2010). How empathy develops across differences is a relatively new frontier (Wexler, 2008). Empathetic connections may be needed to build personal relationships among individuals, thus creating a foundation for relational coordination across role networks at the meso and macro levels. Building these empathetic connections is foundational to the Relational Society Project (Sharma, 2020). Through this multilevel global action research project, we aim to address the epic levels of social fragmentation and isolation that people are experiencing in communities around the world.

Inviting You to Be the Change

We hope you will use relational analytics to foster interdependence and collective self-control among participants, rather than to strengthen hierarchical control. In order to use relational analytics to empower rather than disempower participants, results must be co-owned by those whose relationships are being measured. Once this occurs, there is the potential not only to minimize hierarchical control, but to foster collective self-control for achieving goals that have been identified by the participants themselves through a multi-stakeholder process. This collective self-control is the form of control that Mary Parker Follett identified as being particularly effective in an increasingly complex world.

We thank you for your interest in this growing area of analysis and action that we call relational analytics! We have found relational coordination to be a useful theoretical and practical foundation for doing relational analytics, by providing a way to understand how relationships influence critical outcomes including human well-being, and by showing how organizations can support or undermine these relationships. We welcome questions from you on topics that need additional clarification, and updates about innovations that you have discovered in your work with relational analytics. Please share your questions and innovations by submitting a form at rcsurveyhelp. info and we will respond. With your permission, we will invite the larger community to respond. We look forward to learning with you!

References

Aristidou, A., & Barrett, M. (2018). Coordinating service provision in dynamic service settings: A position-practice relations perspective. *Academy of Management Journal*, 61(2), 685–714. doi:10.5465/amj.2015.0310

Blatt, R. (2008). Organizational citizenship behavior of temporary knowledge employees. *Organization Studies*, 29(6), 849–866. doi:10.1177/0170840 608088704

Bolinger, A. R., Klotz, A. C., & Leavitt, K. (2018). Contributing from inside the outer circle: The identity-based effects of noncore role incumbents on relational coordination and organizational climate. *Academy of Management Review*, 43(4), 680-703. doi:10.5465/amr.2016.0333

Caldwell, N. D., Roehrich, J. K., & George, G. (2017). Social value creation and relational coordination in public-private collaborations. *Journal of Management Studies*, 54(6), 906–928. doi:10.1111/joms.12268

Claggett, J. L., & Karahanna, E. (2018). Unpacking the structure of coordination mechanisms and the role of relational coordination in an era of digitally mediated work processes. *Academy of Management Review*, 43(4), 704–722. doi:10.5465/amr.2016.0325

Dougherty, D. (1992). Interpretive barriers to successful product innovation in large firms. *Organization Science*, 3(2), 179–202. doi:10.1287/orsc.3.2.179

Gebo, E., & Bond, B. J. (2016). Comparing determinants of effective collaboration in a comprehensive crime reduction initiative. *Journal of Policy Practice*, 15(3), 212–232. doi:10.1080/15588742.2015.1044688

Gebo, E., & Bond, B. J. (2020). Improving interorganizational collaborations: An application in a violence reduction context. *The Social Science Journal*, 1-12. doi:10.1016/j.soscij.2019.09.008

Gittell, J. H. (2016). *Transforming Relationships for High Performance: The Power of Relational Coordination*. Palo Alto, CA: Stanford University Press.

Gittell, J. H., & Douglass, A. (2012). Relational bureaucracy: Structuring reciprocal relationships into roles. *Academy of Management Review*, 37(4), 709–733. doi:10.5465/amr.2010.0438

Gutsell, J. N., & Inzlicht, M. (2010). Empathy constrained: Prejudice predicts reduced mental simulation of actions during observation of outgroups. *Journal of Experimental Social Psychology*, 46(5), 841–845. doi:10.1016/j.jesp.2010.03.011

Havens, D. S., Gittell, J. H., & Vasey, J. (2018). Impact of relational coordination on nurse job satisfaction, work engagement and burnout. *The Journal of Nursing Administration*, 48(3), 132–140. doi:10.1097/nna.0000000000000587

Hornstrup, C. (2020) Advancing Relational Coordination Analytics/Interviewer: J. H. Gittell. Personal Communication, Brandeis University.

Hustoft, M., Hetlevik, Ø., Aßmus, J., Størkson, S., Gjesdal, S., & Biringer, E. (2018). Communication and relational ties in inter-professional teams in Norwegian specialized health care: A multicentre study of relational coordination. *International Journal of Integrated Care*, 18(2), 9–9. doi:10.5334/ijic.3432

Kellogg, K. C. (2018). Subordinate activation tactics: semi-professionals and Micro-level institutional change in professional organizations. *Administrative Science Quarterly*, 64(4), 928-975. doi:10.1177/0001839218804527

Kellogg, K. C., Valentine, M. A., & Christin, A. (2020). Algorithms at work: The new contested terrain of control. *Academy of Management Annals*, 14(1), 366-410. doi:10.5465/annals.2018.0174

Kuebart, A. (2019). Geographies of relational coordination in venture capital firms. *European Planning Studies*, 27(11), 2206–2226. doi:10.1080/09654313.2019.16 20696

Lee, H. W., & Kim, E. (2019). Workforce diversity and firm performance: Relational coordination as a mediator and structural empowerment and multisource feedback as moderators. *Human Resource Management*, 59(1), 5-23. doi:10.1002/hrm.21970

Manski-Nankervis, J. A., Furler, J., Young, D., Patterson, E., & Blackberry, I. (2015). Factors associated with relational coordination between health professionals involved in insulin initiation in the general practice setting for people with type 2 diabetes. *Journal of Advanced Nursing*, 71(9), 2176–2188. doi:10.1111/jan.12681

Olaleye, O. (2020). *The Nature of Invisible Work: Role Stratification and the Impact of Relational Coordination*. PhD Dissertation, Brandeis University. Working Paper.

Pagell, M., Klassen, R., Johnston, D., Shevchenko, A., & Sharma, S. (2015). Are safety and operational effectiveness contradictory requirements: The roles of routines and relational coordination. *Journal of Operations Management*, 36(1), 1-14. doi:10.1016/j.jom.2015.02.002

Schein, E. H. (2013). *Humble Inquiry: The Gentle Art of Asking Instead of Telling*. Oakland: Berrett-Koehler Publishers.

Sharma, S. (2020). *Building a Relational Society*. Report to the Topol Family Foundation.

Singh, B., Selvarajan, T. T., & Chapa, O. (2019). High-quality relationships as antecedents of OCB: Roles of identity freedom and gender. *Equality, Diversity and Inclusion: An International Journal*, 38(8), 793-813. doi:10.1108/edi-08-2018-0148

Stephens, J. P. (2020). How the show goes on: Using the aesthetic experience of collective performance to adapt while coordinating. *Administrative Science Quarterly*, 000183922091105. doi:10.1177/0001839220911056

Wexler, B. E. (2008). *Brain and Culture: Neurobiology, Ideology, and Social Change*. Cambridge, Mass.: MIT Press.

Wilson, D. S. (2019). *This View of Life: Completing the Darwinian Revolution* (First edition. ed.): New York, NY: Pantheon Books, a division of Penguin Random House.

Index

Page numbers in *italics* refer to figures and those in **bold** refer to tables.

For Product Safety Concerns and Information please contact our EU
representative GPSR@taylorandfrancis.com
Taylor & Francis Verlag GmbH, Kaufingerstraße 24, 80331 München, Germany